D1291626

Tim Draper

Tim Draper and Sari Ostrum. Courtesy of Jacquelyn Ostrum.

Tim Draper

From Eastman Theatre's Muses to the Founding of Rochester City Ballet

Wendy Roxin Wicks

For Barbara,
Enjoy!
Warmly,
Wendy Roxin Wicks
Jan 6, 2015

MELIORA PRESS
An imprint of the University of Rochester Press

Copyright © 2014 by Wendy Roxin Wicks

All rights reserved. Except as permitted under current legislation, no part of this work may be photocopied, stored in a retrieval system, published, performed in public, adapted, broadcast, transmitted, recorded, or reproduced in any form or by any means, without the prior permission of the copyright owner.

First published 2014

Meliora Press is an imprint of the
University of Rochester Press
668 Mt. Hope Avenue, Rochester, NY 14620, USA
www.urpress.com
and Boydell & Brewer Limited
PO Box 9, Woodbridge, Suffolk IP12 3DF, UK
www.boydellandbrewer.com

Hardcover ISBN-13: 978-1-58046-499-4
Paperback ISBN-13: 978-1-58046-502-1

Library of Congress Control Number: 2014951778

Cataloging data may be obtained from the Library of Congress.

This publication is printed on acid-free paper.
Printed in the United States of America.

For Tim and Britt, Dave, Gary, Mom & Dad

*Enrico Cecchetti and Nicholas Legat of the Imperial
Ballet School of St. Petersburg trained Olga Preobrajenska.*

❧

*Olga Preobrajenska, Prima Ballerina Assoluta of the
Mariinsky Ballet of St. Petersburg, trained Kathleen Crofton.*

❧

*Kathleen Crofton, Anna Pavlova's "Baby," and Olive McCue
of the Eastman Theatre Ballet trained Timothy Draper.*

❧

*In returning to Rochester to restore ballet to the Eastman Theatre stage,
Tim's students inherited his own rich artistic pedigree. Theirs is the direct
lineage to the Mariinsky Theatre and the classical Italian, English,
and Russian balletic traditions.*

CONTENTS

ARTIST REMINISCENCES

ACKNOWLEDGMENTS

Coming of age in Rochester, New York, during the 1960s, where a fifteen-minute drive connected a rural cornfield to one of the three top music schools in the nation, I was always fascinated by the seemingly disproportionate amount of culture that resided within our region. For Mom and Dad, however, who had for so long flourished under George Eastman's largesse, sheet music had equal value with food in our household and thus afforded my siblings and me a rare behind-the-scenes sense of ownership of all things Eastman. My first thanks, therefore, go to my late, beloved father, Paul Roxin, ebullient family man, music aficionado, impresario, clarinetist, Rochester Philharmonic Orchestra board member, aviator, and humorist whose early founding of the University of Rochester's Hillel Symphony led to his courtship of and sixty-one-year marriage to an Eastman School cellist; and to my equally dear mother, Beatrice Caro Roxin, ESM '49, whose artistic and literary sensibilities led to wonderful memories of weekly trips to the Rundel, piano lessons with Vincent Lenti, ballet class with Thelma Biracree, and eventually ballet class for my daughter with Tim Draper. Thank you, Mom!

A giant debt of gratitude goes to Tim's family of origin, who welcomed me into their home with coffee, stories, laughter, tears, and photos. I am especially grateful to Tim's older sister, Donna Draper Hansmann; her late husband, Art Hansmann; Tim's younger sister, Jaye Draper; and his late mother, Hazel Draper. It is also quite safe to say that had it not been for Tim's beloved life partner and my trusted friend, Randy Stringer, who provided me with the broad "who's who" during the earliest days of this project, this book might still be sitting in a sorry state on my to-do list.

I am also thoroughly indebted to Tim's much-loved star dancers from 1986 to 2003, who took time from their busy lives to contribute the rich reminiscences that precede each chapter of the book: Erin Bellis, Chelsea Bonosky, Kristi Boone, Tina Brock, Janelle Cornwell, Jonathan Davidsson, Kathy Joslyn, Sarah Lane, Alanna Lipsky, Natalia Malley-Masten, Jill Marlow, Hayley Meier, Brittany Monachino, Jillian

Nealon, Jim Nowakowski, Sari Ostrum, Brittany Shinay, Cindy Van Scoter, and Rebekah von Rathonyi. Tim truly loved the members of his professional division, and their stories are the true heart and soul of this work. I would also like to provide a special thank-you to Tim's first Cavalier, George Orosz, for sharing his memories and personal collection of photos and memorabilia from the early years when the school and company were just being launched.

On the publishing side, a profound thank-you to the exceptional talent at the University of Rochester Press and Boydell & Brewer, Inc. Very special thanks go to the University of Rochester Press's founder and provost emeritus of the university, Dr. Brian S. Thompson, for his exceptional support and championing of this project at every turn; to Robert Kraus, chair of the Editorial Board for his early and sustained enthusiasm and numerous thoughtful contributions throughout the process; to Sonia Kane, editorial director, for her tremendous assistance and generosity of spirit in bringing the manuscript to life; and to Sue Smith, managing director; Julia Cook, assistant editor; Ryan M. Peterson, managing editor; and Tracey Engel, production editor, for their invaluable knowledge and suggestions.

I wish to acknowledge the generosity of Tim's many friends, colleagues, board members, parent volunteers, and admirers who graciously gave of their time and support: Peter Anastos, Dona Bellis, Nancy Bielski, Janet Boeff, Michelle Buschner, Susanne Callan-Harris, the late Edward A. Charbonneau III, Sarah Jane Clifford, Dr. Bertram (Bud) Coleman, Julianne Deming, Tory Dobrin, Fiona Fairrie, Anita Bartolotta Garland-Cox, Malcolm Grant, Gay Grooms, Deborah Hess, Melinda Lane, Kate Lipsky, Stuart Low, David Manion, Kevin McKenzie, Mike McKinley, Janet Meier, Gayle Miller, Mary Mostert, Cathy Nealon, Brian Norris, Jacquelyn Ostrum, Wendy Perron, Anthony Rabara, Donna Schoenherr, Herbert M. Simpson, Sally Stepnes, Karen Ventura, Victor Trevino, Penny Warenko, Marie Carapezza Welch, and Pamela Wilkens-White. A very special thank you goes to Donna Ross for her extraordinary memory and immediate long-distance responses to my endless questions; to Michelle Buschner, for providing me invaluable insights about her long-term friendship with Tim as well as decades' worth of recital programs from Little Red and the Michelle Buschner School of Dance that both chronicled Tim's passion for his art form from the time he was a young boy as well as provided the crucial names and dates required of an undertaking of this kind; and to Jamey Leverett, artistic director of Rochester City Ballet and Tim's brilliant artistic heir, for sharing her thoughts about her late mentor while the two of us sat with legs kicking in the amphitheater of Spoleto's two-thousand-year-old Teatro Romano, excitedly awaiting the 9:30 p.m. performance of her protégés, who included Jim Nowakowski and my daughter, Brittany Shinay.

For my questions about the origins of the Eastman Theatre Ballet, the Eastman School of Music, and the Mercury Ballet Company, I am grateful beyond measure to the following individuals, who graced the Eastman stage over various decades with their artistry and whose vivid recall of the Theatre Annex years shed inimitable light on what made Rochester such a special cultural mecca: my first cousin, Tara/ Francia Roxin Stepenberg; Elizabeth (Bette Purvis) Power; the late Earl Kage; Katherine Wilson Whitelaw; Eleanor Gitlin Lange; and Lana Gitlin Rouff.

I have been fortunate to have access to three major sources of archival material: the Ruth T. Watanabe Special Collections and Eastman School of Music Archives, Sibley Music Library at the Eastman School of Music; the Local History and Genealogy Division, Central Library of Rochester and Monroe County; and historical newspaper pages available through the Old Fulton New York Post Cards website. For this, I am completely indebted to David Peter Coppen, Special Collections Librarian at the Sibley Music Library and Eastman School archivist, and his assistant, Matthew Colbert, who were unfailingly generous in allowing me to spend week after week examining the Eastman Theatre scrapbooks; Gabriel Pellegrino, Librarian of the Central Library of Rochester, for providing me with a wealth of old newspaper clippings; and Thomas P. Tryniski, whose Old Fulton New York Post Cards allowed me to piece together many missing pieces of the puzzle.

I am additionally indebted to the esteemed Eastman School of Music historian, author, and member of the piano faculty, Vincent Lenti, for his brilliant scholarship and for so kindly giving me a private tour of Eastman and its environs, including accompanying me up multiple flights of stairs during my quest to determine if the Eastman Theatre dressing rooms had changed at all from the 1920s (they had not!); and to my University of Rochester Warner School advisor, Professor Andrew F. Wall, whose agile mind, extraordinary motivational skills, and exceptional good form kept this project completely on track even when our discussions occasionally diverged from the manuscript to the very best of the Great White Way.

A special thank-you goes to the superb photographers whose artistry so thoroughly enriches the manuscript and who generously provided permission for use of their work: Richard Finkelstein, Ed Flores, John Hanlon, Mirka Kleemola, Christine Knoblauch, Travis Magee, Cameron McKinlay, Rosalie O'Connor, Ken Riemer, Nancy Sands, Adam Silversmith, and Jade Young. The cover photo is courtesy of Kathy Joslyn, Elizabeth Power, and Gary Wicks; the back cover photo is courtesy of Charles "Chuck" Monachino.

A huge thanks to Ellen Zuroski, where after forty-three years of friendship, I've quite decided that whether it takes place in Pop's Place, the Temple of Zeus, or the Pit, there is never better conversation to be had anywhere, and I am so grateful for the ongoing encouragement of this project; and to Bob O'Leary, a special thank-you for the great years we had together in the Assembly and for reminding me early on about the many virtues of the New York State Supplemental Budget in the funding of nonprofits. A very special thanks to veteran journalists, Stuart Low and Herbert Simpson for the generosity of their time in reading my manuscript and for their many thoughtful contributions, and to my wonderful indexer and proofreader, Maria Sullivan.

Finally, I need to express my heartfelt gratitude and love to those who are always the brightest part of my day: my husband, Dr. Gary Wicks, for his patience, superb editing and photographic talents, and for bringing me to Corsica so that I could bring this book home; my multitalented son and favorite cheerleader/critic, David Shinay, who never fails to bring a smile to my face as he urges me to eat more quinoa, go early to the library, and stay late; my daughter, Brittany Shinay, whose exquisite artistry is trumped only by her deep-down good soul and BFF companionship shared over a Shot in the Dark, Extra Hot; and my extended family, Logan, Ted, Jen, Mike, Jeff, and Ludia. Last, I want to thank my friend, Tim, who entrusted me with his story when he was no longer able to tell it. Everyone who knew Tim had a story to tell, and there are so many other artists, friends, family members, collegues, and others who should be a part of this memoir. Please know that I gave it my best, Tim, but if memory serves and some "cleanup/polishing" is required, you know I will have your back.

Wendy Roxin Wicks
January 15, 2014

INTRODUCTION

A rtists do not create in a vacuum. Rather, it is through the voices of their mentors that they characteristically find their own voices, whether by brushstroke, the shaping of a foot, or the placement of bow on string.

This was assuredly the case for the late ballet maestro Timothy M. Draper, whose early training and performances in connection with the Eastman School of Music of the University of Rochester, one of the most celebrated music schools in the world, left an indelible mark on the man who would one day transform the teaching of ballet in America and whose students would appear on the world's most fabled stages.

To understand Draper and his genius fully, we must examine the community into which he was born. That community was Rochester, New York, and although at first glance it might seem unlikely that a midsize city of fewer than four hundred thousand would be capable of creating ballet artists on a par with the great cultural capitals of the world, that is, in fact, precisely what happened.

The story unfolds on the pages of seventeen heavy, fragile, and fastidiously curated scrapbooks of early Eastman Theatre history, which date back to the years 1922–28. It is in these priceless volumes, which reside in the Sibley Music Library, that the reader truly can begin to discern the unbridled excitement that accompanied the opening of the Eastman School of Music in 1921 and the Eastman Theatre one year later, funded by the Eastman Kodak Company founder and philanthropist, George Eastman, "for the enrichment of community life."

The enthusiasm was not limited to Rochester and its environs but was palpable across the United States and indeed the globe, as every news service fed daily on the vaunted descriptions of Mr. Eastman's impeccable taste in creating what was to become the most magnificent music hall ever constructed in the United States. Only two others were larger at the time—New York's Hippodrome Theatre with its seating capacity of fifty-three hundred and the Capitol Theatre, also in Manhattan, a lavish movie theater that seated four thousand.

There is no question that the grandeur of Eastman's eponymous theater behaved a bit like a siren, compelling the greatest dancers of the day to make a stop in Rochester. Such stars as Anna Pavlova, Ruth St. Denis and Ted Shawn, and Pavley and Oukrainski were always seeking out the most glorious of venues for their popular US tours.

But it was the imagination of Enid Knapp Botsford, a precociously talented young woman, who with her mother's encouragement had left her childhood city of Rochester to pursue ballet training in New York City and London at the highest levels because it wasn't available back home, that led to the popularization of ballet training in the United States, a tradition developed some five hundred years earlier in the Italian courts. Fortunately for the legions of Rochester-trained ballet dancers who now dance, choreograph, teach, coach, judge, and direct companies worldwide, appendicitis forced Botsford to return to western New York and make the transition from award-winning, Pavlova-trained student and performer to teacher. Recognizing the potential of the Eastman Theatre to be a most spectacular backdrop for the pieces she was creating in her mind, and with a distinguished training background, she enthusiastically and successfully prevailed on Mr. Eastman in 1922 to launch a high-quality ballet school housed in the Eastman School of Music, with an eventual ballet company that would draw on the most promising of its ranks to perform on the Eastman Theatre programs. Due to concerns about the suitability of dance for official curricular endorsement by the University of Rochester (whose trustees at the time were of the Baptist faith and therefore considered the practice of dance taboo), Eastman elected to keep the ballet school and company at somewhat of an arm's length from the authorized Eastman School of Music payroll while endorsing it heartily. Mrs. Botsford thus became the head of the Eastman Theatre's first ballet school in April 1923 with six students, just seven months after the opening of the theater.[1]

Shortly thereafter, articles began appearing in local and regional newspapers about the new Eastman Theatre Ballet, featuring Enid Botsford's most talented students, most of whom were still teenagers. Rochester quickly began to gain traction as a serious center for the study of ballet, and young dancers began flocking to the Botsford studio, having attended the exciting performances taking place on the Eastman stage and themselves wanting to perform. Among these were the Misses Thelma Biracree, Olive McCue, Betty MacDonald, Evelyn Sabin, and Dorothy Saunders. Miss McCue would one day become Timothy Draper's teacher and the cofounder and codirector of the Mercury Ballet Company, in partnership with Miss Biracree, giving Tim his first exhilarating taste of performing on the Eastman Theatre stage in Tchaikovsky's holiday classic, *The Nutcracker*. Even Mrs. Botsford herself would later guide Tim in the late 1960s into the early 1970s, providing him with performance opportunities and exposure to many of the great artists of the day, who would help fuel his transition from student to professional. And herein lies the inextricable link that binds today's extraordinary dancers of the Rochester City Ballet (and previously, those of Draper Dance Theatre) to the legendary Eastman School of Music: three of Mr. Eastman's young muses, Enid Knapp Botsford, Thelma Biracree, and Olive McCue, became enamored with all that the Eastman School of Music and the Eastman Theatre had to offer in its nascent years and transmitted that passion to the next generation.

In exploring Tim's own growth as an artist and his desire to restore ballet to his hometown of Rochester "to fill a void"[2] when he finally returned to the area in the mid-1980s after having a professional career that took him all over the world, we will come to understand in almost pentimento fashion how pivotal the Eastman School's influences and those of the theater's ballet mistresses were in training dancers in Rochester to the highest professional standard and launching them into professional companies, Broadway careers, university-based dance programs, and eventually careers as independent dance teachers and mentors themselves. In 1988, one year after Draper established his own professional ballet company, Draper Dance Theatre, he created an evening of dance to pay homage to his former teacher, Miss McCue, by asking her to restage on his company one of her many works, *Emperor's Waltz*. Clearly, the same voices that had inspired the Eastman Theatre Ballet, and then the Mercury Ballet Company some twenty-five years later, would now inspire his own company long after the Eastman Theatre had originally opened its doors.

When Tim asked me to write his memoir just a little more than a year before his untimely death, we had been sitting at the long, antique farm table in Java's Café, the popular bohemian coffee shop on Gibbs Street, located right next door to the Eastman School of Music. Tim had been regaling a group of parent volunteers who had come together to bid farewell to his well-liked romantic partner of several years, the Canadian-born Randy Stringer, whose career was taking him to Richmond, Virginia. On the exterior at least, Tim was in fine form, forcing all within his midst to lean in very close to him to catch every word as he told us tales of the various onstage hijinks of his beloved Ballets Trockadero de Monte Carlo (or the Trocks, as they are affectionately known to their devotees worldwide), the fabulous comedic, all-male ballet troupe that parodies spectacularly *en pointe* the great classics of the Ballets Russes de Monte Carlo, with which he had previously performed and later served as ballet master. As we were forced to clutch our stomachs when the hilarity became too intense, I got a good look at the man who was the most transformative teacher of our children, many of whom were routinely being accepted into the very best dance companies and competitions of international renown. At this particular moment, however, we were being asked to consider the clatter and generalized pandemonium wrought by a group of muscular "mallerinas" clad in white swan tutus, bolting offstage to find anything that resembled a bucket because some food poisoning earlier in the day was wreaking a little havoc with their onstage *fouettés*. Yes, clearly Tim was in his element.

As the laughter began to die down, he turned to me and asked me what I thought of his story. I told him that it was hilarious and that everyone thought it so. He then told me that he had hundreds of these stories and that maybe it would make sense to write them down. The next thing I knew, he was asking me to write his memoir, laying everything out in some detail. I remember being perplexed by this, teasingly suggesting to him that he was perhaps a little too short in the tooth to be thinking of such activities. He laughed and then proposed that we all pose for a group shot. It wasn't until a year and a half after his death, as I was staring vacantly outside a hotel room window in one of the most beautiful parts of the world—Banff, in the Canadian Rockies—that I remembered this conversation even taking place.

I had first become acquainted with Tim Draper in 1999 after enrolling my daughter, Brittany Shinay, in his satellite school, which was located at the time on Route 31 in Perinton, east of Rochester. I certainly never imagined that he and I would ever come to know one other well, especially after an initial fleeting meeting in his downtown facility office. In somewhat bemused fashion, he took my proffered hand as I attempted to introduce him to my then nine-year-old (I didn't know that most parents of beginning students didn't do this sort of thing). That we would come to share endless laughs, phone calls, e-mails, and strategy sessions regarding the future of his company, the Rochester City Ballet, over a too-short but intense period of time I attributed in part due to our being nearly the same age and even sharing the same birthday, January 25 (his in 1954, mine in 1953). We clearly also shared a passion for his success, and that was the catalyst for our closeness. I simply enjoyed aiming for sold-out audiences whenever I could get my hands on the tickets, because I believed in him and his extraordinarily talented company. However, I knew that something more had forged such a tight kinship between us. I then began to recall that in the 1950s and 1960s, my cousins on my father's side of the family had studied ballet with Miss Thelma Biracree, one of the early Eastman Theatre Ballet stars. The first one to do so, Tara Stepenberg (née Francia Roxin) was favored with multiple balletic gifts and brains. She enjoyed singular success as a student of the legendary Miss Biracree, and then went on to study at the prestigious Boston Conservatory and the Juilliard School. She eventually provided the initial inspiration to one of the most inventive choreographers and artistic directors working today, Stephen Petronio (Petronio took his very first improv class with her), as well as a platform for others to pursue their dance passions, including the Bessie Award winner Marta Renzi and Dr. Martha Eddy, the founder and director of the Center for Kinesthetic Education.

After Mom and the other aunts saw what Tara had accomplished with Miss Biracree, the rest of us cousins were told to "suit up," and so we dutifully climbed the three flights of stairs to a small studio in the Eastman School of Music's Theatre Annex at 50 Swan Street. Miss Biracree and Miss McCue shared Annex Studio B on alternating days. Miss McCue was in residence on Mondays, Wednesdays, and Fridays, with Miss Biracree having Tuesdays, Thursdays, and Saturdays. Perhaps what bridged the space between us was Tim's and my conjoined but unspoken memories of racing down Swan Street after class on different days and in different years to devour the prized white-cream-filled, chocolate-frosted donuts at the White Tower restaurant, where the Eastman parking garage now sits at the corner of East and Swan. Sometimes I think it was just pure propinquity at work. Other times I hear the whispers of childhood that follow me just as surely as George Eastman's portrait, gazing from the mezzanine stairwell of the Eastman Theatre, tells me Tim's and my alliance was sealed beneath the Eastman marquee, which continued to list Tim's name each *Nutcracker* season for the last several years of his life. Regardless of its origins, I am grateful beyond measure that Tim reached out to me in life and in death, and that a publisher of impeccable standards and with intimate ties to the Eastman School of Music thought enough of his talent to bring this book to fruition. That Timothy Draper's world-class ballet company, the Rochester City Ballet, celebrated its twenty-fifth anniversary year during the 2012–13 season is testimony to the legacy of what began in earnest decades ago on George Eastman's stage and in his Theatre Annex studio. It is regrettable that with all of the technology that has been at our disposal over the past quarter of a century, no one videotaped each and every one of his classes and rehearsals, for each one was a jewel. In those two-hour segments, given multiple times a week for over seventeen years, we all were the beneficiaries of the intellectually agile mind this great artist brought to his craft—not just the excellent technique he was passing on to his students but the rich history of his art form and of the arts in general. His dancers were imbued with the names of the luminaries who had preceded them; the music to which they performed; the composers and the choreographers with whom they collaborated; the legendary costumers of opera and ballet; the designers of the striking sets; and the scene painters from whose canvases sometimes sprang full-length works on the stage. Essentially, Tim provided context for his young charges, who may or may not have been able to absorb all that he initially dispensed but who would one day come to appreciate the breadth of their training, which went far beyond "dance class" as most people think of the term. Although Tim Draper never knew the great Hollywood director Rouben Mamoulian, who from 1925 to 1926 directed the Eastman School of Dance and Dramatic Action, Olive McCue of the Eastman Theatre Ballet knew him very well. She ensured that intergenerationally at least, Mamoulian's wondrous fusion of all the art forms—the defining centerpiece of his short time at Eastman—was passed on for future generations to know and appreciate.

Throughout his lifetime and even beyond, Draper always inspired others to do their very best work. His artistry always drew people in. Everyone wanted to be a part of the magic, because his most talented students were winning international ballet competitions and contracts with some of the most prestigious companies in the country, including the American Ballet Theatre and the New York City Ballet. They set great store by what he did. When his inspiration was coupled with his enormous charisma, affability, and loyalty to those who were loyal to him—all of which defined his personality—he was irresistible and very well loved. He also had a heart of gold, something that not everyone realized because he didn't go about broadcasting it. It would be revealed when he gave a full scholarship, with no questions asked, to a hard-working talented dancer of limited financial means, or when he would dig into his own pocket to come up with money for studio air conditioning instead of taxing the formal budget. Of the former, if pressed, he would simply say, "You don't think I would deprive Annie/Bethany/Christine of her dance lessons, do you?" or of the latter, "You don't think I do all of this all because I plan to make money, do you?" And that would be that.

Along with a level of perfectionism that permeated every element of his being, and knowledge (that he mostly kept to himself) of ravaging heart disease, which meant he probably would die very young, came a temper that would erupt instantaneously at times, always bringing terrible hurt in its wake. He wanted—he demanded—excellence, and he would simply not tolerate any less. These aspects—his perfectionism and his temper—were his yin and yang. A funeral parlor filled to overflow capacity could mean only one thing, however—that he had engendered a most deeply felt love, devotion, and for some, forgiveness, to the extent that even ten-plus years after his death, many would be unable to speak of him without shedding a few tears.

Regarding this book's structure, it should be noted that the chapters begin with individual reminiscences offered by many of Tim's star dancers from the Draper Dance Theatre/Rochester City Ballet years, 1986–2003. These were the company elite whom Tim had hand picked and developed, from the very youngest in his troupe, invited to join only months before his death, to the veterans who had danced for him for several years. Those who knew Tim best knew that his dedication to his dancers was genuine and infinite, and that this dedication did not extend only to his precious company and the studio's professional division but to all of those he trained, whom he considered to be part of his extended family. Never having children of his own, he felt that in some way his dancers were his children. He always maintained that the strict training and discipline he provided them would serve them well in whichever career they ultimately chose to pursue, whether professional dance, law, or academia.

And so, in doing everything within my power to honor his very simple, direct, and enthusiastic entreaty to allow me to capture his life's story on paper, and in keeping with what begins and ends as a labor of love for this extraordinary man who adored and breathed dance, I hope that your life, too, will always be a joyful dance.

Sarah Lane, soloist, American Ballet Theatre. Photograph by
Rosalie O'Connor.

SARAH LANE

Tim was always an intimidating character, not only because of his body-builder look, but also his strict approach and hardcore perfectionism. He pushed us relentlessly to be better. I thought at first that his high demands came from disdain but, as I learned over the years, they came from pride. We were like his children. One day, a distraught, ranting woman with a gun came into the pharmaceutical company on the floor below. The only thing separating all of us young ballet students from this scene was an open staircase. I remember him standing guard at the top of those stairs while everyone was ushered to safety. In that moment, I realized that we were his life. He protected us, scolded us, and believed in us as his own.

Of course, there were *many* days where he just made me crazy, for instance, the day that I excused myself to change into different shoes because the old pair was too worn out. I went into the dressing room next door and, as I was tying my ribbons, I heard the music stop. It was quiet for a few seconds except for an occasional thud like something falling on the floor. I thought it was strange but finished putting on my shoes and went back into the studio. The sight when I walked in was priceless. Everyone was staring at me and Tim was sitting, red faced and angry, in the front of the room with his shoes lying in the middle of the floor. He told me that I needed to learn to change my shoes faster. He had taken his shoes off, thrown them on the floor, and put them back on two and a half times in the same time that it took me to change my shoes once.

He strived in every way to prepare us for a professional company. He used to say, "Don't you know what spring means? It's not just a sea-son. JUMP!" He would say, "I'm gonna have a Starbucks put in here because you look like you're sleeping!" He told me one day, "Dear, the lights are on but nobody's home!" With him, it was *never* okay to stop or be lazy because there were no excuses.

I don't know what possessed him to take me, instead of other, seemingly more talented girls, to the Jackson International Ballet Competition. When he told me that he was taking me, I thought, "Me? The little girl who was the slowest to pick up choreography and always scared to death before she steps out on stage? I'm not strong enough or good enough." Somehow, Tim had hope for me.

As I began preparing for the competition, I somehow became even more perfectionistic than Tim. I don't think that he really knew how to deal with me. I remember one rehearsal once we were in Jackson that, seeing my frustration with myself, he stopped me and said, as if treading on whole new ground, "It's okay. That's enough. Take a deep breath. You will be fine." I couldn't believe what I was hearing. In a way, it made me want to push even harder than before. He gave me a tiny stuffed animal as a good-luck present when I made it past the final cut. I saw how much he cared and how happy it made him that I had gotten to that point, and I didn't want to disappoint him. For everything he had given me over the years, he deserved to have me do my best. And suddenly, I believed that I *could*, if I just had courage. I ended up winning the highest medal in that competition. Tim gave me the experience that taught me to overcome obstacles. He had higher hopes for me than I had for myself. He wanted me to audition for the American Ballet Theatre, but I couldn't imagine one of the best companies in the world ever being interested in me. Now here I am, a soloist with ABT. Tim never saw my performances with the company, but he did see my first performance with the ABT Studio Company right before he passed away. I was doing a lead in all three ballets that night. I'll never forget the look on his face afterward. He was beaming. That was the biggest reward I could have ever received. I've held that moment close to my heart ever since.

Sarah Lane is a soloist with American Ballet Theatre. She was the ballet double for Natalie Portman in the 2010 film *The Black Swan*. When Sarah won the silver medal at Jackson, Tim reportedly jumped up and down on his bed for joy.

1

SILENCED SLIPPERS

They arrived in various ways on that frigid, uncharacteristically brilliant Rochester, New York morning of February 26, 2003. Some were tucked tightly under an arm; some revealed themselves from a purse not quite large enough to do the transport justice; some were packed in heavy, black drawstring plastic bags; some were nervously held in their owners' hands or, for the youngest among them, in the hands of their mothers. With the exception of the ballet slippers presented by Tim's devoted male students, all were meticulously wrapped with satin ribbons that maybe only days or months earlier had been sewn with the quiet pride or utter frustration that only a new pair of *pointe* shoes can command. The ribbons (if no longer the shoes) were perfect—unnoticeably burned at each end to prevent fraying, sewn into the shoes with many stitches to prevent a dangerous studio or on-stage unraveling. Some of the shoes were inscribed in thin marker with the names of their owners' favorite roles; others were plain, awaiting with anticipation the solos or principal roles that relentless hours at the barre might or might not produce. The effect was perfect. Tim would have expected no less. Although he wasn't going to be conducting any inspections on this particular day, unpleasant memories of arched eyebrows when this or that dancer's tights were beginning to fray were never too far from anyone's thoughts. No, there wouldn't be any admonitions on this day, but how grateful each red-eyed dancer would have been to sustain a full-out Timothy Draper diatribe over the worn tights or mangy ribbons rather than stand in line to say good-bye to the man who had been as much a second father to them as ballet teacher, the man who had the uncanny knack of peering into a dancer's soul and limbs and turning the very best of them into professional dancers. Most of them on this day were "still cooking," still learning, as Tim's alter ego, protégée, and elegant taskmistress Jamey Leverett, was so fond of saying. The lucky ones (or maybe the most unlucky because they had been with him the longest) were off to larger venues and wouldn't have to be reminded on a daily basis of how absent Tim was from the very place that he had created. "Please," they silently implored, "please let Tim give me just one more correction, just one more face, just one more roll of his eyes. Just don't make me stand here saying goodbye to him. No one else ever believed in me the way he believed in me." And with that, twenty-three single *pointe* shoes, one from each member of his beloved professional division, his elite, who had come to pay their unnatural final respects on the side of a serenely beautiful hill that would have been the perfect setting for *Swan Lake* had it not been a cemetery, emerged from their wrappings to be placed on the casket of the man, the artistic genius, the beloved teacher—whose body had given out too soon, at the age of forty-nine.

For those closest to Tim, news of his death, though still a horrific shock, was not completely unexpected. Although he looked on the exterior to be a vibrant, perfectly sculpted athlete, Tim and only a few others knew that his heart was deteriorating, that he was on a wait list for a transplant, that he was diabetic, and that at various times, his doctors had given him only "months to live." He knew that he needed to accomplish his life's work sooner than later. In the five years leading up to his death, it seemed that the worldwide journeys he so enjoyed had begun to take place at an accelerated rate, as did his regular trips to New York City, where he would visit with friends and colleagues and take in the various performances of his blossoming alumni. It was, in fact, customary for Tim to leave town each year after one of his signature works, Tchaikovsky's *Nutcracker*, had been put to bed, particularly in the years when his company, the Rochester City Ballet, collaborated with the renowned Rochester Philharmonic Orchestra for six performances over Thanksgiving weekend. Thus, it came as no surprise to anyone that on completion of what was to be his last "Nut" in December 2002, he was prepared to rejuvenate himself at Lincoln Center and environs, where usually a few of his protégés were performing at the time (Aesha Ash at New York City Ballet; Kristi Boone, Sari Ostrum, and Sarah Lane at American Ballet Theatre). What in retrospect did strike a few intimates as a particularly bad omen was his failure to show up at the *Nutcracker* cast party previous to his leave-taking, traditionally celebrated on the Sunday night following the final performance. Although it was never Tim's style to address the gathering in any type of formal, drawn-out way, his high-profile attendance was not only expected at the celebratory event, but for the younger dancers moving up, a photo, autograph, or kind word from the artistic director was an endorsement of the highest order. The official word that circulated as the evening went on was that Tim was worn out from the rigors of directing six performances in three days. Although to some degree this might have been true, not everyone in his inner circle privately concurred with this assessment. First, there had been a particularly acerbic and debilitating blowup just days earlier during a last-minute add-on Friday night rehearsal for his company members. The dancers resented the extra rehearsal because they had been rehearsing for two weeks straight without a single night off and decidedly felt that they needed time to tend to the rest of their lives. Tim didn't quite view this in the same light. He felt that if he was willing to give up his Friday evening to help them to be the best they could possibly be, then they should be grateful for his attention and arrive with thanks. When the students individually and as a group (still only teenagers, it should be noted) let out their frustrations in class, Tim became highly critical of their collective work ethic. Compounding this, various studio bystanders (the moms), many of whom over the years had managed to be "low-maintenance" relative to their children's dance training, momentarily forgot this unspoken code of support and questioned him over the exclusion of certain key cast members from a postperformance soirée. Tim was starting to feel drained—mentally, physically, and emotionally—and he didn't hesitate to communicate this to anyone who would listen. A few e-mails went back and forth, in which he questioned whether he even wanted to continue developing a company that didn't seem to appreciate him and ventured so far as to say that he might find it more gratifying to instruct dancers of a lower level. Entreaties were made to arrest this train of thought and to assure him that, after a proper vacation and well-earned rest, he would return to continue to develop the artistry of his professional division and steward the company as he had always done.

He never returned. As expected, his travels took him to New York in December as well as to Switzerland in January, to accompany one of his dancers and her mother to the Prix de Lausanne International Ballet Competition. As days turned into weeks, however, and there were fewer and fewer signs of his return, something began to feel askew. Surely, someone had heard from him directly about his whereabouts, which undoubtedly included all of the travel details for which people were hungering. And those e-mails did suggest clearly that he was over his funk and ready to embrace his life's work and loved ones

with the zest for which he was known. However, it was unsettling not
to see him walk jauntily into the studio and up the stairs after the per-
functory two to three weeks' rest. No explanations as to his absence
seemed genuinely to fit. A few weeks later, on Monday, February 17,
a call came from the main office for all members of the professional
division to attend an emergency meeting at the studio, but no one was
expecting catastrophic news. Tim had been planning to meet up with
his dancers along with his associate artistic director, Jamey Leverett,
in New York City shortly thereafter to watch several of them perform
in Jamey's *Push and Pull,* part of her prize for winning the prestigious
New Choreographers on Point: Ballet Builders honor. Twice within
two years, Jamey's works had been recognized nationally. On arriving at the studio, dancers and parents were told to go upstairs to the
main studio to await an announcement, and the gut-wrenching scene
that followed will be forever seared in the memories of everyone in
attendance that day. Had it not been for the extraordinary comfort
that Jamey immediately gave to her dancers, it is hard to fathom how
they would have been able to leave the studio in one piece. In the days
that followed, much had to be decided—among other things, whether
or not the dancers would go forward with their plans to perform in
New York City. Jamey left the decision entirely up to her dancers who,
to a person, thought that this was what Tim would have wanted. It
meant that they would be gone during the normal period of funeral
and burial, but Tim's mother and entire family graciously allowed both
to be delayed until the group could return. The trip thus went on as
scheduled. Unfortunately, it was never far from anyone's mind that
instead of being able to enjoy Tim's celebratory homecoming in the
cultural center of the universe, it would be his body coming home in
a wooden box. In an irony, the coffin was scheduled to arrive at JFK
Airport at the very hour the dancers would be warming up on the stage
of the Florence Gould Hall of the French Institute Alliance Française.

Following the return home from what had turned out to be a wet-
eyed but choreographic triumph for Leverett, calling hours and the
memorial service were filled to capacity in the Diplomat Hotel not far
from Holy Sepulchre Cemetery, where Tim would be laid to rest. The
company's executive director, Kathy Ertsgaard, put on a brave face to
give a heartfelt eulogy interspersed with a little humor to help ease the
pain, and Tim's beloved niece, Melanie Conradt, whose young daughter, Darbi, had performed in his last *Nutcracker,* spoke for the family
in a very moving tribute. Flowers and condolences poured in from all

over the world, including from the American Ballet Theatre, Steps on Broadway, Garth Fagan, the Ukrainian government (which had hosted Tim and his young protégé, Jim Nowakowski, just months earlier), and from the national dance media. It was obvious that Tim Draper had left his mark on the dance world at the very highest level and that that select community was now stunned and saddened to learn that he would no longer be a part of it. In his brief forty-nine years, he had done what perhaps only George Balanchine had done before him— change the manner in which ballet was being taught in America. No longer would the most gifted dancers—those selected for inclusion in the most coveted companies—be warming up audiences at age twenty-one. Through Tim's immense talent as a ballet teacher, his dancers were doing the same but at a much younger age, not unlike the baby ballerinas of the Ballets Russes. He was essentially lengthening their careers on the front end by five or six precious years, extremely important for the short performance life of a dancer. And the world had just begun to take notice.

Jonathan Davidsson, soloist, Estonian National Ballet, Siegfried Variation, 2012 Helsinki International Ballet Competition. Photograph by Mirka Kleemola.

JONATHAN DAVIDSSON

To say that Tim Draper had a monumental impact on all students that took class from him is an understatement. He was unlike anyone else—modest and painfully shy at times, but also blunt and nearly offensive in his countless remarks during class. Not only did he guide us to become better dancers but he also stressed the importance of education.

I remember one of his infamous two-hour classes in the big front studio at the Goodman location. Tim emphasized the importance of shaping our feet in *tendu devant*. Not only should the feet point fully forward but the line also should extend outward, which some people may refer to as "winging." This might seem like an ordinary correction that an absentminded teenager would easily forget. However, it was the way in which Tim delivered his corrections that made them stick like glue in the back of our minds. With the signature look of his raised eyebrow and smirk, the man we all loved stressed the importance of a curvaceously shaped line. "This is a time where you definitely do not want to be straight. (long pause) I never had a problem with that." Then he slowly walked over to the CD player as if nothing had happened, perhaps amused as to whether or not some of the younger ones understood his joke. This was just one of the many memorable and funny ways in which Tim caught our attention and always maintained our full focus, even when the class was running thirty minutes over time.

I couldn't help feeling respect and love for Tim. However, I also remember being very intimidated and sometimes scared of him, which may have been due partly to his powerful stature. But he gave us amusing nicknames, which made us laugh and feel more comfortable. Just at the right time and age, he made me realize how vital it is for male dancers to build upper-body strength for partnering. I was understudying dolls for *Nutcracker* and struggled even with some of the relatively easy lifts. Tim was nice and joked around while working with us, but he made me feel a bit scrawny, which was very embarrassing among a large group of pretty girls. After the rehearsal, he showed me some exercises and directed me to start working out. He hinted that one day, he would like to see me do the "Snow" *pas de deux* from the *Nutcracker*. He made me want to fight. He knew that I could not handle it that my teacher called me weak. Soon after, I made my dad help me get workout equipment for our home. For the next several years, I would hit that bench press religiously every day after coming home from dance. And sure enough, during my senior year of high school, I was able to do the Prince in Tim's version of *Cinderella*, which had lots of challenging partnering and big lifts. The following year, I danced the "Snow" *pas de deux*. Tim planned and pushed me toward these roles several years in advance. At the time, I might not have understood the extent to which he was building me, but he knew how to encourage me to strive for my fullest potential.

During some classes, Tim's corrections turned into speeches that could last for ten minutes. On top of requiring us to be fully disciplined and dedicated dancers, Tim wanted wholesome artists with perspective. His Draper Center required that we maintain a satisfactory GPA in academics. He once told us that his education while touring and dancing abroad was different. He visited archeological sites and museums and encouraged us to pay attention in our academic classrooms and in society. True artists benefit from acquiring knowledge and understanding of the world around us, which is essential in order to deliver believable performances.

Last, there was another correction that I will never forget. Tim frequently told me that my leg was not turned out in arabesque. Some of us were aware of the gravity of his health condition. Our beloved teacher was a bit of a medical miracle and told us that on the basis of his heart values, his doctor was surprised that Tim could even walk up a flight of stairs. Being fed up with reiterating the same correction about my turned-in leg, Tim once said something to this effect: "You know, Jonathan, my doctor says that I may not have very long to live. I would like to see you turn out that back leg now, since I will not be around forever." The light approach and humor that Tim showed to the seriousness of his disease defined him. He was an optimistic, thankful, and genuine person with an extremely generous heart and love for ballet. He sure knew how to catch the full attention of a group of teenagers whose minds meandered. He understood us and believed in us. Tim was extremely special.

Jonathan Davidsson was born in Göteburg, Sweden, and trained at the Royal Swedish Ballet School, the Timothy M. Draper Center for Dance Education in Rochester, New York, and at the Kirov Academy of Ballet in Washington, DC. He danced with the Rochester City Ballet and the Houston Ballet before joining the National Ballet of Canada's corps de ballet in 2012 and the Estonian National Ballet in 2013. When Jamey Leverett created the ballet *Pedestal* as a lasting tribute to her late teacher and mentor, she asked Jonathan to portray Tim. Jonathan turned in a heartfelt performance opposite Sari Ostrum, who portrayed Jamey.

BORN INTO ROCHESTER'S
ILLUSTRIOUS DANCE TRADITION

Timothy Michael Draper was born at St. Mary's Hospital on January 25, 1954, the fourth of five children and third son of Hazel and Lionel E. Draper of 162 Cady Street in the southwest quadrant of Rochester, New York. He was not obviously predisposed at birth to a career in the performing arts. Notwithstanding the familial genes that had propelled his great-uncle, Kenny Draper, into the spotlight as a dancer on the vaudeville circuit throughout the United States,[1] the study of ballet was assuredly not the typical career of choice for boys during this era. Sons in mid-fifties America were normally career scripted for something of a more stable, traditional nature. This would have been especially true for a boy growing up in the midsize, conservative Upstate New York city of Rochester, the thirty-second-largest city in the United States, according to the 1950 US Census. The virtues of government service, engineering, law, medicine, and the skilled trades, were routinely promoted to boys at school, at home, and in the media. Those who did gravitate toward the arts, and dance in particular, typically did so either by having unusually sensitive, broad-minded parents willing and eager to support their children in whichever areas they expressed an interest—popular or not—or in the more time-honored tradition of "accompanying sis to dance class" and then sticking around to give it a personal whirl.

On the other hand, Rochester, being the beneficiary of the cultural largesse of Kodak's founding father, industrialist, and patron saint of the arts, George Eastman, had been singularly transformed into a world-class cultural center on a par with any of the major metropolitan cities around the globe. Thus, by the 1950s, with the most serious students of music characteristically auditioning for one of the "big three"—that is, Juilliard, Curtis, or Eastman—it would not have been unthinkable for a boy to become interested in a cultural pursuit in this environment, anomalous as that might at first appear.

That the young Tim Draper would one day inherit this magnificent pedigree, refine it, and build it to a level that would win the approbation of the world stage also revealed a certain symmetry that would have been no surprise to those who had been a part of Rochester's rich dance heritage from its beginnings. One who knew it well and who had a significant share in that history was Earl Kage, head of camera research for Eastman Kodak Company, World War II veteran, renowned artist, collector, and professional dancer (or as a local journalist once described him, a "one-man cultural institution")[2] who was proud to serve on Tim's Rochester City Ballet board of directors for several years during the 1990s and as an honorary board member for the rest of his life. Kage was only a child when he first became enamored of dance after seeing two of the most popular dancers of the day, the legendary Ruth St. Denis and Ted Shawn, perform at the Eastman Theatre in Rochester. Not long afterward, he became enthusiastically involved with a group of men and women, who in addition to the aforementioned Misses Botsford, Biracree, and McCue, included Elizabeth "Betty" Purvis, a School of American Ballet talent of impeccable technique who had been asked by the very young George Balanchine to join his new company, the New York City Ballet. Others in the group included Earl's long-time partner, Hamilton "Bud" Driggs; Dorothy Toland and her cousins, Peter and Debbie Boneham; Patricia and Jeanne Thomas; Rhoda Young; Paulette Maltalto; Sonja Koch; Marilyn Pike; Sue Wallenhaupt; and the young Katherine Wilson. They and others of Earl's generation always will be known as the custodians of this Rochester dance legacy. When adding to this list the elegant Kathleen Crofton (who had studied with Olga Preobrajenska, danced for Anna Pavlova, and later opened the Ballet Center of Buffalo on the recommendation of Alicia Markova of the Ballets Russes); Bronislava Nijinska, the sister of the famous Vaslav Nijinsky, who had danced with the Imperial Ballet of St. Petersburg and the Ballets Russes and later came to Buffalo; and Rudolf Nureyev, who taught at Crofton's request, it is clear that western New York enjoyed its full measure of balletic prestige throughout the early to middle decades of the twentieth century.

The vivid recollections of Earl Kage and Betty Purvis as well as of the Misses Biracree and McCue provide insight into the environment in which Tim Draper came of age. Understanding the contributions of the central figures who defined the brilliance of those associated with Eastman Theatre dance during that heady period makes it easy to see how their greatness presaged Tim's own and steered him on a path that would one day win him the highest possible accolades.

Enid Knapp Botsford's role in bringing ballet to Rochester cannot be overestimated, and although exceedingly well documented by herself and others, most recently by such esteemed former students of hers as Donna Schoenherr and Mary M. Wilson, her story will find a little more indulgence here.

Mrs. Botsford, or "Botsy," as she was known to her close acquaintances, was born with all of the advantages of being the daughter of a Boston opera singer, who passed on to her a deep-seated love of the arts, and a wealthy business executive, who not only provided the means to fuel her artistic development but also taught her the importance of being savvy when asking for what she wanted. Her mother in particular appears to have encouraged her child in ballet; as an opera singer, Enid's mother understood how indispensable the classical style of dance was to her own art form. Realizing that there was no ballet instruction available to Rochesterians a little over a century ago, the young Miss Knapp was accompanied by her mother to New York City. where she was able to study at the Metropolitan Opera House for several years with Luigi Albertieri, a famous pupil of the celebrated Enrico Cecchetti, the Italian ballet artist who created a method of technique utilized the world over. At the Met, Enid met and performed with many of the great dancers of the age, including Anna Pavlova and Michel Fokine, studying with the former in London after winning the scholarship that bore Pavlova's name.

As mentioned earlier, illness forced Enid return to her hometown of Rochester, and thus begins what is to become a familiar refrain in this book: A talented ballet dancer leaves a promising performance career after suffering illness or injury, then launches a top-tier school in order to eliminate, or at least mitigate, the need for gifted young students to leave home in order to obtain quality instruction. From the beginning, as evidenced by the plethora of articles in local and national newspapers, it is fair to say that Enid's new ballet company, Eastman Theatre Ballet—the first professional ballet company in the United States—was embraced by the community and enjoyed significant success. The company appeared frequently in concert over the next several years, featuring various emerging dancers in pieces that she normally would have choreographed herself or, occasionally, with a colleague. The Eastman Theatre was used primarily as an upscale movie house in its earliest years,[3] featuring the latest vehicles for such silent-screen stars as Mary Pickford, Charlie Chaplin, and Douglas Fairbanks. The choreographed works provided delightful divertissements that closely paralleled the action on screen or aligned with other performances on the program for a given evening or matinee. These programs normally might have included a new full-length feature film, works by the Eastman Theatre Orchestra (later to become the Rochester Philharmonic Orchestra), an operatic work, and the famed organ-concert exit music.

Clearly, it was an exhilarating time for the arts in Rochester. As Enid (by now Mrs. Botsford) described it, many fabulous collaborations and experiments flourished or were abandoned during the frenzied early 1920s, with people literally signing on and off within months as new opportunities came along.

Without question, Mrs. Botsford's entire ballet adventure was enthusiastically received and launched the careers of several of her students/company members. It is well documented that at one point she was teaching at least one hundred students, although there are suggestions that the number was actually closer to two hundred.

Mrs. Botsford's passion for ballet pedagogy and performance clearly seemed matched by Mr. Eastman's own. His fervent foray into the areas of dance and opera in response to their European allure led to his ebullient launch of the Eastman School of Dance and Dramatic Action in 1925. The first inkling that Mr. Eastman even valued dance as an art form was revealed through his inclusion of the Swedish interpretive dancer Ester Gustafson on the program of his historic Eastman Theatre premiere on September 4, 1922.[4] His inclusion of her name next to the names of the stars in the silent adventure film *The Prisoner of Zenda*, to celebrate the grand opening of the splendid theater, signaled to the thousands of patrons in attendance that day that dance would hold an important place in Mr. Eastman's cultural playbook. Miss Gustafson's performance didn't necessarily delight everyone in attendance: "The dancer appealed to those who take their dancing seriously," tactfully stated the New York City–based *Musical Leader Review*.[5] Nonetheless, it is significant that she was featured because three years later in 1925, she would be (at least briefly) one of the two new codirectors of the dance program at the Eastman School of Dance and Dramatic Action. In August of that same year, at Rouben Mamoulian's urging, Martha Graham would become the other codirector,

while continuing part time in New York City with other professional
responsibilities. It is clear that Mr. Eastman was building a faculty and
enterprise of impeccable standards, and had high hopes for its success.

To ensure that the new Eastman School of Dance and Dramatic
Action had adequate space, Mr. Eastman built a five-story building on
the east side of Swan Street, just steps behind the Eastman Theatre.
The new building was named the Eastman Theatre Annex. It contained a ground-floor parking garage for the convenience of the Eastman executives, a palatial ballet studio on the fifth floor for ensemble
work with many windows to allow in natural light, a fourth-floor ballet
studio (eventually relocated to the third floor), and studios on other
levels for operatic and orchestral rehearsals, theatrical set design and
construction, costuming, and storage. And between 1923 and 1926,
the Eastman Theatre Ballet and Eastman Opera Company flourished,
replete with costumes, lighting, and sets unrivaled in their day to create a host of memorable performances that added immeasurably to
the Theatre's concert program.

From the excellent scholarship of the Eastman School professor of
piano and historian Vincent Lenti, we know that the Graham appointment was a marvelous adventure of sorts. One can sense the playful
allure of the woman who quite captivated most, if not all, of her students, when recalling her time in Rochester many years later:

> Ester Gustafson, the teacher who preceded me in Rochester, was what
> was then called a nature dancer, emphasizing all that was natural in
> movement, in clothes, very restrained and proper, no makeup to
> speak of. She gave the impression that she thought eyeliner was an
> instrument of the devil. I entered my first class in clinging red silk
> kimono, with a long slit up each leg, in full makeup, my hair pulled
> back severely yet dramatically. The students, who were used to their
> Swedish teacher's more down-to-earth approach, were in a state of
> shock after the class.[6]

Apparently, behind-the-scene conflicts between Rouben Mamoulian and Enid Botsford led to Mamoulian's recruitment of Graham to
Rochester and the gradual reduction of Mrs. Botsford's influence. It
is regrettable that not a great deal remains of recorded history of the
day-to-day instructional activities that took place during the Gustafson-
Graham period. We do know that performances took place regularly
and that Graham's influence on her students was profound. At least
three of her dancers seemingly worshiped her, referring to her in

rapturous tones as "Miss Martha," and ultimately chose to follow her to New York City. Many other students also were ready to eschew the "natural" look for something far more glamorous.

As quickly as the Eastman School of Dance and Dramatic Action began during those heady times, when money was being spent at a prodigious rate and a mood permeated the institution that anything was possible, success evaporated seemingly overnight with the departures of all three—Mamoulian, Graham, and Botsford—who left within weeks of each other for professional advancement of various kinds.

Mamoulian left for Broadway when he felt his wings beginning to be clipped over his highly ambitious and expensive undertakings (even George Eastman's largesse apparently had its limits). Graham was about to spread her own wings with the formation of a new company.

Documentation suggests that Graham's departure may have been the result of three simultaneous, but independent factors: a falling out with the Eastman School's music director, Dr. Howard Hanson, who had arrived in 1924; a passionate desire to return full time to New York and begin her own company; and some indignation over the fact that local concertgoers didn't always signal an appreciation for her particular style of dance. Regardless, this undoubtedly was the best professional move Graham could make. New York audiences were wildly enthusiastic about her early work, which emanated from "living and working out of a tiny Carnegie Hall studio in midtown Manhattan." She would go on to be considered "one of the greatest artists of the 20th century."[7]

In the case of Mrs. Botsford's departure, it has been suggested that her issues with Mamoulian had to do with the fact that the school program she had created and financed independently had become so successful that he wanted a portion of the revenues to help subsidize his own less financially successful program. Mamoulian's gradual marginalization of Mrs. Botsford is very much in evidence. She ceases to be listed as director of the Eastman Theatre Ballet for the spring 1925 programs, after Mamoulian was given control of the Eastman School of Dance and Dramatic Action. Eventually, an announcement was made that her school would be absorbed into the Eastman School of Dance and Drama Action and that the Eastman Theatre Ballet would give its last performances in 1926.[8]

Mrs. Botsford left Eastman in 1925 with several of her advanced students to run a school bearing her name, an institution that remains in existence in the Rochester region today. It appears that she advocated tirelessly on behalf of her students for their move into professional careers, routinely publicizing their upcoming auditions and various professional successes. Proof of her longevity is that Tim Draper took class with her, along with many of his peers in the dance world, from the late 1960s into the early 1970s. By then she had acquired all forms of professional capital over a long career as well as the financial resources to be able to bring to Rochester artists of international repute. In addition, she always made special arrangements to include her own students in master classes, receptions, and even opportunities to perform alongside these great artists. "She worked to build long lasting relationships with these international companies to provide her students the benefits of influence and connections in the dance world beyond Rochester."[9]

During the 1920s, however, a period of frenetic cultural awakening, two of Mrs. Botsford's original students, Thelma Biracree and Olive McCue, emerged. These young dancers, along with their teacher, defined and essentially become synonymous with Rochester, New York's rich ballet dance idiom over the next half a century or longer. Biracree and McCue cofounded the Mercury Ballet Company in 1950 and codirected the company for the next six years. Eventually, the Misses Botsford, Biracree, and McCue were known as premier ballet instructors, whose students and students' students would bring them national and international fame.

It is indeed possible that not even Mr. Eastman could have envisioned the scores of professional dancers who would one day emerge from his Swan Street Theatre Annex. Nor could he have foreseen the breadth of the classical training provided by these early legends, who built a dance community of the highest caliber for the delight of Rochester audiences and those around the world. During the mid-1960s, for example, over forty years after she had first performed on the stage of the Eastman Theatre, Miss McCue, a woman of high style and flaming red hair, who would "hold herself like a queen even without taking a single step," directed a *Nutcracker* that included the young Tim Draper.

☙

When asked about what distinguished Thelma Biracree from the other dancers of the Eastman Theatre Ballet, Betty Purvis had a simple response: "Thelma was the best." When the Eastman Theatre opened, according to the stories that Miss Biracree passed on to Betty, "it was

Eastman Theatre Ballet, circa 1922. Author's collection.

run like Radio City," more than suitable for the lofty mission of bringing high-quality ballet to the community. The soon-to-be-famous Hollywood director George Cukor was hired to direct one of the stage
shows. "In the early 1920s, he [Cukor] directed a summer stock company in Rochester, New York, in which Bette Davis and Robert Mont-
gomery began their careers."[10] At one point, Miss Biracree found
out that the male dancers were being paid more than the girls. Not
one to let this slight go unnoticed, she corralled the members of her
gender in the wings and just waited. The stage manager called out
"Girls—you're on!" and nothing happened. He gave a louder call,
and again, nothing happened. Miss Biracree then instructed the girls
that they would not be appearing unless they were paid as much as
the boys. The theater director then got involved, and in a singular
impressive coup for Miss Biracree, equal pay was granted. Years later,
when attending a Hollywood party, she noticed Mr. Cukor standing
across the room. Never one to shy away from a little good-hearted
mischief, she went up to him and asked him if he might remember
her. His response: "I remember you, Miss Bearcat!" and they both
shared a good laugh. Young female dancers confronting similar
discrimination in pay today at various nonunion dance companies
might be well advised to apply some of that "Biracree Pluck" to correct this inequality.

In the spring of 1926, Biracree was invited by codirector Martha Graham to perform in *Flute of Krishna*, with the classmates Evelyn Sabin, Betty MacDonald, and Susanne Vacanti, which was captured by Eastman Kodak's laboratory on experimental color motion-picture film.[11] Following this success, "Miss Martha" invited Biracree, Sabin, and MacDonald to New York to become a part of her first company. "At New York's 48th Street Theater on April 18, 1926, the group made its world premiere debut as 'Martha Graham and Dance Group,' performing in Graham's first independent concert as a choreographer." It was by all measures regarded as a triumphant success, with the performance receiving fine reviews.

In 1927, Miss Biracree returned home to open her own school, the Thelma Biracree School of Ballet, in association with the Eastman School of Music, to train the next generation of artists while continuing her own performance career. The Eastman School of Music's director, Howard Hanson, also prevailed on her during this period to provide choreography and performers for productions requested by the Eastman Opera Department. In these productions, she applied the sophisticated knowledge of lighting gels, musical scores, and costumes that she had acquired during her early years with the Eastman Theatre Ballet. At the same time, she continued her work as a dancer and choreographic assistant to Graham in New York City and also as a soloist in Paris at the Gaumont-Palace; it appears that the arrangement worked out very well for all parties. In exchange for rent-free studio space in a most sumptuous location, Miss Biracree not only provided Mr. Hanson with the dancers required for his school's various productions but also gave her own young dancers the essential performance experience needed for their professional careers.

In 1931, she married Dr. Karl Schnepel in the Church of the Reformation at 116 North Chestnut Street in Rochester.[12] That same year, she created ballets to music by American composers for the first Festival of American Music in Rochester; she choreographed and danced for the Festival for the next two decades. She also served as the regional representative for the Lincoln Kirstein–George Balanchine School of American Ballet.

Her studio, Studio B, was located on the third floor of the Theatre Annex, a somewhat challenging climb for those who might have preferred elevators. As Betty Purvis drolly noted, "The hike upstairs was good for the mothers and the daughters!" No wonder those White Tower donuts were consumed furiously after each class! The studio itself, used by Miss Biracree and later by Tim Draper's teacher, Miss McCue, was a relatively small affair, furnished with the traditional mirrored walls and double barres, boxes of rosin in the corners, a chair or two in the center for demonstrating, a chair for the teacher, and space on the left side of the room for the grand piano for Millie Clair to provide the musical accompaniment at Miss Biracree's direction. Adjoining the studio was a changing room for the students, where newspaper articles were frequently posted about current and past students' successes. Often stationed outside the studio was Miss Biracree's other assistant, Earl Kage, who performed double duty as the collector of class fees. According to both Earl Kage and Betty Purvis, what appears to have distinguished Miss Biracree from her peers in this still highly evolving ballet phenomenon in Rochester was her willingness to stretch herself and her students, moving them sometimes in directions away from the works of the iconic classical choreographer Marius Petipa in favor of developing her own choreography to showcase the various talents of her students. Eleanor Gitlin Lange, one of Miss Biracree's students from the 1950s who went on to become a very fine instructor in her own right, has suggested that Graham's influence was very pivotal in this sense. Lange stated, "It is my personal feeling, that since she [Miss Biracree] was such an intelligent woman and a wonderfully creative artist, she instinctively took the 'new dance freedoms' that Graham introduced, later utilizing some aspects of them in her choreography, albeit subtly. If you compare her with Olive McCue, you will find that McCue's choreography was more traditional whereas Biracree had the flow."

There is little question that although Miss Biracree was always willing to experiment with all elements of her art form, her love of classical ballet remained resolute. All her life, she kept a program autographed by the legendary Pavlova, who danced in Rochester at the Convention Hall, now the home of the Geva Theatre, and in the Eastman Theatre. Miss Biracree's young charges were always invested with traditionally scripted ballet instruction, replete with strong classical technique. However, it appears that she did not feel so chained philosophically to this approach relative to the staging of performances as teachers of this era typically did.

Betty Purvis recalled that another of Biracree's defining characteristics was that she wanted her students trained in the correct manner from the very beginning (a teaching method that Tim adopted later on). Biracree thus started her students at a very young age, because mothers were asking her to and because she felt that if she made them wait until the traditional age of seven or eight (the age recommended by ballet instructors of that generation), she would have to fix all of their bad habits. Although Tim's own teacher, Olive McCue, insisted that children come to her only after they had reached the age of eight, he did not allow his young dancers to participate in summer programs at other schools, regardless of those schools' prestige, until after they had completed their sophomore year in high school. He knew that directors of elite schools around the country allowed their students time off in the summer, usually before their own summer programs began, to do "intensives" away from home starting at age nine or ten. Tim, however, believed that his dancers would pick up all kinds of bad habits, which he would then have to spend the next several months fixing. He felt that by the time his students were in their teens, their technique would be secure, and they could benefit from the extraordinary experience of studying with legendary artists and take advantage of the myriad opportunities and connections they could make.

It has been said that Thelma Biracree's landing of Betty Purvis "was a coup" and further explains the depth of dance talent that has always resided in western New York State. Born in Westfield, New Jersey in 1924, Purvis began dancing at the age of five at the Elsa Heilick School of Dance. When she was a senior in high school during the war year of 1942, her father asked her what she might wish to do next. She was unsure. Her mother mentioned that she had heard some good things about a dance school that had opened in New York City just eight years earlier, the School of American Ballet (SAB), run by an emerging Russian choreographer, George Balanchine, and the philanthropist Lincoln Kirstein. Although only three weeks of the regular winter curriculum were left when Purvis's mother called to inquire about the prospect of enrolling her daughter, the school told her to bring her in. Betty therefore commenced her studies during the remaining three weeks of the term, commuting to New York six days a week. After leaving for a summer job to which she had previously committed, she enrolled for the upcoming fall, winter, and summer terms, eventually staying a few years longer, studying with such legendary figures as Anatole Obukhov, who taught ballet and variations (particularly *Le Corsaire*); Muriel Stuart, who had danced with Anna Pavlova and taught ballet and modern; Pierre Vladimiroff, who taught ballet and character (mazurka, polonaise, and waltz); Kyle Blanc; and the great Russian star Alexandra Danilova, who taught her eager students two variations from *Swan Lake*. Purvis recalls Madame Danilova giving these precise instructions to her class about performing: "You entered, you danced, you bowed, and you exited." Madame was also particularly fond of saying, "Don't be afraid to fell [*sic*]!" Whatever the grammatical flaws in this ballet icon's second language, surely no student could miss the passion that to this day remains seemingly at the heart of New York City Ballet's appeal—its stars' willingness to push themselves so far that the thought of an onstage fall is never distant from the minds of the audience. Betty recalls truly loving SAB during those years, and how could she not? Notable among her classmates were Patricia Wilde, Marie-Jeanne, Yvonne Patterson, and Herbert Bliss.

In 1944, a very young promising choreographer, George Balanchine, hand-picked a small group of eight to ten students, including Purvis, to go on a three-month tour. It was entitled American Ballet Caravan (following the 1941 merger of American Ballet and Ballet Caravan). The troupe performed at such venues as the Mexico City Opera Company. After this highly successful tour, Balanchine asked Purvis to join his new ballet company, New York City Ballet, at New York's City Center. Marrying a Kodak engineer held more allure, but Betty did make inquiries as to the best ballet teacher in Rochester, and Thelma Biracree was recommended to her. Prior to leaving for Rochester, though, Betty was invited to audition for a touring company of *Rosalind* and thus left for the South Pacific on Christmas Day, 1945, for six months. Her tour included San Francisco for three weeks, then on to Manila, Okinawa (where she performed in a makeshift theater), Tokyo, Osana, and Agoya.

In September 1946, only twenty-two at the time, Purvis landed in Rochester. She promptly sought out Thelma Biracree, and the arrangements were made. Miss Biracree had told her to come before her afternoon class so that the two of them could talk. Biracree told Purvis that although she didn't have a teaching position available at the time, she might in the future. In no way daunted, Betty sought out a position at Eastman Kodak Company and took ballet class at the conclusion of the workday. She felt fortunate to be given an office job instead of the more customary desk job (a distinction Kodak employed at the time), because the person interviewing her asked her if she knew a dancer named Mary Ellen Bouchard, who was at the School of American Ballet. When Betty replied, "yes," that was it! She recalls having enjoyed her time at Kodak because it paid for her clothes, *pointe* shoes, and other necessities for a young woman pursuing two careers. However, one night after class, "which would have been in 1951, Miss Biracree's husband opened the door and said 'get in here—I want to talk to you.' She [Miss Biracree] is going to teach no more than 70 percent of her classes." (This was a year after Biracree had cofounded The Mercury Ballet Company.) With that, Betty Purvis was officially installed as Thelma Biracree's assistant. She promptly quit her job at Kodak and began teaching barre work in the afternoon classes while also dancing as prima ballerina with the Mercury.

The Mercury's up and coming star was Katherine Wilson, who went on to have a prodigious career as a professional dancer, teacher, and choreographer after graduating with a bachelor in fine arts degree in dance from the Boston Conservatory and studying with the Ballets Russes, the American Ballet Theatre, Luigi Jazz, and Jacob's Pillow.

Other students of note included Carolyn Clair, the accompanist Millie Clair's daughter, a gifted dancer who met a tragic end in New York City; the aforementioned Francia Roxin (now Tara Stepenberg), who graduated from Juilliard, holds multiple advanced degrees in dance, and is presently affiliated with Pacific Northwest Ballet as a staff member of the PNB Conditioning Program; Lana Gitlin Rouff, formerly the executive director of the Binghamton Philharmonic Orchestra; Eleanor Gitlin Lange, Earl Kage, Bud Driggs, and George Francis, a talented dancer who later switched to study with Tim's teacher Olive McCue.

Both Thelma Biracree and Betty Purvis taught on Saturdays, their busiest day, with Biracree teaching the advanced students and Betty and Earl Kage sharing the rest of the class load. Although no longer a part of the day-to-day New York City ballet world, Betty managed to keep up with her contacts there and elsewhere, particularly with three good friends who had been chosen to join the Ballets Russes de Monte Carlo toward the end of that company's run: Bernice Rehner, Shirley Haynes, and Yvonne Chouteau. Purvis recalled, "They did come to the Eastman Theatre when companies were touring everywhere and I invited them to come to my house." She continued to remain in touch with Bernice, and both enjoyed a good laugh a few years back when the latter was cleaning out a storage area and found a box containing eight new pairs of shoes that had been holdovers from her Ballets Russes days!

The Biracree-Purvis arrangement was a positive one. After Betty Purvis arrived, Thelma Biracree became a more talented technician. She was well aware of her assistant's rarefied ballet lineage but was confident enough in her own abilities never to be nervous about absorbing new methods. For example, Biracree traditionally began class in *grand plié*. However, Betty's barre at the School of American Ballet had begun in *demi-plié*, and after seeing the advantages of a more gradual warmup, Biracree changed it. Biracree never lost sight of the true value of what Betty brought to her class, nor did Betty lose sight of the nuanced beauty of the early Eastman Theatre Ballet star, who had been embraced by Martha Graham and whose stature not surprisingly had won her the role of the School of American Ballet's regional representative. Particularly gratifying about the arrangement for Betty was that she was able both to perform and to teach. As Biracree's *prima ballerina*, the company star, she performed a broad range of choreographies, including such originals as *Straw Hat Circuit*, *Au Printemps*, and *All That Glitters*, as well as a few classical ballets, including *Coppélia*. *All That Glitters* actually seems fittingly symbolic of the fastidious care and detail that went into constructing a magnificent onstage performance. Kathy Wilson recalls the thrill of watching "Betty Purvis and Dorothy Toland and all the older ladies beading their eyelashes with hot wax! An ancient art . . . long gone." In addition, Betty appeared with other affiliated programs, including the twenty-fifth-anniversary program of the Festival of American Music, which featured the Opera Workshop of the Eastman School of Music in the critically acclaimed *Merry Mount*, directed by Howard Hanson in 1955.

Betty related how Biracree had uncompromisingly high standards. One time she was rehearsing the corps, and one or two of the girls in the eight-girl ensemble made a mistake. Miss Biracree never made idle threats to her dancers, so it was a matter of some consequence when she informed the group (in a calm voice, as was her way), "We are going to do it one more time and if anyone makes a mistake, they're out of it." Other teachers routinely threatened and then went back on their word. Miss Biracree never threatened except this one time. She confessed to Betty that she was "afraid to watch." But everyone rose to the occasion, focused, and delivered.

On March 21, 1953, a terrible tragedy befell Miss Biracree and her husband. Their son and only child, Karl R. Schnepel, who was in his freshman year at Cornell University, was stricken with a rare acute disease of the blood and died within twelve hours of falling ill.[13] Betty recalls how Thelma, Earl, and she were in the studio when Thelma's husband came in to inform her of the dreadful news. In the wake of incalculable grief, Thelma took a long leave of absence from the studio and company that she and Olive McCue had started three years earlier. Betty describes how she and Earl kept everything going, however, because they knew that eventually, Thelma would need to return, to have something to do as a diversion. Eventually, she did return. It should also be mentioned that her core dancers, who had evolved into her family by that point, had kept her going as well. They all remained lifelong friends.

In 1967, Biracree retired and moved to be near her husband's family in Fort Wayne, Indiana, where she choreographed for the Fort Wayne Ballet Company and created liturgical dances. Following a large farewell party that took place in the Eastman Theatre, Betty Purvis took over the school on a full-time basis and ran it for seven more years in what she describes as a "very satisfying period." Edward A. Charbonneau III, an Olive McCue dancer who starred as the Nutcracker Prince from the 1960s until McCue's retirement in 1974, did choreography for her, borrowing her dancers to create ballets on them while also teaching at the Hochstein School. After Dr. Hanson retired in 1964, Betty tried to convince his successor to utilize her dancers for Eastman Opera Department productions, but lacking the vision of his predecessor, he apparently was satisfied, as Betty recalled, that "the River Campus had modern dance over there and that was good enough." According to Charbonneau, after Thelma Biracree's retirement, Olive McCue moved out of the Eastman School's Swan Street studio to a building located about a block away at the corner of Main and Gibbs that concertgoers from the 1960s would remember as the Rascal Café. While continuing to maintain her second studio in Webster, Miss McCue would have her students and company climb that "steep and narrow stairway" to the second floor of the new studio, where it remained for several years until the building was eventually demolished. It is thought that Tim might have had some limited exposure to the original Swan Street studio, but his friends recall that the majority of his time would have been studying and rehearsing at the Rascal Café location, particularly when he was performing as a soloist with the company, years later.

It might even be suggested that Betty and Tim also shared an interesting connection, that being the Mercury Ballet Company. Although Betty had stepped down from her role as prima ballerina by the time Tim was just beginning his tutelage there, her name and reputation were surely well known to him, as the names of the company stars always are to the up-and-comers.

The last vestige of the Eastman connection, however, remained for a few more years. As Betty Purvis recalled, when Thelma Biracree first began teaching, she typically employed piano students from the Eastman School to provide the accompaniment for class. After Millie Clair went full time, however, there was no longer a need for the students. When Purvis took over the school in 1967, however, she was happy to reinstate the tradition of employing student pianists as accompanists. One young man, for example, played for seven years, completing his master's degree and continuing to play through his doctoral studies. In 1974, Purvis closed the school. Sometime later, she was asked to teach classical ballet for the Rochester Association for Performing Arts (RAPA), which she did between 1978 and 1983.

On May 12, 1997, Thelma Biracree passed away at the age of ninety-three. In the years following her death, Betty and Earl would get together at least annually to celebrate her birthday, February 4, 1904, reflecting the same devotion that Biracree herself had felt for Martha Graham. Her death signaled the end of a glorious renaissance for the arts, not likely ever to return again.

ଙ

During the mid-1920s, a good generation before Tim Draper was born, Earl Kage described how he was "bit by the dancing bug." Although he spent forty-five years in research and development at the Eastman Kodak Company, eventually working his way up to the position of head of camera research, it was the arts—in all their many forms—that were his passion. Kage recalled that his particular love of dance began when he was a young boy, studying tap with Ruby Bohrer of Irondequoit; Bohrer also had been a company member of the Eastman Theatre Ballet. He spoke of how dance had become increasingly popular in Rochester after various European troupes crossed the Pond (i.e., the Atlantic) to perform as well as the feverish excitement that enveloped the city following George Eastman's magnanimous contributions to the arts. After formative training in tap, Earl moved downtown to 10 Elm Street (near Chestnut Street and East Avenue) to study with Florence Colebrook Powers, the wife of Fred Powers, who owned the famous Powers Hotel. Mrs. Powers, who taught "everything from tap to ballroom" was especially well known for her presentation of pageants at the Rochester Exposition. Kage discussed how Powers's primary credentials, however, were derived from the fact that she had been a student of the famous Ruth St. Denis and Ted Shawn, whose Denishawn School of Dancing and Related Arts had become one of the most influential modern dance companies in America and which toured globally, including frequent stops in Rochester. Mrs. Powers was asked to assume the role of director of the Rochester branch of the Denishawn Dance School. With a twinkle in his eye, Earl recalled that sometime in 1935, Mrs. Powers received a call from the Eastman Ballet.

> Marion Tefft was helping choreograph *Maytime* and needed men. Florence, known as Mimi, sent four guys to do the job, including me. I would have been around sixteen at the time. Thelma Biracree saw the performance and said that she would offer the four of us *free* ballet lessons. Three of us took off but one of us stayed. After my first major role in 1938 [doing the annual weeklong *Festivals of American Music*] with Thelma, I had a good review in the local paper.

With this credit in hand, Kage set his sights on New York City. Although he had recently accepted a position at Kodak (no small accomplishment, because it was the middle of the Great Depression, and one out of four people was out of work), he was determined to follow his dream. He therefore boldly took an unpaid leave of absence to go to the Big Apple and try out for the School of American Ballet, then located at 637 Madison Avenue. Mindful of how Thelma Biracree was serving as the Rochester representative to the school, Earl thought it would be a good fit. "SAB put me up at the Winslow, off Madison Avenue, three blocks from the school," he recalled. However, as he playfully related, he did not quite find agreement with the dance code, something that occasionally got him into trouble. "The costume for males at the time was a white t-shirt, black tights, white socks, and black shoes. However, the tights were made of cotton and wool. One had to constantly roll them up and it was a real pain." His solution? Wearing sawed-off tweed trousers. After what appears to have been a failed sartorial negotiation with the artistic leadership, however, he did eventually march himself down to the Capezio store to buy the tights. Not long afterward, he was invited to audition formally at SAB for the advanced classroom. Walking in, he found Anatole Vilzak in charge of the audition class, the dancer who had been brought in as a principal by Balanchine to replace Nijinsky. Vilzak placed Earl at the barre, and at the end of class, assigned him to the beginners' class. Not to be deterred (even if he was a bit disappointed), Earl worked hard and moved up through the levels. One of his classmates was none other than Gene Kelly. Gene had a brother named Fred Kelly who also was in the class. As Earl liked to confide years later with his famous bright-eyed, knowing grin, he never felt that "Mr. Gene Kelly would ever amount to much."

On the appointed day of the official advanced class audition some months later, Earl showed up one more time in what by then had become known schoolwide as the notorious sawed-off trousers. The people warming up around him were smiling, including SAB's registrar, Madame Russo. In fact, whenever he would return in later years to New York, she'd always make it a point to ask him, "Where are your tweeds?" Not unlike the fierce competition that exists today for acceptance into any level at SAB, Earl described how truly hard it was to get into the top level. It is a testimony to the talents of Thelma Biracree that many from her school actually did, including a pretty young girl, as Earl remembered, named Denise Schnurr.

As fate would have it, the legendary, terrifying Russian artist Anatole Oubokov was on hand that day to run the audition. Oboukov had partnered Anna Pavlova in 1914 and "subbed for Nijinsky on occasion and had a reputation that if he asked you to solo across the floor and you did well, then you knew you had really made it." Earl recalled that he "had worked like hell to get there." Finally the day of days arrived. Oubokov pointed to him and said, "You! Solo!" At that moment, Denise Schnurr walked into the room, and that was enough to throw off Earl's concentration. Oubokov's response? "You pig! You do not dance! Do not dance anymore." Alas, that was not one of Earl's favorite memories, but he was quick to add that the widely beloved Muriel Stuart was his favorite teacher and that he also liked Vilzak. It is clear that notwithstanding the Schnurr incident, Kage had considerable talent, but then World War II intervened, and his performance career was put on hold.

Due to his previous employment in Kodak's research laboratories, where he made concrete screens that were utilized by the army in making maps, he initially was given an assignment with the Signal Corps, where he could continue his work on magenta screens. On one occasion, a major and a captain from the Army Engineering Corps in Washington, DC walked onto the train with him. Earl was a private at the time. The captain said, "Soldier, you're out of uniform!" (Earl had been sporting a gold tie clip, eschewing the tradition of tucking one's tie into one's shirt). Clearly, whether it was the tweeds or the tie clip, Earl liked to do things his own way. In any event, the captain was not overly outraged, however, because he told him that when he came back, he should "sign up for the Engineers—we want you with the Corps of Engineers." Earl went to Fort Belvoir, the US army installation near Washington, DC, for five or six weeks. Every day, he tried to contact the major and the captain but was never able to get hold of either of them. He was shipped overseas, landing in England. On his second day there, another major came through and wanted to know if anyone was good with a camera. Of course, Earl was hired on the spot as a photographer for the official US military publication, *Stars and Stripes*, printed by the London *Times*. His first big assignment was to "get a photo of War Secretary Henry Simpson giving a medal to Sergeant Smith." As he recalls, he "took the photo, but nothing happened. Secretary Simpson then turned around and said 'Soldier, you have one more chance.' Fortunately, I got the picture." He eventually was promoted to reporter and sergeant, but he needed to wear his rank. He had a press badge and was treated like an officer until the war ended in 1945.

True to form, Earl continually attempted to bring culture to the soldiers throughout the war. His first interview was with Noel Coward, the English playwright, composer, director, actor and singer, known for his legendary wit and "what *Time* magazine called 'a sense of personal style, a combination of cheek and chic, pose and poise.'" The interview was a success. Afterward, a friend of his, "a British gal who worked at the American Red Cross" was going to try and land him an interview with the British author Rebecca West. The friend, however, said that she hadn't been able to get hold of Rebecca West but got him an interview with someone named Virginia Wolff, if that would please him. So Earl was able to interview Virginia Wolff. Only months later, she committed suicide.

Earl's job while "over there" was to see pilots off in the morning, which forced him to have to always get up early. The good news, though, was that he had the rest of the day to do whatever he wanted to do. One not to waste any time, he went off to Christ's College in Cambridge and became fast friends with Cyril Beaumont, already an internationally acclaimed dance historian and writer. The two men became inseparable, and "that is how I met all the greats in dance in London. We went to the Sadler's Wells and I met Bob Helpmann, Margot Fonteyn's leading male dancer at the time. Through Cyril, I met them all. I also became close to Lincoln Kirstein, who had been born in Rochester, and that was the link that bound us." Earl always was proud that Kirstein gave him an autographed copy of his book, *The Classic Ballet*, which was long a part of Earl's personal collection. In fact, it was the friendship between Beaumont and Kage that started the latter on the road to becoming a great collector, albeit with one great regret. On one occasion, Beaumont brought from his back room two pictures of Nijinsky. He offered them to Earl for ten pounds, but Earl felt that he had to pass. "They weren't small and I had no place to put them." Fifty years later, those Nijinsky treasures ended up selling for almost $5 million, a fact that haunted poor Earl until the end! He also was proud of the fact that he met Sacheverell Sitwell, an English writer and art critic and the younger sister of Dame Edith Sitwell, the literary poet and critic.

Earl returned to the United States in 1945. He did little or no dancing during this time, despite the fact that the School of American Ballet had very few males. Instead, he made the decision to return to Rochester and be a big fish in a little pond. In 1946, he danced in the Eastman Festival Romantic Symphony and was the lead in one of Howard Hanson's pieces. Over the years, he had become extremely fond of Thelma Biracree, who by that time had become "Teddy Biracree" to him. He recalled that after the war, perhaps in the late 1940s, she told him that she and Olive McCue, then another soloist of the Eastman Theatre Ballet, had decided to join forces to codirect the Festival Ballet with the sum of $12,000, which George Eastman had left to Biracree specifically for this purpose. According to Earl, McCue had previously been "studying in New York City with [Mikhail] Mordkin and Miss Biracree invited her to return to Rochester to do a Christmas program with her." Eastman's only stipulation, however, was that the performances had to be held on Friday nights, which unfortunately was anathema to the Eastman School of Music's director, Howard Hanson. Hanson also thought that the twelve thousand dollars could be better spent on hiring RCA Victor to record the music, and "that was the end of that." With that one gesture, the Festival Ballet came to a close. However, this did not discourage Biracree and McCue, who immediately decided to organize the Mercury Ballet Company, a project that came to fruition in 1950 and was housed in the Eastman School of Music's Theatre Annex at 50 Swan Street. Earl danced for many years with the Mercury Ballet, served as Miss Biracree's assistant, and along with Betty, held Thelma's school together on more than one occasion with his vibrancy and kindness. A friend to the end, "he knew how to bring Thelma back to the world of the living" after her great personal tragedy. According to a former student of theirs, Lana Gitlin Rouff, "[Earl] had insisted that the company [the Mercury Ballet] practice her choreography up to the point where she left. He told us to wind up into a close ball! We all laughed when it was presented and so did Miss Biracree."

Earl had also done choreography for Rochester Music Theater's Norene Bride and Suzanne Wiig. When a contract appeared from the Firemen's Fund to stage musicals, Earl asked Thelma to stage everything for the seven musicals that followed. The theater was located somewhere off Hudson Avenue; characteristically, she did a marvelous job.

Throughout his long-term career with Kodak until he retired, Earl continued to share his multidimensional artistic talents. He served as a board member with Tim's Rochester City Ballet. At the Memorial Art Gallery, he served on MAG's board of managers for twenty-five years, chaired its membership and marketing subcommittees, and lent his expertise to organizing countless fund-raisers. He was also a long-time trustee of Garth Fagan Dance, the Aesthetic Education Institute, Friends of Eastman Opera, Friends of the School of the Arts, the George Eastman House of International Photography, Rochester Children's Theater, and the Rochester Philharmonic Orchestra. In 1987, he received the Culture and Arts Civic Award from the Rochester Chamber of Commerce and in 1989, a lifetime achievement award from the Arts and Cultural Council. A quixotically vibrant eight-nine-year-old when he passed away in 2008, he left behind scores of close friends and admirers, with one unfulfilled dream expressed just weeks earlier about launching one more special ballet performance at the Memorial Art Gallery, combining two of his very great loves, portraiture and ballet, in one fabulous locale. He would have been happy to know that on September 22, 2012, his wishes were realized when three principals of the Rochester City Ballet—Jesse Campbell, Megan Kamler, and Brittany Shinay—performed in the Memorial Art Gallery's Fountain Court to the Renaissance music of Eastman School organists as part of a new arts festival, the Fringe Festival. No doubt Earl was smiling from above. He had actually succeeded in scoring the artistic hat trick with that one performance—art, dance, and music.

Earl's greatness, as well as his incomparable sense of ballet history, knowledge, taste, and the overall sensibilities he brought to the Rochester City Ballet and its audiences were not lost on Tim Draper. As an eventual honorary member of Tim's board of directors, Earl was asked to produce a periodic column for the company newsletter, entitled "Kage's Korner," a magnificent glimpse of Rochester's rich ballet scene beginning in the early 1920s. "He was my favorite gadfly," MAG's director, Grant Holcolm, fondly remembered a few years back, conveying how Earl, a creative spirit and proponent of all that was beautiful in the world of arts never stopped agitating with a bright new idea. He was truly a gentleman who made a difference.

◌

Tim's ballet teacher throughout his time at Eastman was Olive McCue, who like Thelma Biracree, began her dance career as a member of the Eastman Theatre Ballet in the early 1920s. Her casting at the time suggests that she rose to prominence rather quickly within the ensemble, frequently appearing in "duets and trios" but occasionally performing solo roles as well. "She carried herself very erect and would make an entrance—a true diva . . . She had long red hair and stood like a queen," was a description of Olive McCue in the 1960s by a former dance student of hers who took class in the old Theatre Annex studio. "She was very demanding and expected nothing but perfection from her students. She taught dance but also decorum—how to be a gentleman and a lady. She did not accept fools—or excuses. If you weren't willing to work 110 percent, you were gone." "McCue had a great sense of theater and drama," recalls a Biracree student who occasionally took class with Miss McCue in the 1950s. "Her act 1 'Nut' was excellent."

McCue's mien was most assuredly an influence on Tim's own later thoughts on deportment. According to Rebekah von Rathonyi, one of the stars of the Draper Dance Theatre (later rebranded as the Rochester City Ballet), he would tell his students, "a true ballerina could step out onto the stage and command a presence without taking a single step. She could give the audience goose bumps just by walking."

After the departure of Enid Knapp Botsford from the Eastman Theatre, Olive McCue, like Thelma Biracree, for a brief time reaffirmed her allegiance to George Eastman and to Rouben Mamoulian by continuing to perform extensively at the Eastman Theatre. McCue's stage photographs from the mid-1920s in particular reveal that she had a very regal, almost goddess-like bearing, with an elegant gown draped around her frame in such a way as to create a "legs for days" look, today's popular sobriquet for the dance-body ideal. When McCue and Biracree had some rare time off, they might have been found walking together up and down the sidewalks of the architecturally significant East Avenue, glamorously made up and dressed to the nines with high heels, hats, and gloves, turning heads, stopping for meetings or refreshment at one of the many lovely city clubs that adorned the area. Or they might have been shopping at some of the tony shops and department stores that were themselves caught up in Rochester's exciting new cultural identity, going to great lengths to import "frocks, furs, and tails suitable for a night at the opera."

When the final curtain fell on the Eastman Theatre Ballet in 1926, Biracree continued to choreograph and perform in many select vehicles at the Eastman Theatre, but Miss McCue's name no longer was mentioned. According to Ed Charbonneau, McCue left Rochester in 1926 to pursue advanced studies and to perform. "I believe that she left for NYC [*sic*] about 1926—she made reference to classes with Fokine and others. She said in later years that during this period she had toured South America with a ballet company and that she toured the USA as an actress in *The Yellow Jacket* [a play by George C. Hazelton and Barry Benrimo]." Mr. Charbonneau also recalls that prior to McCue's 1926 departure from Eastman, she mentioned taking classes under Martha Graham and other notables, as well as taking part in experimental color filming on the third floor of the Swan Street studio. "I think she said she was filmed dancing to the music of [Charles Tomlinson Griffes's] *White Peacock*," Charbonneau noted. According to one of her students, the jovial James Clouser, her post-Eastman studies "may also have taken taken place with the Englishman Aubrey Hitchins, who settled in New York City after the dissolution of Pavlova's touring company. . . . Miss McCue's 'fierce but gentle approach' to ballet could be traced to [him]."[14] McCue also danced with the Metropolitan Opera Ballet during this time. A local census reveals that she returned to Rochester to marry Russell "Peter" Clarke of Greece, New York, in 1941. As mentioned earlier, her former colleague of the Eastman Theatre Ballet, Thelma Biracree, invited her to join in staging the Festival of American Music programs during the late 1940s, prior to their launch of the Mercury Ballet Company a short while later. It is interesting to note that not a great deal remains about Miss McCue's early dance history. Unlike most artistic directors whose biographies typically figure prominently on concert programs, she tended to remain more elusive about her background, granting interviews only on rare occasions and then with a very decided reticence as to what she would or would not divulge. Charbonneau, who later was accorded the exceptional honor of interviewing her much later in her career, attributes her reserve to "a facet of the privacy which theater people enjoyed in her era. The stage and film stars were available for 'photo ops' and interviews pertinent to their latest project, but their private lives were sacrosanct."

As Tim Draper would begin to crave more classical training of his own, during his transition from child to preteen, he would arrive in Miss McCue's studio ready to work. Later, it became apparent how very much he was able to absorb while performing as a student with the Mercury Ballet Company, which enjoyed enthusiastic audiences throughout the 1950s and 1960s at the Eastman Theatre and at multiple venues throughout the region and beyond, guided in no small measure by the muses of a time gone by.

Janelle Cornwell, described as Tim Draper's first true star. Photograph by Stephen Healy. Courtesy of www.communityeconomies.org.

JANELLE CORNWELL

I met Tim when he came to Rochester from Florida in the mid-eighties. I had been at Michelle Buschner's (which is where I first met him—I think I was around seven), and at Botsford's with Lisa Snape as my teacher. When Tim came to town permanently, I was probably eight or nine. I followed him from studio to studio, wherever he was teaching (and collecting students). My parents and I wandered around old industrial warehouses with him, helping to look for studios. The studio on Goodman Street was an absolute disaster, but they saw potential. My mother and father, along with Frank Galaska [Tim's partner], Kathy Ertsgaard, and George Orosz, dumped typewriters, boxes and files out the window into a big dumpster, tore down walls, removed conveyor belts, sanded floors, painted, built a staircase, and mounted barres and mirrors.

Tim did a lot of work, too, but all agreed he was better at teaching than hammering. My parents and I were very close with Tim during those early years. I worshiped him and spent more time with him than I did with my parents. He quickly had a small handful of students (Aimee Litwiller and I were probably the first), and during construction I had a lot of private lessons and small classes.

The school grew quickly. The first performance I remember was at the Lilac Festival. (I was little, probably around eleven years old and danced the Lilac Fairy variation.) Then came excerpts from *The Nutcracker.* I was Clara and a Doll with Cory English. In the spring, we did *Peter and the Wolf* and *Memento.* (I did "The Little Bird" and "Tarantella.") Around this time, Jamey [Leverett], Kathy Joslyn, and some others made up a group of older girls and we had the full-length *Nutcracker*, with Michael Byars and Wendy Whelan (I was Clara), and then in the spring we did *Firebird* with Jamey as the Firebird and Kathy Joslyn as Most Beautiful Maiden. I was Lead Creature, and later that summer in *Hedges*, I was a Girl. Tim and I were having difficulties then, I think because we were so close. We'd probably spent more time together than was healthy.

One summer when I was ten, I'd gone to Boston Ballet's children's summer program, and he *hated* that, so the next summer he took me (with Kathy Ertsgaard and George [Orosz] and maybe Kathy

Joslyn) to New York City, in part to keep me from going away again. That first time it was delightful—he secretly loved it when people mistook me for his daughter and he was always loving and proud of me. The next time, he took me and a few of the older students (Cindy V[an Scoter], Kathy J[oslyn], Laura [Kowalewski], and Jamey, I think) to New York, but this time he and I struggled. I didn't like it when he tried to hold my hand, and I wanted to hang out with the older girls more than with him. . . . We fought, but it was still a good time—he liked showing us off and I loved taking those classes, but I never went back to New York with him.

The summer when I was thirteen, I went to Pennsylvania Ballet's summer program. (Cindy Van Scoter was my roommate.) We had a blast, but Tim *hated* it that we went. (He blamed me for starting the trend of students going away for the summer.) I remember calling him excitedly from Philly—I wanted to tell him about my classes and levels.

That next year, I auditioned for the HARID Conservatory in Florida, a scholarship boarding program, and went for my freshman and sophomore years. Tim was deeply hurt by this (and angry with my parents and me), but I went. I came back for what would have been my junior year in high school, but there was too much emotional water under the bridge (and too many bad habits for him to deal with). I was sixteen and stuck it out for about six more months. I'd dropped out of high school (going to Monroe Community College instead) and took his regular classes (level V or VI, I think) as well as the two classes he taught at SUNY Brockport. I was a semirebellious teenager; Tim and I were variously flirtatious and hurtful toward each other. I didn't understand (until years later as a ballet teacher myself) how difficult (or how necessary) it was for him to assert his authority over me but I ended up leaving one night after a fight and moving to New York City.

I wasn't as dedicated as I could have been in New York (I was, after all, sixteen and living alone there), and Tim knew it. He had sent out his tentacles looking for me and called my mother: "She's *not* going to classes! She could be doing drugs or anything! You don't even know!" My mother at that point was fed up with him (I think she hung up on him a few times) but when I think of it now, he was right! I probably should not have been there!

In any case, after a couple years in New York, I got a job dancing in a small company in Illinois when I was eighteen. I went, toured around with them for a year, and then quit ballet and moved to Alaska. I spent two and a half years in Alaska and then went to finish my undergrad degree in Prescott, Arizona. But I started taking ballet classes again (after about three years!), first in Mexico City (Compañía Nacional de Danza) and then adult classes at Ballet Arizona in Phoenix. I was inspired to take classes again by the opening of a gorgeous new studio in Prescott. When I graduated from college, I began teaching there, and shortly thereafter after their ballet mistress quit and I took over her responsibilities.

It was a fantastic year teaching in Prescott in 2000. I intensified the ballet program and started a children's ballet theater. This is when I reconnected with Tim. He was in my blood when I was teaching. It brought back a flood of memories, and I found myself pulling the same silly tricks that he had used with us as kids.

So, when I returned to Rochester for my friend Aimee's wedding (also his former student), I left an apple on the porch with a note saying I was teaching and often thinking about him. He called me that night at around 9:00 p.m. "Dear! There hasn't been a day that's gone by that I don't think of you!"

We met for few hours that night; I met his partner, Rob, who was very nice. It was so good to see him. He was bigger. He said, "I don't yell anymore, I just lift weights." And he absolutely glowed with pride when he talked about Sari [Ostrum], whom I remembered from when she was a tiny girl.

I loved teaching, but I wanted to do something more political. I went to Denver to obtain my master's at the University of Denver in a program that was combined with the Peace Corps. I did the academic work for one and a half years (teaching ballet for money and taking adult classes at Colorado Ballet for fun) and then headed off to Guatemala for two and a third years for the Peace Corps, which is where I was when Tim died.

When I returned, I first went back to Denver and then came to western Massachusetts when I got funding to study economic geography with my favorite author from graduate school. I take adult ballet classes occasionally for fun, but mostly I balance myself by doing a little yoga and an occasional run.

I'm so glad I reconnected with Tim before he died. It would have left an even bigger hole in my heart had I not gotten that last bear hug from him.

The last time I saw him, Tim asked me if I regretted having left (him), and I told him that I didn't. I know I would have been a better dancer had I stayed with him, but I could never regret the webs that life has woven in me. The lasting imprints that his soul has stamped on mine are a true and loving passion for music, ballet, and beauty, and a desire for conditioned yet unconditional love.

Dr. Janelle Cornwell is a researcher and writer in western Massachusetts. Tim's friend Michelle Buschner remembers Janelle as his first true star during the time he was building his new school and company in Rochester.

TIMMY

If one individual can be credited with fueling Tim Draper's love of dance, it would unquestionably be his highly perceptive, adoring, strict, and yet unfailingly supportive mother, the late Hazel Draper, or "Pete," as she was affectionately known.

Sometime during 1960–61, when Tim was about six, Mrs. Draper, "at Timmy's urging," took her young son to the Alean Charles Dance Studio, later to become known as the Little Red Dancing School, a respected studio on Lyell Avenue. Miss Charles had originally opened her dancing school in 1937 on Lake Avenue, advertising for new students in the monthly calendar of the Riviera Theatre, located right next door to the school. Pictured posing with arms above her head in a little sleeveless fur-trimmed holiday affair as a promotional piece for her school, Miss Alean was a beautiful, svelte young woman with prominent, high cheekbones like Katherine Hepburn's and a flair for the dramatic. Even after retirement, it is obvious in her annual holiday missives that she stayed fit and was a dance instructor to the end.

Studying with Miss Alean, Tim was exposed to tap, jazz, and ballet. Coming home one day from class, he announced to his mother that he didn't "much care for tap or jazz, but I really like ballet." Mrs. Draper knew at that point that he truly "had the bug" because even at a very young age, he wanted her to help him stretch his feet, which she did. She laughingly marveled, nearly a half century later, that she was his first ballet partner. Tim would lift her up in the kitchen while he assumed the role of Cavalier. When we realize that she was a petite, lively woman with engaging, penetrating eyes, it is easy to imagine her as the prototype for the ballet dancer he would later develop at his own studio and company. Although she said that she had had no formal dance training of her own, she "loved to dance ballroom," especially when Uncle Kenny Draper, who danced all over the vaudeville circuit, was around. She was certain that Kenny is the reason why dance came so naturally to Tim—that and the fact that most people in the family eventually felt that Tim had to carry on Uncle Kenny's tradition. She remembered always supporting Tim in whatever way she could. She was proud of having gone to so very many *Nutcrackers* "from the first one he was in . . . and I haven't missed one yet!" With a mother's true love, she never wanted to infringe on his moments, though, so the family followed suit and tended not to attend any postperformance parties—not from lack of desire but because they wanted to honor their mother's wishes. The affection and pride between mother and son was there in abundance. She recalled how Tim would frequently tell her, "Mom, don't you worry about anything—I'll take care of you."

Family was very important to Mrs. Draper, a sentiment that was instilled in each of her five children: Billy, Donna, Mark, Tim, and Jaye. When entering the two-story home of the family compound in Churchville, New York, a quaint village a little less than 20 miles west of Rochester to which the family moved several years ago, the visitor was greeted, while Mrs. Draper was still alive, with an astonishing array of photographs. Every available wall space in the front hallway and on into the living room was filled with portraits of family, friends, and even some of Tim's dance students (a beautiful photo of Sari Ostrum held a prominent place, for example). A most extraordinary but endearing practice, it clearly shows how very precious each and every person in Mrs. Draper's world was to her.

At the time of her passing at the age of 83 on July 3, 2011, she left behind two daughters, a son, a son-in-law, a daughter-in-law, eight grandchildren, eighteen great-grandchildren, one great-great granddaughter, nieces, nephews, cousins, and great-nephews and great-nieces. Tim's devoted sisters, Donna and Jaye, and Donna's late husband, Art Hansmann, who passed away in October of 2013, similarly reflect the importance of family. A small wooden sign adorns the front door of the second home on their lovely property, appropriately labeled "The Gathering Place." This home, too, is one of great warmth, liveliness, and hospitality, Between the garden gnomes, a chocolate Labrador, and an older gray tiger cat that is particularly attached to Jaye, the home is clearly well loved. Familial closeness also extended beyond the parents and siblings. Tim's uncle Gil on his father's side of the family paid for Tim's dance lessons, saying, "You go register him because he's talented. Scholarships will come." Mrs. Draper recalled the great generosity of Uncle Gil, saying, "He would never deny anyone."

Tim and his siblings. *Clockwise from top left:* Tim, Mark, Donna (with Jaye on her lap), and Billy, 1967. Courtesy of the Draper family.

As described by Donna, her parents always worked very hard for what they had and took nothing for granted. In addition to making a home for her growing family, Mrs. Draper also worked full time at night in the factories of Kodak and Delco to assist her mason husband, Lionel, in raising a large family. Without question, Tim inherited his extraordinary work ethic from his parents.

It is also clear that this family has had to endure more than its share of excruciating loss. Mrs. Draper's father, Dominick L. Forkell III, a steeplejack, passed away when she was just seven years old and her mother, Emma E. Forkell, died when she was thirteen. Mrs. Draper was the youngest of eight children. With both parents gone, she initially was cared for by a brother who then went into the service during World War II, followed by another brother, and then another. Eventually she ended up living with an older sister before marrying Lionel E. Draper at the age of seventeen. The shield of familial love could not prevent further tragedy, however; her son and Tim's brother, William M. "Billy" Draper, an exceptionally good-looking and good-hearted young man and the oldest of the five children, was killed in Vietnam in 1968; a grandson, Todd M. Hansmann, passed away in 1972; a great-granddaughter, Victoria Lynn Hansmann, in 1990; and then Tim in 2003. As Donna recalls sadly, their mother had to stay alive to care for Jaye after Billy was gone, but she could not survive Tim's death for long.

It is very easy to determine just how attached Tim's family remains to him to this day, because he is continually referred to as "Timmy," or "Uncle Timmy," rather than "Tim," as the rest of the world, even those dearest to him over his lifetime, called him. "Timmy was just Timmy to us," recalled Mrs. Draper. "We didn't look at Timmy as a world-class artist. He was just a member of our family—he was just himself." She remembers how he would come home for Christmas laden with fancy presents for her. She thought of herself as more of a "sweats and jeans" kind of person, but he told her that he always wanted her to have the best of everything—sweaters, blouses, and slacks. "I want you to have them, Ma," he'd always say. It was always, "Come on, Mom, we're going to go shopping. Let's go to the Highland Diner and then go shopping." Or "Mom, how would you like [this or that]?" His generosity also extended to the rest of the family. On one occasion, Mrs. Draper recalled how he took her, Jaye, Melanie, Billy, and Gina on a plane to New York, and they all had a blast. He took them all to a Mets game and then "Timmy and I took Gina to see 'Annie,'" she recalled with fondness.

The closeness, of course, which was relayed in tongue-in-cheek fashion by Tim's late brother-in-law, Art, often took the form of fist-fights and all-out brawls, usually between Tim and his older brother Mark who, being three years older than Tim, was the sibling closest to him in age. As the "baby" of the family for the twelve years leading up the birth of his sister Jaye in 1966, "Timmy was spoiled." As the youngest for many years, he would have everything to gain by being the provocateur—and provoke he did. "He had a temper when he was little," recalled his mom. "He had his standards."

As Donna and Art recalled, there were times at 66 Harcourt Road (the family home in Rochester prior to Churchville) beginning when Tim was three that "Timmy and Mark bucked so bad, going after each other with a shovel" that Art frequently was called on to break things up. In the back hallway, there was a door whose top half was glass. The glass apparently was broken so often during these fisticuffs that Art became fairly proficient at running down to the store, buying an entire new plate of glass, and installing it before his future mother-in-law would come home so she wouldn't have to know what had happened. In fact, so well did Art accomplish his task, he and Donna recalled humorously, that Hazel would usually make some passing comment, "Oh, good, I see that you were busy today—you cleaned the door." On other occasions, Tim would go into Donna's room, make a mess of all of her bobby pins or go and hide behind her curtains, one time scaring her so badly that she even punched him in the face, giving him a bloody nose. But outside the bosom of the family, as Donna related, "Let anyone pick on him or anyone else in the family, and the siblings would all be their staunchest defenders." This was particularly true later on when "Mark defended Timmy a lot because of Timmy being gay."

One trait that Mrs. Draper insisted on within the family was honesty. She said, "I always told the kids, no matter what you do, bad or good, don't ever lie to me. I will stand behind you no matter what but just tell me how it happened. I will always be there for you because there weren't people to stick up for me when I was little. Just do not lie to me."

The kids were clearly her life, and she always did her best to teach them right from wrong. She was also very practical about her children's prospects. At one point, she remembers telling Tim, "You need to have something to fall back on—go to beautician's school." With obvious respect for her opinion, Tim did just that. He obtained his beautician's license, took a job at one of the well-known department stores of the time,

Tim, his siblings, and mother photographed at Tim's niece, Melanie Conradt's wedding. *Clockwise from top left:* Tim, Mark, Donna, Hazel, and Jaye. Courtesy of the Draper family.

McCurdy's or Sibley's, and then cut her hair and all of his friends' hair. One day he told her "No more dyeing, Ma, you've got pretty gray hair."

One story of family lore that reflects Tim's true character involves how he handled the crisis when his young sister, Jaye, fell into the family pool at the Harcourt Road house in the middle of winter. According to Donna, Jaye had slipped through the ice and their mother began screaming hysterically, struggling to climb over the edge of the pool to fish her out, something that most certainly would have been an impossible task due to her diminutive size. Tim jumped right over her head and pulled his little sister out. In the aftermath of this near calamity, everyone was concerned about Jaye catching pneumonia. Fortunately, she didn't suffer so much as a cold! Tim, on the other hand, did end up with pneumonia, but he was able to recover from it successfully at home. He always remained close to Jaye, who at one point, followed her big brother to dance class at Little Red. "He was very protective of his sister, Jaye," Tim's close friend Michelle Buschner recalled. "She needed some extra help because of an apparent learning disability, which no one ever seemed to recognize in those days." He made sure she received whatever she needed.

Donna best reflects the truest affirmation of Tim's character and how valued he was by the family. She recalls how "if anything had happened to my husband or myself, the kids were to go to my brother Timmy. I love Mark dearly, but he was a soft touch, whereas Timmy would have made them toe the line. Also, education was important to him."

Throughout his childhood and into his early teen years, Tim appears to have become fully ensconced in the world of Little Red Dancing School. His formal elementary education took place initially at No. 43 School on Lyell Avenue, and later at Holy Apostles, also on Lyell (possibly for fourth and fifth grades, recalled Donna), but ballet was his focus. He also began to spend a lot of time with a girl at the studio, Michelle Ilardo, who quickly became his closest friend and confidante. He was six, and she was ten. She took Tim under her wing and always looked out for him. She later became Michelle Buschner, one of the region's most highly respected studio directors, teachers, and choreographers, for whom most of the area's top dance talent taught at some point in their careers. She and Tim remained lifelong friends. He always saw to it that she shared in his success and had at her disposal quality ballet teachers, something very important to her throughout her career.

Once Michelle turned sixteen, she also became Tim's chauffeur. "He always needed rides to and from all classes so I picked him up." Being asked to recall what Tim's home life might have been like at this time, Michelle said that Tim was "very close to and protective of his mom. She was very supportive and positive about Tim's ventures. He used to cut my hair at his house and his mom was always there joining in our conversations." She has no recollection of his father at all.

As Tim's passion for ballet deepened, he became increasingly vocal to Michelle as to what he needed to become the artist of his dreams. He would turn to Michelle, who encouraged him and was his shoulder to cry on when the day-to-day "life in the studio" was sometimes at odds with what he truly yearned for as a young dancer. When he vented to her nightly on the phone, she remembers listening, supporting him, and validating his dreams, even at a very young age.

Not all was venting and frustration, however. Michelle remembers how much fun they all had while at Little Red. "We were all expected to take tap, ballet, and jazz. He was terrible in tap. He was happy, always smiling and laughing. We really had tons of fun together at dance class. He remained friends with most of our classmates from when we were little."

It was Michelle who made his fancy recital costumes so that he might shine on stage, and he, in turn, did her hair from the time he was in his teens. A look back through the Little Red recital programs through the years clearly reveals a traditional, vibrant studio where students bounced into class after school, worked tirelessly, but had the kind of fun that is addictive to young and older children alike when they are able to find a "home away from home," always preparing many days a week for the annual recital. The production usually had a theme that would recognize the entire year's work, with students performing in multiple numbers, from small to large ensemble pieces, as well as in solos, duets, and trios. Because this was primarily a "jazz and tap" recital school (albeit a very good one, a reputation it retains to this day), Little Red naturally could not provide Tim with all of the ballet training for which he so desperately hungered. His quick temper would show itself periodically when he became frustrated over wanting more ballet and wanting it taught to a particular standard. He did, however, single out his teenage dance partner, Marie Reale, as an excellent technician. As Michelle recalls Tim telling her, "She [Marie] was the only one to teach proper technique."

He seemed to sense even back then that the only way a dancer could ever acquire the luscious line, strength, and overall purity of movement "between the beats or spaces" was to have ballet instruction offered on a daily basis, rather than in just one or two classes per week. This, he knew, could separate true dancers from those merely performing steps.

In his later years, Tim stressed the importance of exposing students to various teaching styles and insisted that teachers encourage their advanced students to seek more professional training, even if it meant leaving the schools with which they were affiliated. He did express some regret that Miss Alean did not encourage him to leave and join a ballet school or company. Nevertheless, as his first teacher, she obviously inspired Tim and imparted to him some fine training as well as the performance quality that comes from endless rehearsals and full-scale performances involving props, lighting, exciting multiple offstage costume changes, hair, and makeup. As either the sole male dancer or perhaps one of two at the studio during this time, he was usually positioned front and center for any given ensemble number, surrounded by his female colleagues. Little Red's 1965 program reveals that Tim performed a solo number as the "Toy Soldier" in the *Christmas Ballet* and a couple of group numbers. The next year, the program *Showtime 66* shows that he again soloed, along with participating in a couple of group numbers. The 1967 recital program lists the thirteen-year-old as performing in four numbers, leading off the program in a performance with Janice Marie Batz, Marcia Beale, Laurie Brongo, Fern Carsone, Carolyn Coco, Debbie DeMarsica, Carol Ann Federico, Darlene Lucille Ferro, and Kathy Tarkulich. For dance recital or competition aficionados who enjoy trying to make sense of the groupings by talent, it becomes very obvious that at one point, Tim was promoted out of his former group, one that he might have remained with throughout his training at Little Red, in order to join a more advanced group of dancers.

By the time Tim was thirteen and wanting more ballet instruction as well as company performance opportunities, he was ready to make a commitment to ballet and thus enrolled in the Olive McCue School of Ballet. He continued his affiliation with Little Red, however, obtaining the teacher certification offered by Miss Alean and appearing occasionally on her programs. If his teacher was less than pleased by his desire to move to a new studio, it becomes understandable when taken in the context of not wanting to lose a top student (particularly a male student). Again, Tim felt that teachers should support the growth of their students when the latter required something that the teachers could not provide themselves—and this was something that would gnaw at him throughout his life. It is interesting to note that after Tim owned his own studio and some of his students wanted both to attend the Draper Studio for enhanced technique and maintain at least a partial alliance with their previous studio, they were allowed to do so for one year only, at which time they had to make a clear choice if they were to remain at Draper. (Usually the Draper Studio won.) This wasn't a bad policy, however, depending on what the student's goals were. If a dancer was even considering a professional career in ballet, there was simply no substitute for committing fully to the preprofessional training offered at the Draper Studio. For a very fortunate few—if their natural gifts, hard work, determination, maturity, and luck were all working in sync—there was the possibility of a professional career. Tim thought that if other studio affiliations were competing for his student's time, the student would not be able to train or rehearse to the necessary level, and his or her potential might never be realized. Even if the dancer did not necessarily envision a ballet career but did want a professional dance career, the rigorous training was still essential because it would inform his talent across all other genres. However, for those who wanted to dance just because they loved it, without any future consideration of a career, one has to wonder if it might have been better to allow those students to dance with their other studios, just as Tim had maintained ties to multiple studios throughout his own years of training.

By 1969, for example, while studying with Olive McCue and at this point with Kathleen Crofton in Buffalo, Tim received his second-year teaching certification from Little Red, "awarded annually to those completing the year's study in the Teacher's Course." Also receiving the award was his close friend, Janet Boeff, who would later be the "Nanny" in his company's first *Nutcracker* performance, several years later.[1] Tim was additionally featured on the cover of a 1969 Little Red program as Prince Désiré/Florimund and with Marie Reale as Princess Aurora in the school's production of *The Sleeping Beauty*. Although he had begun studying with Olive McCue two years earlier, there was clearly some overlap in his affiliations. Without question, Miss Alean instilled in Tim a passion for dance and mastery of his chosen art form that was to change the course of his life. He did a lot of growing up at Little

Red and developed the type of invaluable performance experience and poise that is unique to quality recital and competition schools. In addition, he made true lifelong friends, many of whom later became dance-studio directors in their own right and for whom he would teach when his schedule allowed. What is certainly clear is that Miss Alean and her young male protégé had remained on very good terms with one another because he continued to teach and perform for her as late as 1976.

There should be a special place in heaven for a dancer's very first teacher, particularly when that dancer becomes exceedingly good.

Marie Carapezza Welch was a twelve-year old student of Tim's when he was guest teaching for Michelle at the second Little Red Dancing School in Rochester's Mt. Hope Plaza. Michelle had been made the young director of the satellite school and would periodically engage Tim as a guest teacher when he was available. Marie recalls that Tim choreographed and directed a very memorable "Waltz of the Flowers" for her group, which included Michelle's sister, Doris Ilardo; Kathy Bronson; Catherine Dachille; Mary Eadie; Robin Finn; Susan Poppoon; Patricia Siering; and two soloists, Janet Mastrella and Edna Case. As time went by, Tim and Marie enjoyed an excellent teacher-student relationship. He continually monitored her progress, liberally dispensing advice on what shape her future career plans should take. (Sometimes, the conversations took place while he cut her hair at his home on Harcourt Road.)

Several years later, when Marie was getting ready to graduate from high school and Tim was getting ready to join the Trocks, she recalls that he urged her to go to New York City to audition. He said that Marie could stay with him in New York while she was getting settled—the important thing was that she get there. Being only eighteen, Marie never did take Tim up on his offer. Instead, for the next twenty-plus years she was Michelle's respected teacher and assistant, providing a high quality of training that not only enhanced the development of her young dancers but gave them a very good time in the process. She remembers that when Tim returned from Florida several years later, she took classes with him in his own new studio, at a time when regular adult classes were being offered. "He wanted me to be in his original company, but I was getting married in '87 and thought it would be too hard to juggle both new adventures. But I still took classes from him," she recalled.

Rebekah von Rathonyi as Clara. Courtesy of Rebekah von Rathonyi.

REBEKAH VON RATHONYI

Tim possessed an innate sense about every one of his dancers. He recognized that each one of us was unique and special, and he knew us like the back of his hand. He never looked at us in a cookie-cutter way. Instead, we were individuals with different needs. And because he knew each of our strengths and weaknesses, he was able to make them the first priority when training a dancer. Tim was excellent at teaching the technical side of a classical ballet class or choreography, but even more important, he focused on the artistic side, developing us not only as ballerinas but also as human beings inside the classroom.

Tim was very close to his dancers and developed a strong relationship or bond with us. Not as our friend—he never overstepped that boundary. He was our mentor, more of a father figure, which helped when he had to buckle down and be hard or strict with us. I can speak only for myself on this one, but there were times when I felt he pushed me too hard or I didn't understand why he was so frustrated or angry. There were many tears, but he knew exactly what I needed and when I needed it. He gave me tough love all the way. He demanded and expected the very best, even if you were at your lowest. For me, the time I spent with Tim after those grueling rehearsals was special. He was incredibly nurturing, gave me a shoulder to cry on, and gave the best hugs! He always talked to me and explained why it was crucial for him to be so firm and hard on me in class or rehearsal, and then it made sense. I think times like those were what molded me the most and had an impact on my future not only as an artist but also as young woman. If I hadn't had those moments with him, I am confident I would never have made it in the real world of dance, or even just life in general.

I never felt with Tim, as I did with other artistic directors, that he had a stereotypical or ideal view of what a dancer's body should look like. Again, this goes back to the comment on the "cookie-cutter ballerina." We all had different bodies, but he worked with what we had. What I saw in myself as a flaw he was able to see as a strength or turn it into a positive instead of a negative. For example, I thought I had the largest butt on the planet for a dancer. He would say, "Becky, if you didn't have the behind you have, there's no way you could ever jump the way you do. It's what gets you up there, so just use it and stop complaining." It was never about whether or not you had the most amazing feet or the ugliest feet. With Tim, it was about how you used them or presented them, that was the most important detail. I think all of his dancers craved working with him one on one, and of course we all loved getting attention from him. I never felt, though, that it was a competition. I feel he gave us all the same amount, because he noticed the little things. For all many corrections as he would give, he also gave as many compliments, one of the many things that made an RCB dancer confident. You always knew he believed in you even if you made mistakes. He would talk to you at the barre during a combination, asking how your day was, commenting on how beautifully you had done your hair, or how pretty your earrings were. He had the most amazing analogies when he taught class. He would compare a step or a feeling to sports or food; he was incredibly funny and uplifting. Some of the sayings he had were one of a kind! Snow rehearsal usually went like this: "This is supposed to look like snow, not slush." Or "Have you ever seen yellow snow? Not pretty, my dear." And I remember going outside and looking to see if I could find slush or yellow snow, because it helped me visualize how I was supposed to look like as a snowflake in *Nutcracker*! He would often have one of the older girls demonstrate a combination or have her show the rest of the class how lovely her *port de bras* was and that was how he wanted us to do it.

Coaching with Tim was the best! He would pick apart each and every emotion, explaining what you should be feeling and why you should be feeling it in a particular role. Each hand gesture, step, or small movement of the head had a purpose and a meaning. He used to tell me that it was my responsibility as an artist to make the audience feel what I was feeling at that moment on stage without speaking the words to describe it.

Musicality was also very important to Tim. I never really remember him constantly counting out each step for me. Instead, he would say to "feel the music, let it move your body by listening, get lost in the music." Sometimes, if you were trying too hard, he would stop the music and say, "You're thinking too much, just dance."

I think Tim also knew how important it was to have the best instructors possible. The team of faculty members he was able to assemble was a compliment to him, his school, and his company. He realized he needed to expose his dancers to the best, and that is what he gave us in Rochester with the likes of Sally Stepnes, Julianne Deming, and the guest faculty, who included Eva Evdokimova and Fiona Fairrie. Most of all, Tim was passionate about ballet and dance. He instilled that same love, dedication, discipline, and perseverance in each one of us on a daily basis. "Never let anyone in the dance world tell you you're less than what you really are, because you are beautiful."

Rebekah von Rathonyi is the artistic director of Cornerstone Academy for Performing Arts, following many years as the academy director of the Peoria Ballet School. Those who have seen this magnificent artist perform recently have gotten goosebumps, almost sensing that Tim Draper is right nearby, beaming.

MISS OLIVE MCCUE AND
THE MERCURY BALLET

Making the trek downtown to Olive McCue's studio in the fall of 1968 had to be exhilarating for the now irrepressibly determined young dancer. Tim had already had a thrilling taste of performing with the Mercury Ballet in *The Nutcracker* two years earlier, but formal instruction in ballet with Miss McCue multiple times a week would be a new experience for him, and he was ready. As Pamela Wilkens-White, one of McCue's star students recalled many years later, "If you didn't want a recital school, you would go to Olive and Thelma, because by that point, Enid [Knapp Botsford] was teaching ballroom."

Arriving downtown to study at Miss McCue's new studio, no longer at 50 Swan Street but still located close to the Eastman Theatre, must have had a significant impact on the teenager who knew that he would become a professional ballet dancer. Although still in his formative years, Tim knew clearly knew what he wanted from life and had the gumption to seek out the very best place of instruction he could find.

The change in environment for the fourteen-year-old Tim Draper, from the recital studio with its humorous commotion to the more rarefied official training school of the Mercury Ballet Company, had to be profound. For one thing, the Eastman complex and surrounding area alone exuded a feeling of consequence; it was then and remains today the City of Rochester's cultural center. There were still photos on the wall of the various Mercury Ballet dancers who had either come in as stars or had been developed as such, including such early notables as Peter Boneham, who went on to become "Canada's longest serving artistic director in Canadian Contemporary dance"[1] and a leading light of Les Grands Ballets Canadiens; Bobby Blankshine, who enjoyed significant professional acclaim as a featured performer in the Joffrey Ballet; and George Francis, one of McCue's star dancers. According to those who danced with him or admired him from afar, he had extraordinary good looks and a genuine stage presence. Tim did at one point study with the talented Mr. Francis. According to former colleagues, Francis demanded utmost perfection from his students, who tended to remain very devoted to him despite the fact that he would periodically employ a horsewhip on the bottoms of these teary-eyed young dancers if they displeased him in some manner.

After changing from street clothes into ballet attire (at this time, various colored leotards and pink tights for the girls, and black tights and white shirts for the boys), students would enter the studio, go to their chosen spots at the barre, and warm up. Then the pliés would begin. The fun and chatter, or at least the under-the-breath giggles during ballet class that might have invariably been present in another studio, would not have been tolerated in this more formalized setting. Nor would it have been expected by those in attendance because of their passionate desire to become world-class ballet dancers. Tim was very earnest about his studies, according to those who danced with him. After all, he knew that here he would be receiving the serious ballet instruction for which he had been yearning and conducted himself accordingly. All eyes would have been on Miss McCue—or "Madame" as she preferred to be called during class—or on those occasions when for one reason or another she could not make it to class, on her assistant and the prima ballerina of the Mercury Ballet at the time, Pamela Starr Wilkens.

Tim took immediately to this more professionalized level of ballet instruction, offered by the distinguished woman with the flaming red hair. According to the former Mercury Ballet Company star Ed Charbonneau, she "knew how to command the respect and adoration of her students just by entering the room." According to one of the mothers at the time, "What amazed me about Miss McCue was her ability to keep young children interested and listening to what she was telling them. She was actually quite like a martinet—a general!"

Various opinions have emerged over the years to describe Tim's first bona fide ballet teacher, from those who speak of her only in tones of the deepest reverence to those who feel that although her choreography was quite delightful, the actual class instruction she imparted was not always of the highest caliber. What is clear, however, is that by the early 1960s, the ballet studio she shared with Thelma Biracree was the favored studio of visiting out-of-town companies needing class and rehearsal space, and thus she possessed the reputation and credibility to move with authority in the recondite atmosphere of the international ballet world.

Among those who clearly blossomed under the tutelage of Miss McCue, and who became one of Tim's closest friends in class as well as dance partner, was a lovely young dancer, Jacquelyn (Fulreader) Ostrum, who recalled:

> Tim was about fourteen or fifteen years old when I met him. He was one year older than I and that threw us into the same classes and performances. Olive was always on the lookout for men—that is male dancers to perform in her many ballets. I remember Tim Draper started taking class in the fall of 1968 or 1969 and soon became one of her favorites. His greatest asset from the start was that he had a lot of style and in later years after he founded his own school, I saw the same quality and style mirrored in the dancers under his tutelage. Tim was sure of himself, loved being the focus of attention and was gregarious in nature. He made it his business to educate himself in the dance world, becoming well versed with the many companies and exceptional dancers around the world. Names came easily for him and he always had an impressive few up his sleeve. Although he could be critical, he always had the utmost respect for his teachers. In class there was no fooling around. He was focused and extremely serious about his work. Outside of class he was fun and humorous and had lots of stories. He had moments of arrogance and sarcasm but never in reference to his instructors. Our largest performance of the year was *The Nutcracker* and I remember Tim starting out with roles in the first act party scene. In this instance, acting and dance stood on equal ground. He was a great actor thriving in the spotlight, never appearing awkward or nervous. If his career hadn't been geared in dance, he would have made a great actor. His next *Nutcracker* roles were in the Mice corps battle scene and the Chinese dance. Later he would also take part in the Spanish divertissement. We often partnered together but I was also paired with Basil Megna, who was taller and could accommodate my height on point. In 1973, my last year performing in the *Nutcracker*, one of several parts I had was dancing the Russian trepak with Tim. He was always a great focused partner doing whatever it took to make it our best show. During that same *Nutcracker* performance, I danced the pas de deux with Basil Megna as Snow Queen and he danced the Bon Bon with Debbie Bricker, Olive's version of the Sugar Plum and Cavalier pas de deux in other *Nutcracker* renditions. I can't recall where Tim and I partnered one of our last dances together but it was a light flirtatious upbeat piece like a tarantella. I was nineteen years old at the time, making him twenty.

Surely one of Jacquelyn Ostrum's most memorable times with the Mercury occurred when she was one of six McCue students to be selected out of an audition class of three to four hundred in Buffalo by

Olive McCue congratulates RPO Conductor, Samuel Jones, following the Mercury Ballet Company's 1973 *Nutcracker* at the Eastman Theatre. Nineteen-year old Timothy Draper is to the far right as the Bon Bon (Cavalier) with Jacquelyn (Fulreader) Ostrum as the Snow Queen, and Basil Megna as the Snow King. Courtesy of Jacquelyn Ostrum.

the fabled Bolshoi ballet master Asaf Messerer to dance as one of the extras during the Bolshoi's western New York tour. As she describes it,

> Six were chosen from Rochester, all fellow members of the Mercury Ballet Company, including myself. We were also joined by a handful of boy and girl dancers from Buffalo. We rehearsed under his [Messerer's] direction and were able to take class with company members. We were in awe of their prima ballerina, Maya Plisetskaya, who danced alongside us. After touring three cities and performing with the troupe, my mouth dropped open when each of us were handed a paycheck! I felt as though I should hand it right back!

G. Lora Grooms (née Gay Grooms), another of Tim and Jackie's contemporaries and a promising student during this era, loved her teacher very much but describes how Miss McCue could be relentless when she wanted something to be better. To illustrate, she recalls that when she was between the ages of ten and twelve, McCue had spent most of a class singling her out with one harsh correction after another.

At the end of the ordeal, Lora was in tears and quite beside herself. She related the events to her mother, whose perceptive response was, "Why do you think she did this? Because she thinks you are capable of doing better. She cares about you. She sees potential in you." In recalling the overall tenor of Miss McCue's classes, Lora describes a passionate woman who taught with intensity: "Olive was not always the easiest person to deal with. She demanded precision. But this made sense—if you didn't do it right, you would get hurt."

Others who studied with Olive McCue were less certain about her teaching capabilities, however. One labeled her teaching as "confused and wrong." This individual explained that McCue wanted a "perfect second [position], no matter what had to be done to attain it. Second is where the hips and shoulders are in line. If you have to twist your hips, that really isn't second but that is what Olive insisted on. . . . She would have her dancers do anything to get to second position."[2] In later years, Tim, would be concerned about the risks of forcing turnout (the 180-degree outward rotation of the hips essential for executing all of the moves required of a professional ballet dancer) and years later expressed dismay about certain components of McCue's training. He knew at one point that some of the movements she had taught them all "were incorrect" and made sure as a certified teacher in his own right to make the necessary corrections. Although later he always encouraged those students not automatically endowed with natural external rotation to work toward it, he would also engage his close friend Susanne Callan-Harris, a physical therapist well known throughout the area as a "dancer's physical therapist," to assist in this purpose. Tim and Sue had met back in the late 1960s when both were students at Botsford's and remained lifelong friends. He later asked for her help in working with his younger dancers who were "coming up" through the levels to evaluate their external rotation capability and provide them with exercises that could safely and gradually improve on what Mother Nature had not provided.

It is understandable, however, that Olive McCue, with her previous exposure to such greats as the Russian artist Mikhail Mordkin and the Englishman Aubrey Hitchens, would fight hard for her own students to achieve turnout. As the legendary Russian ballerina and teacher Agrippina Vaganova, for whom the ballet method is named, explained in her book *Basic Principles of Classical Ballet,*

> *En dehors* (the "rotary movement directed outward") defines the turned-out position of the leg accepted in classical ballet. . . . The

turn-out is an anatomical necessity for every theatrical dance, which embraces the entire volume of movements conceivable for the legs, and which cannot be accomplished without a turn-out. . . . This is the importance of training the legs of a classical dancer in strict en dehors. It is not an aesthetic conception but a professional necessity. The dancer without a turn-out is limited in her movements, while a classical dancer possessing a turn-out is in command of all conceivable richness of dance movements of the legs.[3]

Another aspect of Miss McCue's training (at least during the early years of managing her own studio) that was not embraced by all of her dancers was her strict prohibition of their training elsewhere or even attending a performance of guest artists visiting Rochester. Two company stars reportedly had to sneak around town to catch a performance of the National Ballet of Canada. As one of the former dancers recalls, McCue made them feel guilty for being there. "From the beginning, it was clear that Miss McCue didn't want people going anywhere else. Part of the reason I went to college was to get exposure to more training." This statement was intoned with just the faintest touch of regret, even though this had happened forty years earlier.

What these and other students were left to ponder under such strict dictates was the degree to which it was worth getting caught. On the one hand, they would feel a sense of culpability in betraying the teacher's wishes. On the other, after seeing the performances of internationally acclaimed companies, they might have had more than a little angst as to whether or not they, too, might have been able to join these organizations had they left McCue earlier.

Quite simply, according to some of the dancers who were with her during the 1950s and early 1960s, McCue did not want her dancers to be influenced by other people and therefore dominated them, even though they were her stars. They were not encouraged to go to New York, despite the fact that this was precisely what she had done in her twenties and what most serious artists dreamed about doing. Not even the very logical and even generous entreaties of her young stars could persuade her that if they were to go and receive advanced training in New York City, they would be of far greater use to her later on, "adding to her own strengths" on their return, as Pamela Wilkens-White put it. Quite clearly, they themselves would have to initiate any leave-taking during this period.

Others at the school, however, did not feel such a lack in their training with McCue, albeit the rigid boundaries did seem to them at the time to be a little nonsensical. As Ed Charbonneau recalled,

[Miss McCue was] very much a teacher of the old school—the training she gave us was excellent, but with peculiarities in terminology and restrictions. For example, we were forbidden to take classes from anyone else, and were not allowed to attend performances by visiting companies. I was summarily dismissed for going to see the Nureyev and Fonteyn film of *Romeo and Juliet* one fall. Of course, a few weeks later I received a sweet phone call: "Where have you been, dear? We're starting *Nutcracker* rehearsals, and you should be here."

Another student recalls how Miss McCue would periodically take one of her advanced dancers to New York City to train with one of the legends. On one such occasion, McCue brought Dorothy Toland with her to take class with Aubrey Hitchins, a class that McCue also took. Miss McCue warned Toland in advance to not look at her during class. She wanted no comparisons.

Many of those who danced for McCue at different intervals over her long career, even those who felt that the classroom instruction might occasionally be wanting, almost uniformly credit her with an excellent sense of choreography. As one dancer recalled, "Olive wasn't a great teacher but she was a fabulous choreographer and I used to love to watch her work. In *Peter and the Wolf*, all of the characters were spot-on."

Several former students suggest that her choreographic talents were most brilliantly on display during the act 1 party scene of *The Nutcracker*, in which she would transform what was traditionally the pretty but predictable dance and dramatic action into a most delightful three-ring circus of sorts, with every single dancer on stage engaging the audience with fully defined characterization and a precision of execution not often found in other productions, even those staged in the major capitals of the world. Whether this took the form of an enthusiastic young Clara mimicking faithfully the movements of the magical dolls, to the scene-stealing antics of her brother Fritz and his friends wreaking every possible kind of havoc on Clara's friends, to an exasperated party parent chastising one of the young male malfeasants, everyone had something to do. This was the work of an artistic director who drew on her own exceptional theatrical training to bring this holiday classic to life, no doubt fueled in large measure by her teacher during the 1920s, Rouben Mamoulian.

Sometimes McCue would import and put her own spin on the ballets she had seen in New York during her annual visits, reworking such popular Balanchine classics as *Serenade, Western Symphony,* and *Peter and the Wolf* into versions of her own. Thus, *Finishing School* was a clear take on *Graduation Ball,* a ballet presented in 1940 by the Original Ballet Russe in Sydney, Australia.[4]

Jacquelyn Ostrum similarly recalls McCue's marvelous choreography:

> During the time I was with her, I performed a wide repertoire of her choreography from very contemporary dance to character dance, which included stylized movement traditional to European countries and then, of course, the purest of classical ballet. Ever year she took on the grand task of choreographing the *Nutcracker* ballet, accompanied by the Rochester Philharmonic Orchestra on the Eastman Theatre stage. From time to time, the RPO would also ask her to integrate her choreography into various operas performed at the Eastman Theatre. I can remember Gluck's *Orpheus and Eurydice* in 1968 where we rehearsed very modern, contemporary dance moves. She would also participate in the Rochester Summer Music Festivals, which were associated with the Eastman School of Music. The Mercury Ballet Company would dance in their "Opera Under the Stars," performed on the Highland Park Bowl stage. A few highlights that come to mind are Menotti's *The Saint of Bleecker Street,* Vaughn Williams' *The Poisoned Kiss,* both in 1973, and in earlier years, the musical, *Brigadoon.*

McCue recognized the importance of touring, so that in addition to the company's own rigorous performance schedule with the Rochester Civic Orchestra, it played to audiences throughout Upstate New York, appearing with the Buffalo Philharmonic Orchestra, the Utica Civic Symphony, the Corning Symphony, the Elmira Symphony, and numerous music and dance festivals with its own orchestra.

These appearances were accompanied by multiple *pro bono* performances for the young people in the area, a practice that Tim later incorporated with his Rochester City Ballet, performing live dress rehearsals for thousands of Rochester City School District schoolchildren on a regular basis. As both student and teacher, Tim knew that an appreciation for the arts needed to be cultivated early in life (not unlike the sensibilities George Eastman expressed during the period leading up to the establishment of the Eastman School of Music and the Eastman Theatre). Thus he had his company perform for these young audiences as frequently as possible.

According to several who studied with her over the years, one of Olive McCue's defining aspects was her expectation that her students would bring an excellent work ethic to her studio. As

Pamela Wilkens-White recalled, "Olive expected you to work. She would rant and rave if she didn't think you were. 'Straighten that leg, straighten that leg,' she would scream at a particular dancer across the room. Then she would walk over to her and say, 'Oh, it is straight, but my, you have funny knees!'" Other dancers would recall her displeasure during certain rehearsals, when she would begin to pound her cane into the floor. Nevertheless, her dancers kept returning or would go off to larger venues. One big complaint heard in the studio during the 1950s and 1960s was that there simply wasn't enough class time. "It was frustrating going to dance every other day," Pamela Wilkens-White commented. "*Every day* would have been better." Whatever frustrations her students felt, however, something far more satisfying was taking place within these emerging young professionals that compelled them to return, year after year, performance after performance. Tim did supplement his study at McCue's by going to Enid Knapp Botsford's when some of the big names, "including Baryshnikov" began coming into town. He would have been fourteen or so when he met the aforementioned Sue Callan-Harris, whose mother, Mary "Ginger" Callan had herself been a dancer in New York and was Mrs. Botsford's (or "Botsy's," as she called her) assistant. Although Sue never felt that she was really the dancer type, her sister was, so the two of them were always taking lessons. It was quite a thrilling time, as Sue recalls, when "Botsy and my mom took the kids everywhere to New York City to see and do it all. There was even a trip to Varna [in Bulgaria] to see the IBC [International Ballet Competition]!"

As Tim improved under McCue's watchful eye and with her ongoing corrections, the barre had to be a place of solace for him, where he could slowly begin to work through his profound grief over his brother's death. With the absolute focus required in a ballet class, there might have been no better a place to help this earnest young man attempt to handle the tragedy that had befallen him and his family. It appears, however, that he mostly kept his feelings of loss to himself. "One thing I noticed when we were young was that he didn't talk about his family," recalls Jackie Ostrum, who eventually spent some "down time" with Tim outside of the studio as they became good friends. "I never knew why. Maybe after his brother passed on, it was too painful, I don't know. But then I don't think any of us really talked about our families—you know teenagers." She recalls one time driving over to my grandmother's home with him and having an in-depth discussion on how to cut men's hair. He was taking courses in hairdressing at the time. He gave me such a clear mental picture of how to do it that I was able to cut short hair successfully from that moment forward without attending a single class. In later years, when he had his own ballet school, he never chose to mention his hairdressing days. I brought it up once backstage when there was an emergency hair issue. I suggested we ask Tim as he had been a hairdresser. He smiled and quickly changed the subject.

The consensus among those who knew Tim well is that he enjoyed this period of training with Olive McCue very much. Her huge impact on him was reflected in the way he later choreographed and staged his own productions. *The Nutcracker* and *Peter and the Wolf* were two classics with which he became intimately connected during his time with her. The fact that he also staged these productions himself reflects just how much he valued her multiple talents and experience. He had obviously paid very close attention to his teacher's unique ability to create onstage magic, something he would embrace in faithful fashion throughout his career.

He also learned in later years about the importance of hiring a strong-willed bookkeeper to manage the books. For a studio owner, a level of business acumen must always accompany artistry in order to have a smooth functioning operation. By all accounts, McCue was not particularly suited to the business side of the venture. At one time, she apparently walked into the studio with a large number of old, uncashed tuition checks in hand and said, "Dear, I found these in a book—do you think you could return them and get new ones?" Sometimes scheduling would prove problematic as well. In the latter half of her career, there were days when she was not up to teaching, and she would prevail on her capable assistant to do the duty. She would say to her prima ballerina, Pamela Wilkens, "Well, dear, this one is on you." Wilkens would then quickly step up to the plate, recalling how inspired she herself had been as a child when such wonderful dancers as Dorothy Toland taught or were the demonstrators. The only time that this last-minute scheduling proved problematic was Visitor Day, when McCue might not have been following what the students were working on in class and therefore quickly had to be brought up to speed. It was during these periodic absences that Wilkens came to know Tim and to teach him. She recalls, "He did well. He wasn't exceptional at that point as a dancer and part of that was because he hadn't had that much classical training. . . . He learned a great deal on form, being at Olive McCue's. Olive had an interest in him."

During this time, Tim would often go back and forth among four studios: his old studio, Little Red; Olive McCue's; Botsford's; and the new Ballet Center of Buffalo. Tim's chief involvement with Little Red at that time was taking a teacher-training course and occasionally performing at the end-of-year recital. The training course apparently was quite a standard practice for the advanced students at Little Red. Although some classically trained instructors would question the validity of entrusting the training of the next generation of dancers to fourteen- and fifteen-year-olds, regardless of their particular talents, the program assuredly had its merits, resulting in the development of some very fine teachers, not the least of whom included Michelle Ilardo Buschner as well as Tim.

There is no question that Olive McCue came to care for Tim very much and was supportive of his goals. He was, in fact, one of the very few students allowed to leave her studio to commute to Buffalo when he expressed an interest in going to study with the distinguished Kathleen Crofton, the Cecchetti-trained dancer who had danced with Anna Pavlova and had established the Ballet Center of Buffalo in 1967. In fact, according to Tim's mother, not only did Olive McCue accept his choice but she also "suggested he apply for a scholarship" with Crofton. That is how he began his additional dance studies as a fourteen-year-old at Kathleen Crofton's studios, a story he later told many times as a reason for wanting to offer exceptional instruction in Rochester.

It is obvious that Tim felt great affection for Olive McCue, honoring her later in life by inviting her to restage a work for his own dancers. Less visible to those who did not know their history was the degree to which he absorbed her grand style, splendid choreography, and her passion for dance, which forever played a role in fueling his own. He always wanted his dancers to be the very best they could possibly be, something that he felt would not happen without a certain level of admonition and sometimes even tears.

Beyond the steps, however, Olive McCue taught Tim about the importance of "living large" professionally. The most vivid example was her establishing, with Thelma Biracree years earlier, the Mercury Ballet Company, which was housed within the Eastman School of Music. While the two women ran the company between 1950 and 1956, it is clear that their strategy of creating a first-class ballet company, with accompaniment usually provided by the Rochester Civic Orchestra under the musical direction of Paul White, was a well-informed one. In the talents of the Biracree-McCue dancers, complemented by the occasional judicious import from a major company, the region had a ballet company in residence of which it could be proud.

Peter Boneham's description of the company drawn from memories of decades past seems to sum up perfectly why the Mercury Ballet flourished as it did. "It was a venture run by two extraordinary women, Olive McCue and Thelma Biracree."

Tim inherited from Olive McCue a draft manuscript on onionskin paper about the Mercury Ballet in which she conveyed how Tim was the "legacy/progeny" of her own efforts. He cherished this document and intended to publish it one day. At a most basic level, it was a reaffirmation that the ballet school and company he established in 1986 and 1987 owed its lifeblood to the Eastman Theatre Ballet and the Eastman School of Music.

Tim Draper and Jillian Nealon at the cast party following 2001's *Cinderella*.
Photograph by Cathy Nealon.

JILLIAN NEALON

"Rhoda! Turnout!" I am in the level 6 Ballet class with Tim, and I look around the room to see whom he is talking to. There is no Rhoda in our class. I meet Tim's eyes and see that he is looking directly at me. Rhoda? Who is Rhoda? Suddenly I realize that he has decided to call me Rhoda, and secretly I am thrilled. Any student of Tim's knows that he loved to give pet names to his students. The names were always ridiculous, and you had to wonder where in the world he came up with them. We all got a big kick out of it, though, and I was happy to join the group of dancers who had acquired one of his famous nicknames!

I had the privilege of studying with Tim Draper for four years, but for me it wasn't nearly long enough. Tim was the greatest teacher and mentor I ever had. He influenced my life as a dancer, performer, and teacher tremendously, and I often wish I had begun my training with him far sooner than I did. Ballet was my life throughout my high school years, as it had to be if you wanted to be a part of the top level in his school. For four years I spent six days a week in classes and rehearsals, and in truth I probably spent more time with Tim than I did with my own family. Tim's students were his family, and I know he cared deeply for all of us.

Tim was by far the toughest teacher I ever had. He could make you laugh, and he could make you cry. Sometimes you hated him, but in the end you always loved him. He expected perfection and nothing less. He never allowed anyone to say "I can't." If he corrected you and you told him "I'm trying," he always replied, "Well, try harder." He would rehearse us *ad nauseam*, dissecting every tiny detail of the choreography and making sure we were perfect and in unison, right down to our fingertips. Tim set the bar very high, and it paid off. There is a reason that the Draper Dancers are known for their impeccable technique, artistry, and versatility. Any student who had the opportunity to train with Tim was truly fortunate. I recognize this quite often as I see the different dance schools across the country and what so many of them lack. I don't think we realized as students how good we had it. Tim was an amazing teacher and therefore, he created amazing dancers.

I would always get nervous before Tim's classes. Every Tuesday, Thursday, and Saturday we would all be waiting at our spots at the barre, watching the staircase to see any sign that Tim was coming up. He would suddenly appear in his tight V-neck shirt and with his big black dance bag over his shoulder, and we would anxiously wait, wondering if he was in a good mood or a bad mood. If he smiled and cracked a joke, we would breathe a sigh of relief, knowing that it was going to be a fun class! I always stood in the second spot at the barre, closest to the stereo where Tim would stand to demonstrate. Every now and then I would try to stand on the other side of the room, especially if I was tired and was hoping to escape his critical eye, but usually Tim would ask why I was standing over there and tell me to move back to my spot!

My favorite times with Tim were in rehearsals. Although it certainly was exhausting to rehearse for hours, running each piece over and over and over, the end result was always worth it. Tim had a way of explaining things to all of us that was often humorous, yet memorable. To this day whenever I hear the "Snow" scene music from *The Nutcracker* I always think back to one particular rehearsal we had for "Snow." We had just finished running the dance, and Tim was not impressed. He pointed out the window to the outside world and said "See that, that is slush, not snow. That's what you all just looked like. I want to see beautiful enchanting snowflakes, not disgusting brown slush that's left-over after it snows." Growing up in Rochester we of course knew what he meant, and the analogy made sense to us! Those little sayings have always stuck with me, but I took so many more important things from rehearsals with Tim. His attention to detail, learning the importance of being an understudy (he loved to put you on the spot and throw you right into the middle of what often turned into chaos!), timing and musicality (something that later proved to be one of my greatest assets throughout my professional career), and the ability to know your spacing on stage—if you happened to be so much as half an inch off of the tape mark you would never hear the end of it! He essentially taught us as students how to be company dancers. He completely prepared us for what we would later encounter in our dancing careers.

Perhaps my most special memory is when Tim asked me to help him critique our rehearsals and take notes. Thinking back on that now, the idea that he trusted me as a teenager to help him clean and rehearse our dances both humbles and astonishes me. He recognized in me as a young student a talent I didn't even know I had, and it is thanks to him providing me with that opportunity to assist him that later inspired me to want to be a ballet mistress. I have great respect for his taking the time not only to train us as students who would become professional ballet dancers but also to teach us the attributes of a teacher, ballet mistress, or director. I wish he could see how much he influenced my career as a company member with the San Diego Ballet, ballet mistress/teacher at the San Diego Civic Youth Ballet, and program manager now at the Joffrey Ballet School. He inspired me and made possible my career in ballet, and for that I will forever be grateful.

I'd like to think that Tim is keeping watch over all of his dancers and that he is proud of each and every one of us. Rochester is truly lucky that Tim opened his school all those years ago, and his memory and legacy live on in all of us.

Jillian Nealon Peschken is currently the registrar, director's assistant, and adult program manager at the Joffrey Ballet School. She is a graduate of Indiana University's Jacobs School of Music ballet department.

OFF TO MISS CROFTON'S

To the impresarios, choreographers, composers, teachers, and students connected with the London ballet universe, she was known as Katie Crofton. But to the rest of the world, including the most passionate balletomanes, she was always "Miss Crofton" or "Kathleen Crofton," a British ballet dancer, teacher, and director of impeccable credentials and taste. "Born in India of British parents, her father an Army officer killed in action, Miss Crofton became famous during the 1920s as 'Pavlova's Baby,' touring the world as the youngest protégée of the *prima ballerina assoluta* Anna Pavlova."[1] Miss Crofton also danced with Bronislava Nijinska's company after training with Olga Preobrajenska, Alexander Levitoff, and Nicholas Legat of the Imperial Russian Ballet. In particular, however, Kathleen Crofton embodied the exquisite training and refinement of the Cecchetti tradition.

As John Dwyer of the *Buffalo Evening News* described her in an interview in 1971,

> There's so much of *Tomorrow* in everything Kathleen Crofton says and does, one scarcely realizes she is a walking history of classical dance. . . . This soft-spoken, firm-willed British artist and adopted Buffalonian is literally a part of the 20th century ballet legend itself. . . . Nowadays it's all about plans for the Niagara Frontier Ballet, four years in the making and shaping under her directorship and already with remarkable results in the record—touring appearances in major cities, a week in the Jacob's Pillow Festival, and a big European tour this summer with the celebrated Rudolf Nureyev heading the star-performer list.[2]

Kathleen Crofton established a ballet company and preprofessional feeder school in Buffalo, New York, in September 1967, with a grand opening attended by Dame Alicia Markova. Markova, a celebrated British ballerina and choreographer, had recommended

Crofton for the job to the Buffalo financier and philanthropist Franz T. Stone.[3] When word got out, students of ballet from all over the country auditioned. At this time, Tim was still dancing at the Little Red Dancing School, shortly before moving to study at the Olive McCue School of Ballet. Gradually, though, as it became conventional knowledge that the legendary artist was working on a grand scale only an hour away in Buffalo, Tim spoke with Miss McCue about commuting back and forth, and she agreed that this would be the right thing for him to do.

Tim thus arrived at Crofton's studio, the Ballet Center of Buffalo, reportedly a "gorgeous huge studio" located on the top floor of the Marine Midland Bank at the corner of Elmwood Avenue and West Utica Street.[4] Undoubtedly, Tim knew immediately that this was the place to continue on his path toward becoming a professional. Within the next two years, while Tim continued to enjoy training and performance opportunities with Olive McCue, the commuting ended (save for the weekends), and Tim was fully enveloped within Crofton's world. By August of 1970, he was sixteen years of age and a resident student at the Ballet Center of Buffalo. There he struck up a close friendship with a particularly gifted young ballet dancer two years his junior, Donna Ross. When she was fourteen, Donna had begged her parents to send her the nearly 2,000 miles from her hometown of Midland, Texas, so that she could study with ballet legends. She had been attending pre-professional dance training camps during the summer months for quite some time. She gained immeasurably at the hands of world-class ballet instructors but then slipped frustratingly back into old habits six months later. Midland in 1970 was a relatively small community of less than sixty thousand, and the quality of training available could not rival what was taking place in the major preprofessional training programs. From the time she was very young, Donna had become passionate about ballet and knew, as youngsters often do, that she had something special. She thus did significant research into the best residential programs of the day, narrowing it down to four: Interlaken, North Carolina School of the Arts, Mary Day's Washington Ballet School, and Kathleen Crofton's Ballet Center of Buffalo. The first three, despite their excellent professional qualifications, presented some concerns to the Ross family relative to the availability of accommodations. Donna followed the recommendation of a young woman from Texas Christian University (which had a program that placed a good deal of emphasis on ballet) who said that Miss Crofton's dancers were very good. Donna went to Buffalo, she auditioned for Crofton and was accepted.

The year 1970 was unquestionably a time of great national angst. College campuses were in full-throttle rebellion over President Nixon's prolonged involvement in Vietnam, invasion of Cambodia, and the shooting deaths of four innocent student protesters on May 4 at Kent State University by members of the Ohio National Guard. A hundred thousand marched on the nation's capital to protest the Vietnam War. The Chicago Seven were found guilty of inciting a riot at the 1968 Democratic national convention. Daily studio life at Crofton's, however, projected a vastly different sensibility. Debussy, not The Who, permeated the workday surroundings, which must have been beyond anything for which Tim might have hoped. The winter before he arrived, for example, Crofton had prevailed on her dear friend of half a century, Madame Bronislava Nijinska, or "La Nijinska," of the Ballets Russes, to travel to Buffalo to mount three ballets for Crofton's company: Tchaikovsky's *Sleeping Beauty*, Poulenc's *Biches*, and *Brahms Variations* (Paganini-Boutnikoff).[5] Nijinska had choreographed *Les Biches* for the founder and impresario of the Ballets Russes, Sergei Diaghilev, in 1924.[6] Kathleen Crofton had also danced in Nijinska's company, and thus in addition to friendship, knew her work firsthand. As the December 18, 1969, issue of the *South Buffalo–West Seneca News* described it, "Kathleen Crofton, Artistic Director of the Center Company and Melvin Strauss, Director of the Festival have joined forces with the famous ballet figure, Bronislava Nijinska to mount three ballets by the legendary choreographer. Madame Nijinska, great Russian ballerina of the Imperial Theatre of St. Petersburg, beloved by Stravinsky, Diaghilev, and dancers all over the world as a choreographer, now in her 79th year has come to the Center Ballet from England's Royal Ballet and the Rome Opera to re-create three ballet classics for the Buffalo audience."[7]

The collaboration was apparently a spectacularly successful one, as evidenced by the fact that it was then restaged at Jacob's Pillow. The timing of this special historic reunion among friends was particularly poignant; less than three years later La Nijinska was dead.

Tim and Donna seem to have made the most of their time together as friends and fellow students at Miss Crofton's. In addition to the rigorous ballet training offered, the Ballet Center of Buffalo had established an affiliation with the State University of New York College at Buffalo to enable students who would ordinarily still be going to a traditional public or private high school at this time in their lives to have a full academic program that would enable them to complete their studies at the appropriate time. Donna recalls, "Tim and I took a Shakespeare course together at Buffalo State. We played the roles of Romeo and Juliet in the reading and our professor was delighted to have two teenagers of the same age as the fictional R and J." With the scholarship he had received from the studio, Tim was able to attend college, dancing for half a day and attending school for the other half.

Donna recalls one especially enjoyable day off that they celebrated with another of their friends, Debbie Gladstein of Rochester. The trio packed a picnic lunch and went across the Peace Bridge into Canada. Debbie had previously trained with George Francis of Rochester, as did Tim for a brief time, and all seemed to come to the conclusion that he was "a kind of dark, but charismatic and interesting man." They all lived in a brownstone dormitory called the Residence, with students who lived not too far away, such as Tim and Debbie, occasionally going home on the weekends.

In a letter addressed to her mother a little over a year after arriving in Buffalo, Donna provides special insight into what it was like for her and Tim to study with the extraordinary Kathleen Crofton.

Dear Mom,

Ah, how frustrating are unfinished tasks, especially when they are meaningful and enjoyable occupations! But, it was only another meaningful experience that has kept me from carrying them out. Last night, I was all prepared to spend a nice quiet evening in the solitude of my room listening to music, doing some work on a term paper, and reading. Well, needless to say, my plan wasn't carried out, instead, around 10:00 I went downstairs to bring a pillow to Miss Crofton who was staying the night because Mrs. Collingwood went to Toronto for the weekend, and ended up having tea with Tim, Nancy, and herself, and talking until 12:30! But now, I wouldn't have traded any amount of time for that wonderful experience. What a wonderful woman she is! In those few hours, so many ideas sprung forth in my mind and with all of us there was genuine pleasure in sharing our thoughts. I know that we made her very happy. . . . I want to dance more than anything in the world. Dance is the most total form of life in existence. It is sound, stillness, light, dark, movement, high, low, feeling, thought, sexuality, sensitivity, solitude, flight, depth, precision, fluidity, separation, unity.

Love—

In class, Donna remembers Tim sometimes being a "sad, shy, scared, and occasionally hostile young man. He was not very advanced

in Buffalo. . . . I think most of us thought he was a sickly young man. . . .
He used to hang in the back of the class against the barre and look
sullenly at the other dancers. Never in a million years did we think
he would go on to become such a fine dancer and a great teacher/
director! He once told me that he and some of the other dancers
'hated' me because I was so quick and well coordinated." Donna's talent was independently corroborated years later by Sue Callan-Harris,
who "remembers Donna Ross as being able to do everything and that
she was going to be fabulous someday (because she already was)." She
remembered Kathleen Crofton as well, "sadly, because she came here
and died shortly afterward."

But Donna remained a good friend to Tim, well aware that her new
comrade in arms was still mourning acutely the death of his brother
during this period. "Tim spoke sadly and lovingly of his brother, William, who had been killed in Vietnam shortly before he came to Buffalo. . . . [He] also complained constantly of migraine headaches and
took Darvon for the pain. He seemed depressed in Buffalo. . . . I attributed it to the loss of his brother and to the headaches."

On other days, however, Tim's demeanor would be quite different—most studious, where he would be learning, absorbing, imbibing
every movement including the slightest nuance, grasping it all from a
big-picture perspective. Donna describes Tim as the "most dedicated
of all the students. [He] did love it a lot."

Donna has very vivid recollections of Miss Crofton, who to this day
remains her greatest artistic influence. She recalls how Crofton

> used to teach in a dress, stockings, and pumps. She usually had a
> piece of jewelry around her neck. That is how they dress in Russia—
> they don't wear practice clothes. She also wore her hair in a classical
> bun over her ears in the small nape of her neck. She was very soft spo-
> ken but she could get angry (usually at the male dancers) where she
> would stomp her feet, put her hand in a fist, and in something that
> sounded like a screech, bellowed "NNNNooooooooooo. You are not
> getting it because you've been out making whoopee."

Whistling the classics was another part of this legend's standard (if
somewhat unusual) teaching *modus operandi*, helping to create genuine
dancers by showing her students the steps and combinations with her
arms while whistling the strains of Tchaikovsky, Vivaldi, and Stravinsky.
While doing so, she would focus particularly on épaulement—the use
of back, head, neck, and shoulders—to create the magnificent *port de*

bras, oftentimes in lunge position with movements coming deep from the back, that was often cited by critics as a distinguishing feature of her students and company members.

As Donna explains,

> Miss Crofton instilled in her dancers the artistically pure *port de bras* and style of the Imperial Ballet School of the Mariinsky Theatre. It was not only technique, which she gave us, though she did that in spades also, but a true purity of style and technique such that I was doing four pirouettes *en pointe,* consistently, as a fifteen-year old in Miss Crofton's school! We could all jump, do complicated, intricate *batterie* [rapidly "beating," that is, crossing the feet or lower legs while in midair] and all with the lilting, lyrical expressive upper body, épaulement, and strong, athletic backs that was the style of the Imperial Ballet School, Pavlova's and Nijinsky's Alma Mater! Indeed, Tim, Deborah [Gladstein], and I were the direct descendants, artistically speaking, of Anna Pavlova.

Crofton's faculty included Frank Bourman and his wife, Rosalia Kurowaka; Elizabeth Cunliffe of the Sadler's Wells Ballet; David Gayle of the Royal Ballet; and others.

Donna went on to say that Crofton liked Tim, even if he was not, at first, very advanced. But he absorbed it all and ended up becoming just that. The fact that he routinely described himself as truly "taking off" with Nancy Bielski at Harkness House in the early 1970s is a testament to how much attention he had been paying at Miss Crofton's. Echoing these sentiments was Janet Boeff, who recalls, "I believe this [Miss Crofton's] was where he received his best training."

Donna Ross also describes how Crofton would expect a bit of fearlessness from her dancers when it came to pirouettes.

> We would be in *tendu croisé,* with our heels down in back in preparatory position in fourth [position]. Then there would be a pirouette *en dehors* in *attitude,* plié in arabesque, pull in and do another in *retiré* and land one foot with the other in *coup de pied.* And then a *bourrée* turn. She would give us lots of turns in *attitude* and arabesque. Students were fearless and full-bodied in their movement—so dramatic and very athletic also. What she did was create dancers. This was the Russian style and one actually might say it was the pre-Vaganova instructional style since Pavlova, with whom Miss Crofton performed, died in 1931, while Vaganova didn't publish her instructional system until 1934.

Crofton liked to refer to her female students as "duckies" and "sweeties." Her observations would often conclude with the encouraging "All right, sweetie," or "Okay, duckie." Revered by her students for her extraordinary pedagogical technique and kindness, she was also admired for her inherent bravery, both the consequence of being a loyal British subject who gave up performing in order to contribute fully to the war effort during World War II and for being raised as a Christian Scientist, which meant that when she broke or badly sprained her arm (as she did at one point), she would just "carry on" with a makeshift sling and nothing more.

In the summer of 1971, Crofton's company, the Niagara Frontier Ballet, enjoyed a highly acclaimed European tour with the legendary Rudolf Nureyev and other stars. Among this elite troupe was the internationally accomplished Deborah Hess, who recalls that she "stayed in Europe after our European tour with Nureyev and Eva Evdokimova, etc."

Notwithstanding the tour's resounding artistic and professional success, however, "the cost of mounting such an undertaking was exorbitant, because shortly thereafter, rumors began to circulate that the school and company were mired in deep financial problems and both might have to be shut down. On December 21, the rumors became reality when Franz T. Stone, the president of the Metropolitan Buffalo Association for the Dance and the company's original sponsor who had brought Miss Crofton to Buffalo, stated that the MBA had "suspended operations due to a pressing financial deficit." In the same article, it was announced that the ballet company's official training school, the Ballet Center of Buffalo, which had also received aid from the association, would be closing as well.[8] Not missing a beat, Tim and Donna "packed their bags and traveled to the Big Apple." Donna describes the adventure:

> I was all of fifteen and Tim was seventeen and off we went in a rented car, I think, but perhaps it was the bus, I do not remember exactly. At any rate, we got to Manhattan from Buffalo and for the first couple of days we found an apartment, inconveniently located on the Upper East Side, which belonged to the sister of a classmate of ours from Buffalo. She had done the NYC "thing," you know, oh, "I'll leave my key at the pub downstairs and when you get in, just go to the bartender and tell him that you are friends of mine and ask for the key and don't forget to lock the top inside lock at night, leave a light on when you go out in the morning and be careful, etc. etc." Tim and I decided that we would try our luck in the Big Apple so that we would have a place to go even if Miss Crofton's School did close.

We set up auditions at three of the four major dance schools . . . all but SAB, since neither he nor I were the Balanchine ideal, although, in retrospect, I regret not giving NYCB a try, since many people tell me I bear a resemblance to Melissa Hayden, one of Mr. B's lead ballerinas and that Mr. B would probably have liked me. The first day we went to the Joffrey School (I was fifteen going on thirty-five in those days). . . . I recall vividly what I wore to the audition . . . a red, woolen "midi skirt"—this was 1971, and a red, white, and cranberry colored scarf and putting a safety pin in the back, thus making a halter top ensemble, then red, high-heeled, platform sandals, which were all the rage at the time. Feeling very confident, Tim and I walked into Mrs. D's office, introduced ourselves, and went to change clothes for class. After a class taught by Meredith Baylis, we were told that we were both accepted! Not only accepted, we were both given full scholarships! Next stop was ABT. Leon Danielian, wheelchair bound that day due to problems stemming from arthritis years earlier, could not take his EYES off of TIM! He was mesmerized. He wheeled his chair around vigorously, right in front of Tim, and watched him with an ardor, an intensity that was almost frightening! (I am sure that he was as fascinated by this handsome young man's face and body as by his obvious dancing talent.). . . . Again, victory! We were both given full scholarships! Oh, the joys of ACCEPTANCE! They LIKED us!

The third and last stop for us came the next day when we went to Harkness. There, Tim was given a partial scholarship. I do not remember more of that trip to NYC with Tim (one of several) except that we spent our last night there at a discount bookstore with Tim complaining the whole time that we should be going to a show, that he had not come all the way to NYC to spend the evening in a bookstore. I agreed that it was unfortunate, but pointed out to him that we were quite running out of money and that unless he had a great idea for how to PAY for the tickets to a Broadway show and supper, we had better hang out someplace cheaper!

On returning to Buffalo, Tim and Donna, along with their classmates and company members, learned that alternative funding arrangements were in the process of being made. The two were thus faced with a difficult decision: remain in Buffalo with an extraordinary teacher, albeit in a school with a shaky financial situation, or move to New York City and jump-start their careers with a larger and more stable, nationally renowned organization, something that was obviously within their grasp. After much deliberation, they elected to remain in Buffalo with Katherine Crofton, despite the fact that their "road trip" had met with singular and stunning success.

On April 4, 1972, it was learned that the reassurances had indeed been well founded with the announcement that officers and directors had been named to a newly formed organization. The Great Lakes Association for the Dance would be stepping up to rescue the company. It would be the known as the "parent organization for a new ballet company, Festival Ballet of New York, and a new ballet school."[9] The president of the new organization, its "white knight," as it were, was Arthur C. LeVan, who had recognized months earlier that this company and school were worth saving and thus had the foresight to establish a committee, the Friends of the Ballet, install himself as chairman, and do everything within his power to save Crofton's company and school after the previous sponsoring organization had suspended it.

Perhaps the most intriguing aspect of the bailout was that in large measure, it was owed to the tenacity and spirit of the woman who had given the neighboring city of Rochester its very first taste of professional ballet nearly fifty years earlier—the former Enid Knapp Botsford, now Mrs. Enid Botsford-Orcutt! As the newly installed vice president of the Great Lakes Association for the Dance, Mrs. Orcutt—in collaboration with her husband, Brent, Arthur C. LeVan, Earl W. Stokes (the treasurer), Kathleen Crofton (the secretary, artistic director of the company, and director of the school), and numerous board members culled from the Buffalo music community and from industry—began working indefatigably, calling on corporations, foundations, and individuals to ensure that a great artist of Kathleen Crofton's pedigree would remain with the school and company that she had founded only four years earlier. They stressed how she had given the Buffalo community an extraordinary gift of ballet in drawing on her international reputation to develop the next generation of artists by exposing them to the greatest of the greats in the ballet world. An initial goal of $40,000 was sought for first-year operating costs of the new company as well as to "acquire the costumes, music, and scenery valued at $100,000 from the suspended operations of the Niagara Frontier Ballet Company's parent organization, Metropolitan Buffalo Association for the Dance." New plans also called for "an educational thrust into the community for lecture-demonstrations, as well as mini-performances and full-scale productions for sponsoring groups. In addition, salon-type presentations at the studio itself," at this time listed as being at 267 West Utica Street, were to be offered to the public to experience and become involved in ballet through rehearsals and preparation for an actual performance.[10] This was another tradition that Tim Draper carried on years later as artistic director of his own company and school.

And for a while, the new ballet company, Festival Ballet of New York, exceeded everyone's expectations. By that time, though, Tim had made the decision to leave Buffalo for New York City, after a remarkable two years of training with Kathleen Crofton. Donna Ross later averred that Tim's outstanding professional success as a dancer and teacher was a direct result of the exemplary training that Crofton had given him in Buffalo. Donna knew that by the time he began studying with Nancy Bielski in New York City, he was already at a sufficiently advanced level to be able to take full advantage of Nancy's rigorous classes. One downside for Donna, however, was that with Tim's departure, he wouldn't be able to witness her meteoric rise. A 1972 *Union-Sun Journal* review of the Festival Ballet of New York's *Nutcracker* by Dennis Harrison states, "Among the adult members of the Festival Ballet of New York the excellent debut of Donna Ross in the *Nutcracker* Friday earned her the warm enthusiasm the audience gave her."[11] The headline "Dame Margot, Festival Ballet Score at Eastman" announced another success. In a review on April 1, 1973, George H. Kimball, the arts critic of the *Rochester Times-Union*, noted Dame Margot Fonteyn and Heinz Boesl's visit to the Eastman Theatre in a joint appearance with Crofton's Festival Ballet of New York to perform *Sleeping Beauty*, *Les Sylphides*, and six other ballets. Kimball stated, "The relatively young Festival Ballet, directed by Kathleen Crofton, was doing respectable work when I first saw it about two years ago. Last night, the corps de ballet was coordinating with smooth precision, resembling the New York City Ballet. Among the evening's soloists were James Bogan, borrowed from the New York City Ballet, and Donna Ross, the Festival Ballet's own, who together made the *pas de deux* from Heisted's *Flower Festival in Genzano*, a mid-program brightspot."[12]

Donna had by this time risen to the role of principal dancer with Crofton's company. In addition to the Heisted piece, she also danced alongside Margot Fonteyn throughout both of the featured selections. For *Sleeping Beauty*, she danced the role of the Enchanted Princess in the Bluebird Pas de Deux in 'Aurora's Wedding' and for *Les Sylphides*, she performed the role of The Waltz. Attendance at this sensational Eastman Theatre performance was near capacity in the three-thousand-seat auditorium.

In a heartbreaking incident, and unknown to many in attendance at the Eastman Theatre or to those attending the program at Buffalo's Kleinhans Music Hall a short time thereafter, the company had sustained a fire less than a month earlier. The blaze destroyed all of the costumes, sets, and musical scores. It was ironic that at a time when the company should have been celebrating a sensational artistic triumph, an abrupt announcement was made that the company would be shutting down for good.

As reported in an Associated Press wire story on April 28, 1973, "The Festival Ballet of New York, whose Buffalo studio was destroyed by fire last month, has decided to disband, its director disclosed Friday. Kathleen Crofton said she was resigning her directorship and going to England. She said her company might be revived sometime in the future, but not in Buffalo. 'We tried very hard in this locality, but there doesn't seem to be quite enough financial support here,' she said."[13] The article went on to say that the "troupe was formed in 1967 as the Niagara Frontier Ballet and in 1971 toured Europe with Rudolf Nureyev. Last year, it went through bankruptcy proceedings and was reorganized as the Festival Ballet. Sponsored by the Great Lakes Association for Dance, the company had close ties with dance interests in Rochester." What the article did not say was that Kathleen Crofton insisted that the Eastman Theatre show go on as planned, despite the catastrophe that had just befallen the company, and had engaged the efforts of multiple volunteers to sew new costumes. Donna Ross and James Bogan actually had not been in Buffalo when the fire broke out but were rehearsing for the Margot Fonteyn Eastman Theatre performance at the School of American Ballet studios in Lincoln Center (coached by Hector Zaraste for the *Bluebird pas de deux*, and Stanley Williams for *Flower Festival in Genzano*). This type of stoicism was one more example of Miss Crofton's extraordinary grace under pressure.

Regardless of the sad setback for Miss Crofton and those who supported her, she left quite a legacy during her relatively short time in Buffalo. As Donna Ross states, "many of us went on to dance with bigger professional companies."

> *Tim Draper* had a performance career with Les Ballets Trock-
> adero de Monte Carlo before serving as the artistic director
> of the Rochester City Ballet and later the ballet master for
> Trockadero.

Joanne Zimmerman danced for about twenty years with the Dutch National Ballet.

Mary Barres danced for a number of years with the Hamburg Ballet, then went on to get her bachelor of arts in art history from Harvard and a PhD in dance from the University of Utah, writing her thesis on John Neumeir.

Debby Hess is now ballet mistress at the National Ballet School of Canada after having an international performance career.

Lynn Glauber danced for the Joffrey Ballet and was a soloist with Maurice Béjart (who referred to her as "my little Pavlova").

Debbie Zdobinsky danced with the San Francisco Ballet and San Francisco Opera

The *Pinowsky* sisters danced in Europe.

Rodney Gustafson danced for a number of years with American Ballet Theatre and now has his own company, the State Street Ballet in Santa Barbara, California.

Valerie Feit danced with Eliot Feld and Alvin Ailey American Dance Theater.

Debra van Cure danced with Kathleen Crofton's Maryland Ballet in Baltimore.

Michael Matinzi and *Katherine Collingwood* danced for the National Ballet of Canada. Later, Katherine was dancing with the Royal Winnipeg Ballet when she was stricken with and died of ALS (Lou Gehrig's disease).

Raymond Lukens, who toured with Kathleen Crofton has been a faculty member of American Ballet Theatre's Jacqueline Kennedy Onassis School since 2005. With ABT's school principal Franco De Vita he coauthored the ABT National Training Curriculum and created the syllabus for the New York University masters degree training curriculum in ABT ballet pedagogy.

Deborah Gladstein, after graduating from Bennington College, acquired extensive training and professional experience in the Alexander Technique and t'ai chi ch'uan.

Diane Lewis presently is the dance department cochair (classical ballet) and choreographer at the Hochstein School of Music and Dance in Rochester.

Donna Ross danced with Joffrey II, the Joffrey Ballet, and the Dallas Ballet.

No doubt Kathleen Crofton would be delighted to know that several members of this special group began holding reunions a few years ago, meeting twice yearly in New York City. The reunions involve grand camaraderie over shared meals and attendance at the ballet performances of American Ballet Theatre, New York City Ballet, and other companies. Organized initially by Donna Ross, this group has loosely included Deborah Gladstein, Lynn Glauber, Valerie Parnelski, Valerie Feit, Lynn Rifkin, Donna Fargnioli Romer, Ray Lukens, Diane Lewis, and Deborah Hess. Hess performed throughout the United States and Europe, working directly with Bronislava Nijinska, Rudolf Nureyev, Hans Brenna, Asaf Messerer, and Anna Marie Holmes. She is also well known as a juror on the international ballet competition circuit, and as a noteworthy faculty member at Canada's National Ballet School.

Ms. Hess recalled that she didn't know Tim as a fellow student: "We did not cross paths as students with Katie Crofton. He came to study with her after I left." But, she said, they did

> meet up many years later when he came to meet me in Toronto and see me teach at NBC. He invited me to guest teach in his school a few times, and unfortunately, it never worked out schedule wise. We had talked about me coming to Rochester shortly before he died, and we were excited as we thought it was going to work out that time. I was so shocked to hear of his passing. It was easy to instantly like him, he had so much energy, that we did feel an instant bond, sharing Katie Crofton stories.

In a further cruel irony, almost mirroring the catastrophe of the studio's collapse in the wake of triumph, Donna Ross herself would soon confront agony of her own after consenting to ill-advised surgery on her feet, a decision that forever changed the course of her life. She went on to have an excellent career with the Joffrey Ballet and quite likely also would have with the Stuttgart Ballet as well, had John Cranko not passed away shortly after auditioning her. However, those who were aware of the highly nuanced quality of her talent generally agree that had she not had the surgery or sustained any other "surprises" in the form of accidents, illnesses, and so on, she very likely would have been one of the greats in the ballet world, performing with the American Ballet Theatre, the New York City Ballet, or the Royal Ballet on the same level with Rebecca Wright, Martine van Hamel, and Georgina Parkinson.

Thus, in 1973, within a short seven years after an auspicious beginning, Buffalo lost its distinction as a center for extraordinary ballet with the closure of Crofton's Festival Ballet of New York and the Ballet Center of Buffalo. Its neighbor to the east, Rochester, was facing a similar fate with regard to its ballet fortunes, if not for the same reasons. Olive McCue herself was but a year away from retiring; 1974 saw the staging of her very last *Nutcracker* for the Mercury Ballet Company.

Years later, Tim Draper reflected on his time with Kathleen Crofton, saying that despite the exceptional training he received from her, living away from home was not easy for him. He often emphasized that one of the reasons he opened a first-rate training program in Rochester was to enable young dancers of clear potential to be able to receive high-quality instruction while remaining at home with their families.

Fortunately, all was not lost when the costumes of the Festival Ballet of New York went up in flames. Enid Botsford-Orcutt, a long-time supporter of Kathleen Crofton and a fellow board officer who had earlier invited her esteemed colleague to guest teach at her own facility, now extended the welcome once again. It proved to be a fortuitous move for Mrs. Botsford-Orcutt, who was in the process of bringing in international stars to her facility during the mid-1970s, including Tim's previous Crofton teacher, David Gayle of the Royal Ballet; Mikhail Baryshnikov of American Ballet Theatre; and Patricia Wilde, Jurgen Schneider, Anton Dolin, George Zoritch, Miguel Lopez, and Fernando Bujones. Kathleen Crofton assuredly would be a most favorable complement to this faculty roster. Crofton did, in fact, take up Enid Botsford-Orcutt on her offer, occasionally reuniting with Tim Draper during the time he was commuting back and forth between New York and Rochester. Shortly thereafter, Crofton was named artistic director of the Baltimore-based Maryland Ballet Company following a nationwide search. She remained in Baltimore from 1973 to 1978 while also teaching ballet at the University of Maryland and occasionally guest teaching back in Rochester. Among her top achievements was landing the legendary Russian prima ballerina Natalia Makarova to guest in the role of Juliet in April of 1977. This role had been choreographed for Makarova seven years earlier by Ivan Tchernichova of the Kirov Ballet before Makarova's defection to the United States. With the help of Baryshnikov, who had practiced the ballet with Makarova in Russia, and the choreographer's former wife, Elena Kittle Tchernichova, who had met Crofton in San Francisco, the details were arranged, and the ballet was performed as a benefit to help Crofton's new company of sixteen dancers.[14] Years later, Crofton was credited by blogger George Taylor with overseeing the company's growth from an amateur dance group into a respected professional, regional ballet company: "From the 1950s to the 1990s there were: Baltimore City Ballet, Maryland Ballet, and Harbor City Ballet. Directors included Danny Diamond, Kathleen Crofton, and Petrus Bosman. The peak years were Maryland Ballet's under Crofton."[15]

In 1978, Crofton was entreated to return to Rochester, this time by the wife and daughter of Chester F. Carlson, the American physicist who invented Xerography. According to Earl Kage, Dorris Carlson and her daughter, Catherine, were passionate about ballet. Because both the Festival Ballet of New York and the Mercury Ballet Company had folded by that time, there was a serious abyss in Rochester's ballet scene. With the backing of mother and daughter and the involvement of several others who agreed to serve as board members, Ballet Concordia was established and Kathleen Crofton was installed as its artistic director. A press release was circulated, delineating plans for the formation of Ballet Concordia, Inc. by the company's board of directors. The article went on to state that gala performances would be set with the Rochester Philharmonic Orchestra at the Eastman Theatre and the Buffalo Philharmonic Orchestra at Shea's Buffalo Theatre for the spring or fall of 1980.[16] Natalia Makarova sent another warm expression of support, offering to do a guest performance for her friend. Unfortunately, Kathleen Crofton passed away on November 30, 1979. According to the Monroe County Medical Office, she died of a heart attack in her offices at 50 West Main Street in Rochester.[17]

The Rochester community, as well as all of Upstate and western New York, was now be deprived of the incomparable gifts of this internationally renowned dancer and teacher, even further discouraging the likelihood of a ballet renaissance for the region in the foreseeable future. She was "a truly great lady, a great teacher, a great director, a great woman," were Donna Ross's parting thoughts on Crofton. "She is my role model and my inspiration . . . all that she did, she did on her own. An amazing woman . . . an extraordinary contributor to the arts of the twentieth century!" It would be up to Tim Draper to fill the very significant void his teacher had left behind, the Englishwoman who had helped shape a young man into the artist he was destined to be, all from the back row of a beautiful studio in Buffalo.

Tina Brock Cannon. Photograph by Cameron McKinlay.

TINA BROCK

You could say I met Tim in the nick of time. I was about twelve years old and didn't know if I wanted to continue dance. I enjoyed it, but I had been dancing since I was three. I was contemplating quitting to explore other interests, like soccer and volleyball. My mom was a stickler about finishing what I started. So she said we could have the discussion about what I wanted to do after I finished this new summer intensive dance program I had just signed up for. However, we never had that conversation. That summer, I met Tim Draper.

I was nervous about my first class at Draper Dance Studio. (I think that's what it was called then. It went through so many name changes. I always just referred to it as "Tim's" throughout the years!) That first class from him was . . . well, the first word that comes to mind, intimidating! I remember being a little afraid of him. Somehow he demanded so much respect without even saying anything. He was super strict, yet he had a charm about him that was magnetic. He spoke with an air of confidence and was an excellent teacher. I had never taken a ballet class that was so disciplined, structured and fun! I learned so many new steps and concepts that summer. Precision, technique, turnout, alignment, transitions, musicality . . . he knew exactly what he wanted from his students—in one word, perfection. I had so many corrections to tackle. I was really enjoying this challenge.

Tim had just introduced a whole new world to me. Even though I was completely discouraged by how far behind I was with my technique and training, I was hooked. Tim pushed me so much. He saw my potential that I never knew I had. I saw myself growing and improving so quickly. I was so grateful for his belief in me, because it was then (and because of him) I chose to become a professional dancer.

Tim was opinionated and temperamental. His ways weren't always the easiest to swallow. He rarely sugarcoated anything and could be pretty harsh at times. I think every student in my class was temporarily kicked out of the studio at least once just to prove the point that he was still in charge. Tim's nickname for me was "Louise." It was after Gypsy Rose Lee, because he used to tell me my dancing was trashy, but that he would transform me into a beautiful dancer. (And I'm so grateful that he did!)

I was one of the first generations of Tim's dancers. I think there were kinks he was working out in terms of running a dance school for the first time. As I am sure, dealing with a bunch of emotional teenage girls is not the easiest either. Despite Tim's unorthodox ways sometimes, he was a very caring man. We developed a close relationship over the years. He truly was like my second dad. I trusted him and confided in him. He looked out for me and invested so much time into my growth and development as a dancer. Even after I graduated and left the studio, I would still call him and ask his advice. His opinion always mattered.

Tim Draper will always have a special place in my heart. I loved him like a father. I am so grateful he saw something in me that summer because I am still dancing professionally, eighteen years now and still going! Without him, I wouldn't be where I am today. Thank you, Tim.

Tina Brock Cannon is a Cirque du Soleil dancer who performed in the Beatles LOVE theatrical production in Las Vegas. She was also the lead dancer and dance captain in Celine Dion's *New Day*, performed as a Radio City Rockette, toured the United States with the Broadway show *Fosse* (under the direction of Ann Reinking), and performed nationally and internationally with Hubbard Street Dance Chicago and River North Chicago Dance. She danced at the movie premieres of Disney's *Pocahontas* and *Hercules* and was featured in the PBS special *River North Rising* and the film *Soul Survivors*. Tina not only put a smile on Tim's face but was one of his most versatile dancers. In his 1992 *Nutcracker,* she was both his Snow Queen and the Russian Trepak!

6

TRAINING FOR TROCKADERO

After leaving Kathleen Crofton's sometime in 1972, Tim traveled back and forth to New York City quite a bit, enlisting the very best teachers possible to help him bring his dreams to fruition. It is almost inconceivable that one of Tim's very favorite teachers who helped further refine his technique during this time period—the world-renowned Nancy Bielski—still remains ballet's most iconic instructor, the crème de la crème teacher among New York's dance community, whom the stars of New York City Ballet, American Ballet Theatre, and Broadway cannot go a week without. Tim additionally trained with Nanette Charisse, the sister of the dancer Cyd Charisse. Tim had also won a dance scholarship to the Joffrey Ballet School in 1974 and began studying there that summer, when the company itself was still located in New York. In the beautiful circle of life that seems to permeate the ballet world in particular, one of Tim's star dancers, Jillian Nealon Peschken, would later become the registrar, director's assistant, and adult program manager at the Joffrey Ballet School after graduating from Indiana University and having a professional ballet career with Ballet Austin and the San Diego Ballet.

Nancy Bielski's daily 11:30 a.m. class at Steps on Broadway, or just "Steps" as it is known by the dance community, continues to be a sold-out affair for which every single space at the barre is claimed. Over the years, such artists as Julie Kent, Sarah Lane, Jenifer Ringer, Diana Vishneva, Sophiane Sylve, Vladmir Malakhov, and Mikhail Baryshnikov have routinely found their way to this exceedingly popular class, perhaps best summed up by Pacific Northwest Ballet's artistic director, Peter Boal: "Nancy's personality combines humor, friendship, and an underlying authority that reminds us we are all there to work."

It is evident to even a casual observer that Nancy is much more than a revered instructor to these dancers; she is also their mentor and dear friend. It is not at all unusual to see her rushing backstage after one of their performances to offer her congratulations.

Dance Magazine's editor in chief, Wendy Perron, found this to be the case when profiling special teachers in the business. In the August 2006 issue, she mused

> We all remember our favorite teachers fondly—their tone of voice, the way they demonstrate, their corrections. That time in class with a teacher you trust is precious. And their insights and values go with you wherever you go. For this issue, we asked 18 top dancers who their favorite teacher was or is, and what that person means to them. In the case of Nancy Bielski, master ballet teacher at Steps on Broadway (and also a company teacher at American Ballet Theatre), we interviewed four dancers who take her class religiously and got four different sets of praise. In Bielski's class Anna Larghezza got help for her jumps, Elizabeth Walker improved her adagio, Melissa Morrissey strengthened her work, and Jenifer Ringer improved her placement. A good teacher helps where help is needed—and has the eye to see where the weak spots are. At our photo session with Bielski, I decided to get some corrections for my own port de bras, and she gave me a gentle litany of reminders: 'Chin up, hips forward, ribs in, earring to the ceiling.' I got a taste of the Nancy Bielski experience. These are the constant reminders that help us bring our thoughts into our bodies.[1]

Tim was eighteen when he originally met Bielski at Harkness House for Ballet Arts, where he studied as a trainee on scholarship for the next two to three years. She actually was not that much older than he, having begun teaching at a young age following a performance career with the Boston Ballet, the Harkness Ballet Company under the direction of Ben Stevenson, and the Cincinnati Ballet. Her earlier training had been with Esther Brooks of the Cambridge (Massachusetts) School of Ballet, the Royal Ballet School, and the School of American Ballet. Recalls Nancy, "Tim stood out in class as a serious dancer, a superbly clean dancer who worked carefully. . . . He could turn and jump with considerable strength." Although he was not blessed with great feet, Bielski credits Tim as being a "very good dancer" who stood out in class for his clean lines and for the fact that he loved to talk ballet long after the music had stopped.

With family and friends back home in Rochester, Tim would naturally return frequently during this period of the early to mid-1970s, always juggling many projects at once. In addition to taking class and performing in lecture demonstrations at the Orcutt-Botsford studio where he was able to continue to train with the Royal Ballet's David Gayle and other luminaries, he also attended the State University of New York (SUNY) College at Brockport in pursuit of his bachelor's degree. Tim's sister Donna remembers his determination to obtain a degree. At one point, she recalls, he had missed his ride to Brockport, so Donna got right in the car, along with her year-and-a-half-old baby, Melanie, to pick him up so that he wouldn't miss his class. Obtaining a degree is never an insignificant matter for a ballet dancer, with rehearsals, performances, and teaching consuming the majority of the dancer's waking hours. Tim was determined to complete it, however, often taking classes online, and eventually he obtained his bachelor's degree from SUNY Empire State College.

When not working on his undergraduate degree, he had the unique opportunity to study at Orcutt-Botsford's with members of American Ballet Theatre and the Boston Ballet as a felicitous result of the school's new satellite program with these world-famous organizations. Once again, Mrs. Botsford-Orcutt was demonstrating her mettle as an arts visionary, bringing in the top names in the ballet world, sponsoring performances by the world's most famous companies and soloists, and providing her students with every opportunity to study with the very best. The late 1960s into the 1980s proved to be a true renaissance for the school, out of which came many world-class dancers. Some from the Rochester region fail to appreciate or even realize this because from the late 1940s through the late 1960s, Enid Botsford was more singularly focused on teaching Rochester's young ladies and gentlemen deportment, ballroom dance, and those social graces deemed essential to a cultured existence. Although few would argue the importance of those activities, particularly when they seem at times to be much in absence today, the consensus of the time was that serious ballet training in Rochester was exclusively within the purview of Thelma Biracree and Olive McCue. Only later did the Botsford studio regain its status as a serious venue in the development of ballet dancers. Local newspaper articles from 1959 bear this out. "Boys will be boys, and girls will be girls for a while," began a story in the *Avon Herald-News*, "but they soon become young socialites and want to know ballroom dancing and social niceties. Mrs. Enid Knapp Botsford of Rochester has organized a program of 30 years standing, which includes ballroom dancing lessons and the learning of social forms for youngsters in grades 6 thru 8."[2] The article went on to say that ballet lessons would also be offered in Avon if there was sufficient interest and that a well-attended summer camp offered by Mrs. Botsford had just concluded at her Pittsford facilities on the grounds located adjacent to St. John Fisher College. A student of the Brighton Schools affirms Mrs. Botsford's professional interests at the time, stating, "I attended BHS between 7th and 9th grade. . . . [I] would have graduated in 1963. For some reason I thought of Miss Botsford's School of Dance this week. . . . I remember coming in one evening and saying, 'Good evening, Miss Botsford, I am Pam Whittemore.' BIG MISTAKE. As Miss Botsford informed me, the correct introduction is 'My name is. . . . You may be a garbage man, but your name is . . .'"[3] From the late 1960s on, however, it is clear that the Botsford's School of Dance was once again a bastion of serious training. The elite of the ballet world taught in her beautiful studios at 3646 East Avenue in the Rochester suburb of Pittsford. It was a marvelous set of circumstances in which vision and financial resources were most happily aligned.

During these pockets of time when Tim was commuting back and forth between New York and Rochester, he loved teaching and performing in the various opportunities that came his way. Among those for whom he taught was his old friend Michelle Buschner, who at a young age had become the director of Little Red Dancing School's second location on Mt. Hope Avenue near the University of Rochester. The proof of Tim's happiness during this era is his smiling face in many of the photographs that remain behind.

One of Tim's special partners and fellow dance instructors at Mrs. Botsford's was his old friend from the Miss Crofton days, Donna Ross, whose passion for dance he successfully reignited after a postsurgical infection left her in despair over future prospects.

> While in Stuttgart, I became distracted from ballet and discouraged because my infected toes were still causing me pain, especially *en pointe*, despite the fact that I was taking very strong antibiotics for the infection. I announced to the director of the school that I was quitting to go to college and study philosophy and become a writer. My parents told me to stay in Stuttgart at least until Christmas time. I did and learned to speak and write German fluently. I gave English lessons on the side to German and Swiss executives and traveled around Europe, staying at youth hostels. When I came home, I studied for the SAT and Achievement tests and took them. I lived at home with my parents and took courses at Midland College . . . and then that summer, I went to Colorado College for summer school. That fall (1974) I transferred to the U of R [University of Rochester]. While there, I began taking classes again at the Botsford School where my

teacher from Buffalo, David Gayle, was teaching. I also began teaching classes there. I danced a performance with Tim Draper (Peasant Pas de Deux from *Giselle*), at a school lecture/demonstration and it got me back into the ballet mode. My feet had almost completely healed by then.

Once Tim pulled her back in, Donna went on to enjoy a highly successful performance career with the Joffrey, earning high marks from the founding artistic director, Robert Joffrey. "Donna's range proved enough to encompass works by choreographers as diverse as Arpino and de Mille, Ashton, Tudor, and Araiz. She danced prominent roles in such ballets as *Kettentanz, The Dream, Façade,* and *Rodeo,* and also in our sole 19th century ballet at that time, *La Vivandière Pas de Six.* She was a fine dancer for the Joffrey, thoughtful and conscientious about her work, and strong."[4]

Two of Tim's other close friends and dance partners during this period were Anita Bartolotta and Karen Ventura. Anita recalls how "even though we lost touch in later years, he [Tim] was my best friend, my roommate in Manhattan, and dance partner during our Botsford years and I loved him dearly."

Anita recalls how she and Tim met at Botsford's in 1974, when she was fourteen years old and he was twenty. "It was a very exhilarating time for the studio with guest stars from all over the world coming in to teach, such as David Gayle, Lorenzo Monreal, Leon Danielian, Pat [Patricia] Wilde, Peter Martins, Fernando Bujones for a summer, and even Mikhail Baryshnikov." In fact, Tim and Anita trained with Baryshnikov's own trainer, Jurgen Schneider, who had taught at the school for several years. Tim and Anita performed numerous school demonstrations together on the small stage on the upper level, frequently dancing the "Peasant *Pas de Deux*" from *Giselle* (to the extent that, Anita laughingly remembers, "we were sick to death of it!") and also doing the "Bluebird *Pas de Deux*" from *Sleeping Beauty.* Summer "ballet boot camps" had also become the norm for dancers of the Orcutt-Botsford School of Dance during the 1970s. Tim and Anita were becoming quite inseparable, "hanging out all the time. He would talk a lot about Olive McCue and the Mercury Ballet . . . with a particular recollection of having accidentally dropped his friend and dance partner, Debbie Bricker, into the pit of the Rochester Civic Orchestra, with his running offstage." As evidenced by the fine career Ms. Bricker went on to have, it appears that the mishap did no lasting damage.

Anita Bartolotta and Timothy Draper, performing "The Peasant Pas de Deux" from *Giselle.* Courtesy of Anita Garland-Cox.

In addition to the natural camaraderie that developed as a result of kindred spirits and many shared laughs, Tim was always drawn to exceptional talent. This was quite consistent with the fact that Anita was quickly coming into her own at a precocious age. After one performance during this period, Jurgen Schneider pulled her mother aside to tell her that her daughter "was going to be a great ballet star."

Anita recalls that Tim was involved romantically at the time with a young man named Jim Clark, who was well liked by both family and friends. According to Tim's sister, Donna, "He and Jimmy were together for a long time." She says that her kids remember Jim well; he reportedly loved animals. "They used to own some Siamese cats, a pair from New York City. Timmy always had cats. One of them, Simey, had multiple litters, which helped pay for dance lessons." Eventually a couple of Simey's offspring went to Donna and Jaye with Donna keeping Lawrence and Jaye keeping Adam. They also had parrots, one of which, Charlie the Parrot, allegedly ate spaghetti. Donna recalls that the parrots had something to do with the actress Erica Kane of *One Life to Live* fame. Apparently, a friend of hers "had the parrot and gave it to Timmy." Donna recalls humorously, "All of the things that were brought home 'temporarily' all ended up staying with my mom." Tim also continued to supplement his performance and teaching earnings with money he made as a hair stylist.

Anita Bartolotta's recollection of Tim, born out of a friendship that developed over thirty-five years ago, perhaps best exemplifies the passionate hold he had on his loved ones during his lifetime, a feeling that has not abated throughout the years that have passed since his untimely death. "He was always so kind and encouraging. They [the Botsford School] had wonderful ballet legends teaching us, people such as Patricia Wilde and Fernando Bujones. At the same time, however, they also had some 'sickos,' some real 'pieces of work.' Knowing how sadistic some of these people could be, Tim would always go out of his way to be kind to me about my talent." Years later, after Tim had launched his own studio, he would recall in a *Times-Union* interview just how cruel this behavior could be: it nearly sidelined his career.

> Draper's career progressed smoothly, with scholarships to the Joffrey Ballet and the Harkness House of Ballet Arts. But his ambitions were dashed during a period of recuperation in Rochester, where "severe criticism, by teachers of a ballet school here made me feel rotten about myself. Instead of correcting me, they humiliated me. So I said I guess I'm not good enough. I'll never make it in the dance world. I quit."[5]

Fortunately for the dance world, this never came to pass. The cheerful Anita played a large role in the cure. The positive aspects of the studio also restored Tim to performance level and allowed him to move forward toward a professional career.

By the time Anita and Tim met, Anita had already been dancing at Botsford's for several years, beginning as a child of eight, after previously studying tap and ballet at the Fairport Fire Hall. After a performance, someone approached her mother and told her that she should bring her daughter to Botsford. Anita describes Enid Botsford-Orcutt as a "fabulous teacher, a true force of nature"; however she could at times be "really, really tough and really cruel but she taught me the art of the dance—to never make a movement without thinking about what your eyes are doing, what your face is doing." Anita quickly learned that this was a "whole different ball of wax." By the late 1960s, Botsford-Orcutt was in her fifth decade of teaching and was still informing her students with the "pedagogical screaming" that assuredly had been a part of her own instruction. By the time she was nine, Anita had become Botsford's protégée and was on full scholarship with the school, a mark of distinction that lasted throughout her tenure there. Because the studio was actually Botsford's home, Anita often found herself in her teacher's living room, lying on the floor, trying to pull her kneecap up with every bit of detail she could muster. Anita recalls, "She was a wonderful teacher, bringing out the love of music, living the music, learning the art of the dance, mind control, muscle control, and the way your face looks." Possibly the most memorable part of Anita's years at the Botsford Studio was taking class on one occasion right next to Baryshnikov. As she explains,

> One summer when his [Baryshnikov's] trainer taught at Botsford, Baryshnikov took classes, and I stood next to him at the barre. He was still dancing at ABT. Leon Danielian [a legendary ballet star from the 1940s and fifties] was teaching at ABT, and Enid prided herself on not being "a dance factory that can crank out twenty-five pirouettes." It was a place to obtain exceptional Cecchetti technique and [with the hiring of several Russian faculty] strict Russian technique, as well.

Botsford-Orcutt was "big on ABT" and utilized her vast background and resources to make Botsford a satellite school for American Ballet Theatre, much as the Biracree School of Ballet had been a satellite school for the School of American Ballet a generation earlier. Icons of the ballet world made their way from Covent Garden and 890 Broadway to Pittsford, New York on a regular basis. One can only imagine the excitement this generated, not only in the studio but also for those locals who followed ballet. One never knew if a famous dancer might be in a nearby shop or restaurant. In addition to providing guest artists with superior teaching accommodations, the Orcutt-Botsford school also played host to major ballet companies on tour, providing them with rehearsal space and lavish postperformance receptions. At one such soirée, Dame Margot Fonteyn, still actively performing into her mid-fifties, offered up to Botsford students her own personal secret to maintaining her lithe figure: "Just eat steak and salad, dears, and you'll stay thin your entire life." The legendary Rudolf Nureyev was at the same party.

Another classmate and dance partner of Tim's during this period was Donna Schoenherr, now the founder and director of the

London-based Ballet4Life. Like Tim, she went on to have a noteworthy international performance career. Donna's formative training on full scholarship at Botsford's included studying with all of the same luminaries as Tim, Anita Bartolotta, and Donna Ross, and performing with American Ballet Theatre and the Boston Ballet through the satellite program Botsford's had established with both companies. Subsequently, she joined the Cleveland Ballet at the peak of its success.

> I met Tim when I was a young and a very innocent ballet student. I always thought of him as a big pussy cat inside a lion's exterior. He was easily wounded and had a wickedly sharp sense of humour (much of it way too sophisticated or catty for me to grasp; I am sure of that when thinking about it now!). I recall him as a very sensitive and soft soul but with a sense of holding and hiding behind a foundation of strength and fortitude and persistence. As a dancer, the positive aspects I remember him possessing include being a hard worker in class and a musical performer, having a nice sense of working with others around him and supporting the younger, less experienced dancers.[6]

Among her favorite recollections of Tim, drawn from memory so many years later are the following:

> Loved jumps!
> Good partner, good with quick steps
> Gave the younger dancers support and advice
> Making us laugh with his silliness and antics and comments
> Committed and devoted to the art form

She also recalled that Tim had "trouble with artists he did not get on with, had trouble finding a way to work through the conflict and that did affect his output. He was a bit too quick to make judgments, which he then held onto." Her affection for him was genuine, something true for nearly all who knew him, warts and all. "I was sad to not have collaborated with him when we were both all grown up and established professionals in the field," she noted. "How ironic that he was on his way back to Rochester having just been in London."

In the summer of 1977, Tim went to New York with Anita Bartolotta to audition for a professional job. Due to Tim's many friends and connections, he arranged for them to stay in Manhattan with other dancers in tunnel apartments (often referred to by New Yorkers as railroad apartments), buildings with long hallways and bathrooms in the kitchens, which were located in a nice West Side neighborhood. Their days were essentially consumed with taking classes and auditioning.

Both Anita and Tim were accepted into the Israel Ballet Company, a troupe that had been founded by Berta Yampolsky and Hillel Markman. It "began from nothing in a country where modern dance ruled." Berta Yampolsky, the troupe's choreographer, is praised for her "work in contemporary neoclassical style. She excels in aesthetics and clarity, demanding a high level of technical skill from dancers. Her repertoire includes dramatic, abstract and contemporary ballet."

Anita was too young to obtain working papers and thus had to decline the contract. Tim did go to Israel, however, although the experience appears to have been far from satisfactory. Because he had to be hospitalized almost from the moment he arrived, his mother, sister, and best friend were worried. Anita recalls the situation vividly, sharing the following letter she received from Tim dated July 7, 1977. He wrote to her while convalescing in the hospital from a virus he contracted shortly after arriving in Tel Aviv. Because this was long before the convenience of e-mail, the effort and pathos of the letter are all the more meaningful. One notes, however, that amid these travails, Tim's droll sense of humor is still alive and well.

Clearly, Anita had become a most close and trusted ally to whom Tim could fully unburden himself. Ultimately his letter proved prescient, because his stay with the Israel Ballet was short. Although the company had paid for his airfare from the United States, it appears that an issue arose over his passport. After conditions failed to improve generally, Tim, then twenty-three, made the decision to leave his first professional company and return to the United States. "Ma, I'll be on the plane tomorrow," were his parting words from Israel.

July 7, 1977

Dear Anita,

First of all, I've been sick most of the time I have been here. I spent 3 days in the hospital. I had some virus. They fed me intravenously because of dehydration. So as you can see, I have started things off well. You should be darn lucky you didn't come! The company leaves a lot to be desired. The studio (only 1) is small and hasn't any air conditioning. The heat makes it unbearable. I must confess that the ballet mistress (Rose) is a gem. You would love her and her classes. But one good thing isn't enough to keep me happy. The repertoire is awful. They are doing a lot of new things. The ones I've seen, I don't like. Rose doesn't teach all of the time, which puts it a little more gray here. Tell me about the performance. I hope all went well for you. I'm waiting to hear what happened in Pittsburgh. If things don't look brighter here soon, I will return home. What I will do then, I'll never know. Tell everything that's happening with you.

Write soon,
Take care, I think of you often. Tim

Tim Draper c/o Hillary Yesmer, 11 Prag Apt. 5 Tel-Aviv, ISRAEL

Anita Bartolotta was well on the way to having an exemplary career of her own. By the time she was in her late teens, she was dancing as a company member with the Boston Ballet, rehearsing for the Boston Pops season. She had previously caught the company's eye while still a student at Botsford's, performing "Marzipan" and the "Spanish Dance" in the *Nutcracker* and the Waltz in *Les Sylphides*.

Returning home to Rochester for a visit, Anita recalls how when visiting her old studio she "blew out her knee" during a particularly demanding class taught by Tim's former teacher, the guest artist Kathleen Crofton, who was filling in for the studio head. In an instant, everything changed. Enid Botsford-Orcutt assured Anita that she would always have a job teaching there, because the studio founder had meant for the school to live on forever. Anita did teach for the 1978–79 season, but the "forever" part was not to be. In the aftermath, she was understandably distraught, having been preordained for greatness with the brightest of futures by Baryshnikov's own trainer. Anita lost contact with Tim and most of the others in her dance circle. Nevertheless, she went on to have a marvelous professional career as an actress, spokesmodel, singer, and dancer. She remembers attending one of Tim's performances with Trockadero, but that was the last time she saw him. The shocking news of his death came to her from their dear mutual friend from the Botsford days, Karen Ventura. To this day, Anita holds on to a cherished pair of haircutting scissors that had once belonged to Tim, probably acquired during their time together while training and auditioning during that one pivotal summer in New York City. Although the scissors had cost fifty dollars and had previously traveled with him wherever he went, they are now retired permanently, at least from professional use.

❧

By 1978, feeling once again restored, Tim began a more permanent residence in New York. Returning to Nancy Bielski at Harkness House for continued classes, he also performed during this period with the Puerto Rican Dance Theatre (now known as Ballet Concierto de Puerto Rico) and the Garden State Ballet, two highly acclaimed institutions. Ballet Concierto, founded in 1970 by Lolita San Miguel and Julio Torres, enjoyed critical acclaim by Clive Barnes of the *New York Post* and Anna Kisselgoff of the *New York Times*. In the January 1980 edition of *Ballet News*, Walter Terry described Puerto Rican Dance Theatre as "only partly Latin in personnel, and only partly folkloric in repertory materials, but although its key technique is that of classical ballet (and very good classical ballet at that), its flavors, its timbres, its kinetic dynamics are unmistakably Hispanic."[7]

Also during this period, Tim became acquainted through a mutual friend with David Manion, the artistic director of the Riverside Dance Festival at the Theater of the Riverside Church in Manhattan. Well known and respected throughout the dance world, Manion became one of Tim's lifelong friends to whom he regularly turned for advice. The Riverside Dance Festival was "known as the most eclectic of the city's dance-producing programs, offering a traditional proscenium stage at an affordable cost to small companies performing ballet and modern, ethnic, tap and social dance."[8] When the much-loved venue of impeccable taste closed, it left a true void for New Yorkers and out-of-town companies alike.

In 1978, Tim also met Tory Dobrin, a young man his own age, who would change his life. Dobrin, who is now the artistic director of the world-famous Ballets Trockadero de Monte Carlo, a position he has held since 1997, recalls, "I met Tim within the first week of arriving in New York City about 1978. He and I became close friends right away. . . . I joined Trockadero in 1980 and recommended Tim for the job to the management." What Tory actually did was quite noble—one might say atypical in the fiercely competitive world of professional ballet. He recommended Tim to the Trocks' management as a temporary replacement for himself, having just sustained an injury that would prevent his going on tour for several months.

Despite the fact that the company was essentially still in its infancy at this time—having been founded only six years earlier by Peter Anastos, Natch Taylor, and Antony Bassae—the Trocks were literally an overnight success, notwithstanding the fact that their debut took place in a second-story theater in Manhattan's Meatpacking District. Expectations were managed appropriately. "With only two proficient classical dancers among them they didn't imagine that the group would outlast the two weekends of its first season."[9] However, Arlene Croce of the *New Yorker*, the "doyenne of New York dance critics" as she was known at the time, clearly *got* the brilliance of these all-male ballet dancers *en pointe*. With their collective tongues held firmly in cheek, they alternately worshiped and skewered the troupe that was their life-blood and after which they fashioned their name, Les Ballets Russes de Monte Carlo. With their nostalgia for Diaghilev and the grand affectations of his august stars on full display, this over-the-top parody appealed to both balletomanes and the general public alike. Croce's praise quickly led to more raves from the mainstream media. Now in its fourth decade, Trockadero was off and running. It is clear that the company's staying power has been the result of several fortuitous events, best summed up by Joan Acocella, who wrote in the *New Yorker*, "The Trocks' business is comedy, and the basic joke, of course, is that men are dancing women's roles. Just to see those size-10 shoes, those yawning armpits, that chest hair peeping up over the bodices—I do not mention what greets you when the ballerina turns and her skirts fly up—is to laugh."[10] As Jill Sykes of the *Sydney Morning Herald* describes the troupe, "Hairy chests peer over tutu bodices. Garish make-up gives comic expressions enough power to bounce off the back row. Dancers don't just fall down, they push each other over. The competition is intense: upstaging is a way of life."[11]

With its unparalleled ability to go from the sublime to the ridiculous and back to the sublime in a matter of seconds—all with impeccable technique, deep reverence for the classics amid the send-up, and the comedic timing worthy of a Jack Benny or a Rodney Dangerfield—the Trocks have tapped into the ballet-going public's insatiable appetite for the continual reenactment of splendiferous ballet warhorses. As Dobrin points out, the troupe is selling itself as an old, dusty touring Russian ballet company that the modern age doesn't have anymore. With more and more ballet companies these days devoting several weeks of each season to more contemporary repertoire, Trockadero has, in addition to everything else, met a market need. The Trocks' audiences include ballet aficionados, dance critics, and stars of traditional elite ballet companies. An aficionado's eyeliner may be all askew after watching "Paul Ghiselin . . . the much loved Trock who forever moults in 'The Dying Swan.'"[12] A dance critic who is first to notice impending on-stage disaster reports that "it's only a few minutes into the show when I spot the tiniest of wobbles on the far right of the stage. The wobble grows, quickly becoming a teeter that knocks into the next dancer, and, before you know it, they've all keeled over this way and that."[13] Traditional ballet stars frequently find their way backstage postperformance to extend their congratulations to these magnificent performers. Even the average ballet fan seems happy to take his or her *Swan Lake* either straight or with a little travesty thrown into the mix.

There could not have been a better company fit for Tim than the Trocks. Comedy done well requires an intellectual nimbleness. Tim's own wry sense of humor was supremely suited to an organization that affixed to its dancers such deliciously memorable stage monikers as Marina Plezegetovstageskaya and Maya Thickenthighya. A few of these names are announced as "cast changes" at the beginning of each performance with full-bodied Russian pronunciation to humor the conceit along even more. The brilliant choreography of Peter Anastos, men with personalities larger than life who could also dance *en pointe* ("technical mastery and outrageous camp"),[14] and a chance to be utterly submerged in the classics made famous by Les Ballets Russes, added up to a match made in heaven.

What Trockadero gave Tim was a superb knowledge of and appreciation for the feel, history, and nuances of each classical ballet in the repertoire, from the choreographers and legendary casts to the theaters in which they were staged. Of course, the Trocks have long been known for their steadfast commitment to mastering the original choreography *before* dissecting it for humor potential. As an article in the *Cleveland Plain Dealer* explains: "The dancers always begin with the original choreography, if available, which then is tweaked to add the idiosyncrasies for which the Trocks are so feted." Dobrin further describes the process: "Setting the original choreography is important because it gives it a kind of legitimacy and makes it interesting for us as dancers. We try to keep the rehearsal process relaxed. The guys in Trockadero tend to be funny. Things unfold as we shape the material."[15] As a result, it is not a stretch to suggest that the Trocks dancers may be even more intimately acquainted with the attendant histrionics and possibly feel them a touch more deeply than those who perform the roles in the more conventional manner.

According to Dr. Bud Coleman, associate professor and chair of the Department of Theatre and Dance at the University of Colorado at Boulder and a member of the Trocks during the 1978 and 1979 seasons, Tim joined the company in the summer of 1980. Dr. Coleman's PhD dissertation chronicles the history of Les Ballets Trockadero de Monte Carlo.[16] He describes how Tim was hired right after the company returned from its July engagement at the Spoleto Festival, a significant international event founded in 1958 by the noted Italian-American composer Gian Carlo Menotti. At that time, the festival was located in the ancient, cobblestoned Umbrian hillside town of Spoleto, Italy, with its magnificent plazas and narrow streets about 60 miles northeast of Rome. Performing there was a huge feather in Trockadero's cap, because Spoleto had "introduced to the international dance community some of America's most prominent dancers and choreographers, including Jerome Robbins, Mikhail Baryshnikov, and Twyla Tharp. To illustrate just how far the company had come since its inception only six years earlier, the troupe was visited at the festival by one of the world's leading ballerinas, the Italian Carla Fracci. "[She] agreed to have her photo taken in the Taglioni pose with two Trockadero dancers, dressed in Pas de Quatre costumes."[17] This photo was added to the press kit under "Stars Who Love the Trocks," joining photos of the Trocks with Natalia Makarova in 1976, Shirley MacLaine in 1977, Mikhail Baryshnikov in 1978, and Sir Robert Helpmann and Joan Sutherland in 1979. Although not on this tour, Spoleto would later be an important triumph for Tim's protégés years after his passing.

"After almost non-stop activity—the company had already logged 116 performances in 1980," writes Coleman, "the Trocks finally had a chance to take a break. With the fall tour not starting until 24 October, the company had time to rehearse some new works, especially since only two new dancers (John Devaney and Timothy Draper) had to learn the repertoire. . . . With a smaller turnover, it was easier to prepare the ten ballets which were scheduled for this tour, which included a revival of *Giselle*, Fialkow's new *Lamentations of Jane Eyre*, and a premiere of his [Fialkow's] new solo, *Quintessential Prairie*."[18]

Michael Patrick McKinley, who hails from Austin, Texas, was one of Tim's multitalented colleagues. McKinley joined the Trocks in 1978 and was accorded the dual personas of Tatiana Youbetyabootskaya and Igor Teupleze (the former appellation ceremoniously retired after a fabled run). He recalls Tim as someone he always liked and whose dancing he respected. Mike remembers how at one point, both of them were cast in *Giselle* in two of the soloist roles in the corps, "Monte" and "Zuma." Three decades later, it still isn't completely clear who was "Monte" and who was "Zuma," but Mike knows that Tim's role involved an *assemblée six de vole* and that he excelled at it. "Tim had lovely legs and awesome *batterie*." Tim would reportedly come to rehearsal wrapped in layers and layers of clothing—a complete head-to-toe garbage-pant ensemble, as it were, concealing his callipygous figure. That get-up would have been amusing years later to his own advanced dancers, who had to contend with his absolute insistence on sleeveless, skirtless leotards as suitable classroom attire. Although he claimed that the extra bundles were needed to keep him warm, it was more likely that Tim was actually embarrassed by his calves. In fact, according to McKinley, they were regarded by many as quite beautiful.

Mike notes that he didn't know Tim terribly well due to the fact that their overlapping time at the Trocks was brief, but he does remember him as a "delightful" person with a good heart and sardonic sense of humor, willing to step up to the plate even when the circumstances were less than favorable. This behavior was on full display during the time he was charged with driving the Trocks' very strict and inopportunely nauseated ballet mistress back to New York City from whatever city they were performing in at the time, despite the fact that a long road trip was probably not the perfect antidote for the passenger and not much fun for the driver, either. Indeed, whatever social capital might have been accruing for this junior company member over the long trip back to civilization, it surely evaporated on the spot as he reportedly assessed his hapless charge in the immediate throes of ill health with full theatrical aside, "and here I thought you were chic."

According to Coleman, the six-week fall 1980 tour (October 24–December 17) was a strenuous one, comprising twenty-seven performances in nineteen cities, with Tim thrown right into company life with all of the chaos, hilarity, and high drama that could be expected from the world's most famous send-up troupe. The tour began in Birmingham, Alabama for a two-night engagement with the Alabama Symphony Pops Orchestra. The music critic Emmett Weaver (Birmingham *Post-Herald*) thought the Trocks' Birmingham debut was "magical entertainment elixir, which bubbled and fizzled so delightfully with mirth)."[19] On October 28, at Dickinson College in Carlisle, Pennsylvania, the company premiered *Quintessential Prairie*, a work by Roy Fialkow, a company member and choreographer. "The story of one incipient pioneer woman's odyssey from Pinsk to Dodge—searching the American wilderness for a nice place to set up a home and bring forth life" was how the ballet was billed. "To the strains of Sir Edward Elgar's 'Pomp and Circumstance,' Aggrippina Proboskovna lifts her worshipful face to the heavens in prayer for a good harvest and is rewarded with a shower of plastic vegetables and (salvation!) a child. Aggrippina is so excited with her tiny charge that she whirls it about the stage with such abandon that she sends the little tot flying back into the wings."[20]

Some critics loved it; others were less enchanted. Diana Haithman of the *Detroit Free Press* was "delighted with this 'gleeful attack' on American choreographers, with all the stiff-legged, flailing American-Gothic-in-dancing-shoes movement that has become a popular expression of the pioneer spirit. This dance neatly illustrates that trying to adapt the prairie to the *pointe* shoe is like trying to stuff a pelican into a shopping bag." On the other hand, Marilyn Tucker of the *San Francisco Chronicle* described it as "a devastating putdown of 40 years of American ballets from the likes of Agnes de Mille, Eugene Loring—even Martha Graham." Fialkow himself defended his work to the *St. Paul Sunday Pioneer Press* by calling it "in the genre of Agnes de Mille. It's a character dance that's very American, in the style of *Rodeo,* and *Billy the Kid,* or the dream ballet from *Oklahoma.* If you're doing satire, you must be very precise. Comedy is the hardest form of art there is. You have to be so deadly serious about it in order to be true to the art."[21]

The highlight of the tour, however, was Trockadero's debut in San Francisco, home of what is considered to be America's oldest ballet company, the San Francisco Ballet. Their local promoter, Don Thomson, booked the company for four performances in the 3,252-seat War Memorial Opera House, from December 10–13. It appears to have been a love fest for critics and audience alike:

> Allan Ulrich of the *San Francisco Examiner* concluded that a "heap of terpsichorean legends and conventions was destroyed last night as the Trocks adroitly danced on the Opera House stage." Noting that the capacity audiences got the laughter and sophisticated parody they had come for, Ulrich announced that the Trocks were staying for two more performances of "hilarity" if "success hasn't gone completely to their heads." Janice Ross of the *Oakland Tribune* clearly seemed to understand this troupe's motivation ("underneath all of the Trocks' brilliant spoofing . . . is a deep love of the classics and a thorough understanding of their motivation and intent").[22]

Heuwell Tircuit of the *San Francisco Chronicle* was also effusive in his praise. "Genius! Sheer Genius! Beyond dance, this is doubtless the world's finest comic ensemble,"[23] he proclaimed to the city. In addition to the raves, the four-day stand was also a huge financial success for the organization. Sheldon Soffer Management purchased a full-page advertisement in *Variety* (January 28, 1981) announcing that the four performances grossed $133,324. The tour concluded in San Jose on December 17, followed then by the commencement of the winter tour, which included three performances at the Detroit Music Hall on January 8–10, 1981.[24]

It bears mentioning that notwithstanding the spectacular onstage triumphs that most Trocks performances garnered, in true ebb-and-flow fashion, the special challenges of logistics were occasionally given voice by the dancers (perhaps with just a bit of higher amplification when considering that this stable of stars made its livelihood by embodying the prima ballerinas of imperial Russia). These would typically begin and end with the all-important question of who had which dressing room. "Dressing rooms? Oh God," recalled Michael Patrick McKinley in mock horror when posed the question. "It got to the point where the stage manager would assign them and put up signs because it was always a mad scramble and we all knew the fallout if Sanson [Candelaria, the company's gentle, beloved star] did not get the best one."

In later years, Tim would thoroughly crack himself up when regaling others with stories of how Trocks corps members would tear after the costumes to get the most flattering one. Sometimes, in the course of onstage emergencies, as when a broken toe or overlong toenails would prevent the completion of a performance, whoever could pour himself into the costume would be the one to finish out the role. Tim's key roles, according to Anthony Rabara, who also danced with him at the time, included one of the four "Little Swans" in *Swan Lake* and dancing in Anastos's *Go for Barocco*.

One of Tim's future students, Cindy Van Scoter, recalled how Tim always loved to tell his Trocks stories, remembering three in particular.

"Whenever someone would jump," he'd tell the group, "there would be a big THUD backstage—so that it sounded like someone weighed three hundred pounds." Another time a bunch would be completely nauseous with food poisoning from something they'd eaten earlier in the day. They'd go onstage and perform, go backstage to throw up, and then go back on. And when it was really hot, "they'd stand in the toilet and flush it because there was nothing better than the cold whirlpool water."

Following Detroit, Trockadero launched its European tour (January 13–February 26, 1981, including twelve performances in Germany and twenty-eight in Italy. Tim performed on the night of his twenty-seventh birthday in Frankfurt at a small, 150-seat house that had been built primarily for avant garde troupes. The Trocks' management was angry at the poor audience turnout, particularly after learning that the venue not only failed to advertise its productions but actually seemed to take pride in doing so. Therefore, few initially knew of the performances. By the time they were done at this theater, however, it was filled to capacity, all by word of mouth. Gerhard Rohde, the dance critic for the *Frankfurter Allgemeine Zeitung*, appreciated "the Trocks' technical skill as dancers but truly understood their excellent sense of parody. Trockadero are actually not wicked about their subject; they are, rather, secretly in love with it and drawn to it." Echoing this sentiment was Renata Leimsner, whose review in Main-Folo warned "readers not to confuse the Trocks with drag revues. They are great satirists, and they take their subject seriously. They take it seriously as only something one loves sincerely can be, and their satire is based on sincere love of ballet. They never distort more than is necessary to twist the matter into distinctly perfect sauciness, so it amuses, never criticizing it. They have mastered the lessons of high parody, knowledgeably exploding and imploding what they parody. The gentlemen can dance, often better than those who put on airs."[25]

Italy was next up, with the Trocks performing in Rome, Pisa, Taranto, and Prate. Although he was not mentioned by name, it appears that Tim's work in *Giselle* was rewarded. "In *Giselle*," according to Irene Freda Pitt of the *International Daily News*, "they even manage to outshine technically a number of dancers who have appeared in reach-me-down productions." Pitt also cited Mike McKinley's work: "The most brilliant item after *Giselle* was the closing for *Go for Barocco*, with Suzina LaFuzziovitch [Natch Taylor] and Tatiana Youbetyabootskaya [Michael McKinley] as two zanily contrasted soloists (one gigantic, one tiny) in this clever send-up of Balanchine by Peter Anastos, the group's previous director."

Amusing to most of the Trocks on this European trip was Tim's seeming inability to grasp the nuances of the Italian language. No matter how many times his colleagues would attempt to fix his phraseology, nothing seemed to work. However, he was able to make his needs known by using one phrase with reckless abandon in a sing-song voice that set the group atitter each time it was employed, "Scusi mi, toiletty?"

After the last show of the European tour on February 28, the troupe flew to West Lafayette, Indiana, to perform at Purdue University. Following this, they returned to New York City for two weeks before leaving for a month-long tour of the United States from March 12 to April 10, 1981.

Because it was the wont of the Trocks in their early years to periodically launch tours that played in cities proximal to their dancers' hometowns, the company performed in what Tim might have considered his "home away from home," Buffalo, New York, where he had resided during his years with Miss Crofton and the Festival Ballet of New York. Thus, Trockadero arrived in Buffalo in 1981. Several friends and former students attended the performance, including Michelle Buschner and Marie Carapezza. After the performance, many went out with Tim, enjoying a great reunion.

Subsequent to this US tour, the troupe headed north to Toronto. Sometime during this period, a representative from a major ballet company, having seen Tim perform, discussed a contract with him. Then he injured his Achilles tendon. Although the injury would not completely sideline his dancing at this point, performing at the level required by a major company was out of the question. With the Trocks on a four-month hiatus, he assessed his options with his partner, Frank Galaska, and they made the decision to move to South Florida.

Tim had no trouble finding employment. He was now an accomplished dancer with global touring experience under his belt. Distinguishing him further were his handsome, lean sculpted look, a natural gift for teaching and choreography, irresistible charisma and a sarcastic wit that would engage all within his midst, and a sensibility reflecting precise, uncompromising standards that ensured beauty and excellence in all that he undertook. Trockadero had been a turning point for Tim, providing him with a chance to live his art in an unconventional yet most riveting way that only years of classical training at the barre and center could have fashioned. The possibilities ahead were intriguing. That he would continue to perform and teach was a given, but a wider canvas seemed to be beckoning, as well. Those who knew Tim best recall that from the time he was young, he knew precisely what he wanted and what was or was not acceptable to him. He was also thinking about how he could improve on his chosen art form from the vantage point of teacher, choreographer, and director. The next few years would give him the chops to eventually do just that.

For all of the many possibilities that lay ahead, however, Tim always had "an unfinished feeling about his performance career," recalls Victor Trevino, a close friend of Tim's and fellow dancer from his Florida days. He continued to dance for a while but did so with the knowledge that ultimately his body, not his mind, would call the shots.

Alanna Lipsky. Photograph by Christine Knoblauch.

ALANNA LIPSKY

Tim was committed to helping me grow as a person and as a dancer, and he always challenged me to try harder, practice again, and keep pushing to perfect my craft. He never missed an opportunity to test our abilities and stretch our determination. He knew that there was always more of ourselves that we could give and somehow knew how to bring that out in each of us. With very little background in ballet, I initially struggled to perform at the level of others in class. Through his instruction, I grew stronger and came to exceed my own expectations of what I could achieve. Drawing from those experiences, I adopted the belief that I could always surpass the expectations I set for myself.

Tim had a unique way of motivating us to improve our technique. I will never forget the time when he announced that all of the dancers in our class needed to get stronger and increase our stamina. Although that was a frequent occurrence, there was one instance that stood out. On that day, Tim decided that all of the dancers would stay after class once a week to do tae bo cardio boxing. He insisted that the many hours of class and rehearsal were not nearly enough, and that for us to build the necessary strength, tae bo was the answer.

So there we were, twenty dancers, in leotards, tights, and sneakers, gracefully kickboxing away. At the time, although I didn't realize it, Tim imparted one of many lessons to us within that exercise. In essence, his message was to do and try whatever you can to be the best you can possibly be. In spite of his unorthodox style, his extraordinary passion and commitment to our improvement was resolute. He had this special way of pushing us to jump higher, stretch further, and reach beyond what we thought was possible. It is in this light that I remember and honor Tim's spirit.

Alanna Lipsky graduated from the Ailey/Fordham Bachelor of Fine Arts Program in Dance where she worked with such notable artists as Bill T. Jones, Jennifer Muller, Kazuko Hirabayashi, Joanna Mendl-Shaw, and Debbie Allen. She has performed with the Alvin Ailey American Dance Theater, AdrienneCelesteFadjoDANCE, and KDNY Dance Company. She was chosen to perform as a guest artist at the 2004 Youth America Grand Prix

Gala. Alanna has also performed on national television for *LIVE! with Regis & Kelly* and danced commercially for companies including Equinox, Moncler, Paul Mitchell, and First Niagara Bank. Alanna is a certified GYRO-TONIC trainer currently in graduate school at New York University, where she is studying to become a school counselor.

COCONUT GROVE

Arriving in South Florida in 1981, Tim appears to have more or less continued the pattern he had established previously: performing, teaching, taking class, choreographing, and directing any and all projects that took his fancy. Soon he was dancing with Fusion Dance Company in South Florida, teaching for Florida Regional Ballet, serving as ballet master of both Dance Miami and Ballet Etudes, choreographing for Miami Dance Theatre, codirecting and choreographing for the Fort Lauderdale Ballet, and teaching at Ballet Florida in West Palm Beach. Also, he finally was getting a taste of what it was like to put his own work on display. Edward Villella's Miami City Ballet was not yet a part of the cultural mix—that would not happen until 1986.

For someone who had grown up in a location where winter and overcast skies were mostly a nine-month affair, Tim's being able to further his dream in the "Sunshine State" had to be glorious. His gregarious nature drew everyone in. If he wasn't directing, rehearsing, taking class, or performing, he was entertaining a host of friends who knew that there could be no better person with whom to pass the time, catch up on the latest gossip, and dissect any subject (especially involving dance).

An old and very dear friend of Tim's stretching back to childhood, Janet Boeff, got together with him in Florida whenever the opportunity presented itself. Although she was a little older than Tim, their shared love of dance and laughter had brought the two close, first at Little Red as students and certified teachers, and then throughout the years when Tim would invariably corral Janet into being a part of his productions. The two somehow always managed to stay in touch, no matter where his travels took him. She recalls, "I used to visit him when I was traveling for Bausch & Lomb [during the 1980s]. They used to drag me to all these crazy dance clubs. We had a blast!"

Mike McKinley, Tim's former Trocks colleague from Austin, remembers running into Tim toward the end of 1981. Mike, Tim, and Tim's partner, Frank Galaska, met for drinks, where they had an enjoyable reunion. Hilarious conversation ensued at a restaurant that boasted a mechanical bull—"the height of Texas chic," as Mike humorously remembered.

The British ballerina Fiona Fairrie also recalls meeting Tim in Miami in 1984. A nationally renowned master ballet instructor and coach to numerous national and international competition winners, she came to America in 1975 after performing with the Royal Ballet and the Stuttgart Ballet. When they met, she was the ballet mistress for Momentum Dance Company, a modern dance organization, and she taught Tim from 1984 to 1985. Her recollections are that he really loved her class and that the two of them would frequently brainstorm afterward about the teaching of ballet. An old condition, Achilles tendonitis, had become increasingly troublesome to him at this point, so she helped him with his *plié*.

Tim had been teaching at the Magda Auñon School of Ballet in Fort Lauderdale for its highly regarded founder, who had studied with Alicia Alonso, the Cuban *prima ballerina assoluta* and choreographer. After a time, however, Auñon's best students elected to leave the studio to follow Tim, a pattern that became inevitable because he was just so good. Students and parents alike were smitten. He pushed his students harder than they had ever been pushed before. He did it with such passion, humor, and genuine desire to make them the best they could be that they came to crave this particular brand of medicine and would follow him to the ends of the earth. An illustration of his commitment to bring out the very best in his young charges may be found in an article published in 1985 in the *Boca Raton News*. The subject of the piece was one of Tim's students with enormous potential, Rachel Chastine, who later performed as a guest artist with Tim's own company. The article also provides a very enlightening glimpse into Tim's overarching philosophy of dance at the time:

"Rachel is incredibly talented," said her instructor Tim Draper, who worked with Rachel for two years at Magda Auñon's School of Ballet in Fort Lauderdale and spent some time with her and her mother in New York. "She is so musical, so dedicated, so hardworking; all the qualities a dancer needs. Of all my students, she has improved the most over the past two years. And she has the ideal body for a dancer. As a member of the ballet corps of the Fort Lauderdale Ballet Company, Rachel portrayed Columbine in *The Nutcracker* and danced in *Moonlight Concerto* and *Les Sylphides* last year. However, Rachel is still at the beginning of her apprenticeship. . . . She has improved a great deal in terms of her technique," said Draper, who formerly danced with the Festival Ballet of New York and the Ballets Trockadero de Monte Carlo. "She's only 14, and she's just beginning to develop as a dancer and a person. These next years will be crucial as to how she develops her performance on stage. I stress the good points of the profession with my students but I tell them the bad things, too," said Draper. "They must know that there are other things . . . they must grow not only as a dancer but as a person, as well. The inner growth is what helps them communicate with the audience. You have to reach inside yourself—and if all you have in your life is dance, you're going to be a shallow person."[1]

Fiona had also been a teacher at the Magda Auñon studios. Although she was put in the somewhat awkward position of having to hear about "Tim's naughtiness" (in taking Auñon's students), Fiona adored Tim. Several years later, when she was teaching in Bradenton and he had already launched his own studio, she looked him up out of the blue and they engaged in a far-ranging conversation about ballet, his new school and budding company, and his summer intensive program. "I asked him if he needed summer teachers and that was that," recalled Fairrie. Terms were reached immediately, and she began teaching the following summer. To the delight of both, in true *Casablanca* style, the "beginning of a beautiful friendship" was rekindled on the phone that day. As a result, some of the most legendary names in the international ballet world came to Rochester, New York, summer after summer.

One particularly exciting element of Tim's art form that came to life during the latter part of his Florida years was choreography. His creation *Devenir* was selected for the 1985 Gala Performance of the Southeastern Regional Ballet Festival in Charleston, South Carolina and garnered Tim a nomination for the upcoming 1985 Moretti Award for Artistic Achievement—Broward County (Florida) Cultural Arts Awards. This early-career choreographic triumph later was restaged by his own company, Draper Dance Theatre. Equally rewarding, however, was the fact that Tim had become an exceptional teacher, and that didn't go unnoticed. Nancy Bielski paid him the highest compliment in this regard by routinely inviting him to guest teach for her at Harkness House, Hebrew Arts, and Steps. Once his teacher, she was now pleased to consider him her very gifted colleague.

By late 1985, despite the many successes and public affirmation that Tim was receiving in Florida, the pain of his Achilles tendonitis could no longer be ignored. He simply was no longer able to jump. As he later explained, "In Florida with the Fusion Dance Company, I woke up one day and my ankles were totally enflamed." Describing the condition as a buildup of scar tissue from poor early training and years of dancing on hard surfaces, Tim's doctors said, "If you continue to dance, they (the tendons) are going to rupture."[2] Even before that time, however, possibly as far back as 1982, Michelle Buschner remembers many phone calls back and forth between them, usually on a biweekly basis, about the idea of Tim's return to Rochester. "From the early 1980s, I begged Tim to move back to Rochester. I told him that he could take over my studio and I would teach for him!" By 1985, with his performance career unhappily over, the logical options seemed to be to remain in Florida; return to New York City, the place that always rejuvenated him; or come home and build his own organization from the ground up. After the crushing diagnosis, he decided to remain in Florida, at least initially. "I was bitter but at least I was still in dance," he recalled a few years later. "I had something to occupy me. If I didn't, I'd be devastated." This experience colored the rest of his life. From that point on, he was on a mission to ensure that dancers would never have to quit before their time because of potentially preventable, career-ending injuries. From his exhaustive time in physical therapy, Tim began to apply his knowledge by "bringing scientific prevention techniques to his teaching in several Florida companies. As he revealed to a reporter a few years later, "I was always told, 'Grin and bear it. Dance and get over it.' I tell my students, 'This is your body. Take care of it. You can't buy another one.'"[3] He also always made sure, as he had confided to his mother, that his studios would have proper flooring to prevent what had happened to him from happening to his dancers and to do his best to help them have long-term, sustainable dance careers. He told his mother, "Mom, these students are my children, and I want them taught the right way. They will never dance on concrete, since it will ruin their feet."

It was during this time that Tim met the young, talented dancer Victor Trevino. Both were affiliated with Ballet Florida—Tim as instructor and Victor as company member. Victor was every bit as passionate about his art form as was Tim, and the two quickly became close friends. Tim confided to Victor that he had been having trouble with the artistic leadership team at Ballet Florida, as he had with previous institutions, because he did not want to compromise his standards. Victor, who was enormously impressed with Tim and the excellence he brought to the organization, agreed that his dominating personality could be off putting to certain people. He thus began urging Tim to establish his own school and company, where he would be able to run the show on his own terms. For his part, Tim saw in Victor a highly talented individual who should be traveling the world. He thus recommended Victor to Trockadero, just as Tory Dobrin had once done for him. From 1986 to 1994, Victor rose to become one of its stars. The two remained lifelong friends, crossing paths frequently in the years ahead.

After a time, Tim decided that it was time to return to the Northeast, and arrangements were made. Tim and Frank had been subletting their New York apartment while in Coconut Grove. It was therefore their original plan to return to New York City. However, after learning that they had lost their apartment lease, they changed their plans. Instead, the two moved to Rochester, at least for the short term. Tim had remained in close touch with loved ones back home over the years, always keeping an eye on the local dance scene. He had, of course, been in touch regularly with Michelle Buschner. He also knew that because Olive McCue had closed her Mercury Ballet a little over a decade earlier, Rochester no longer had a professional ballet company. Tim's roots in Rochester were deep. Unlike so many artists of his generation, who would travel from place to place, make friends, and then move on again to further their careers, he carefully tended those relationships that were important to him. If he did not immediately see himself in Rochester, perhaps something did strike him about the sadness inherent in Kathleen Crofton's final days—passing her last hours in a downtown studio thousands of miles from her place of birth—and he did not want the same for himself. During visits back home, in addition to spending quality time with his family, he made sure that he got together with old friends. But what was pivotal in making Rochester home again was the extraordinary outpouring of affection and admiration from students and parents alike, demonstrated immediately as he began to guest teach for his old friends. When coupled with the valued counsel he received from his dear confidantes in New York, Nancy Bielski and David Manion (and later Gayle Miller), the idea of being in Rochester just began to make sense. These three friends not only became a sounding board for him regarding fund-raising, finding a board of directors, and managing a company but also later had official titles as members of his new company's advisory board.

With the culturally oriented community of Rochester no longer having a professional ballet company in residence, the timing was right for Tim to bring his considerable talents home. He knew that founding his own school and company from scratch would not be an easy task. For one thing, having performed himself with the Mercury Ballet accompanied by the Rochester Civic Orchestra, he was acutely aware that those world-class arbiters of the most refined artistic sensibility, the Eastman School of Music and the Rochester Philharmonic Orchestra, would be watching his every move. Their extensive history with dance in Rochester presaged no less. The long shadow cast by Eastman's muses was always palpable. It might be experienced by a fourth-generation dancer attempting to apply a little extra makeup in an upper floor backstage "Tower" dressing room before the fast descent down multiple flights of stairs; or when facing a singularly unimpressive parking lot that once was 50 Swan Street, housing the rehearsal studios, equipment, and gels used to produce ethereal magic onstage; or when traveling up the long driveway to 3646 East Avenue where once a mystical woodland studio stood, no longer inhabited by a Misha, David, or Leon.

But an opportunity such as this would not come along twice, and although unfortunate leasing arrangements in New York City might have been the cause for Tim to give his home town a good second look, he must have felt the pull of destiny. If a void was going to be filled, he would be the one to fill it.

Chelsea Bonosky. Photograph by Travis Magee.

CHELSEA BONOSKY

Tim Draper. Such a large name for such a powerful human being with such a giant heart—that beat for everyone else. Everyone has their own stories to tell, but one thing that unifies them all is the extreme impact he made on everyone's life, not only as dancers, but as full-hearted artists and developed human beings.

One of the biggest things I will ever remember about him was his unending confidence in me. I would doubt myself and question myself, but he wouldn't hesitate for a split second in dismissing those fears. That was—and still is—the hardest thing to find within myself since he has left. But if he saw even a small kernel of confidence in me, I'm constantly reminded that it still has to be in there. I always wanted his constant approval, respect, and attention. He gave all that—and more—in a way that ultimately made me realize it wasn't for him, rather for myself, for that voice inside that said, "This is what I'm meant and destined to do." That voice that said it doesn't just pour out of my dedicated muscles and trained ability, but from my veins, and it's meant to flow out and never stay bottled. He saw that shining in a ten-year-old girl, and I will never be able to fully comprehend how his eyes could transcend all else and see that.

It's ironic that this memoir is in honor of him and his memory. I'm tempted to say he would argue that it's more about us as individuals growing—as it always was for him. I hesitated for a very long time in attempting to write this, because I didn't know how to put on paper how someone's actions affected my development as a person and an artist, yet I can look back with humbling tenderness at the man that made me and continues to mold me into the person/artist I am today.

It goes without saying I would not be who I am and what I am if it wasn't for him entering my life nearly sixteen years ago. . . . I hope everyone cherishes the time they had with him and all he has left behind, and continues to treat it with the meaningful respect it deserves. His memory is unending. I hope that I can make him proud.

Chelsea Bonosky is a graduate of New York University's Tisch School for the Arts. After working under the direction of Alonzo King with LINES

Ballet, she apprenticed with Stephen Petronio during his touring schedule and multiple Joyce seasons. She has worked with Christopher Williams, Cherylyn Lavagnino Dance, Choreo Theatro Company, Jessica Lang, Patricia Norowol Dance, Curt Heyworth, and Sidra Bell. She presently works with Adam Barruch Dance, where she is engaged as a performer and as Mr. Barruch's assistant at major venues throughout the country, including the Yard in Martha's Vineyard. She is also on contract with the London-based Punchdrunk's production of *Sleep No More NYC*, and models for Estée Lauder and *Pointe* magazine. She was an absolutely stunning Arabian in Tim's *Nutcracker*.

8

COMING HOME TO BUILD A DREAM

Wrapping up his commitments in Florida, Tim returned to Rochester in 1985, taking up the offer of his two close friends, Michelle Buschner and Karen Ventura, to guest teach at their studios. Both teachers were enormously popular. To this day, it would be difficult to find anyone with a connection to dance in Rochester during the mid-1980s who hadn't been either a student or colleague of these two dynamic women.

Michelle had many of the region's most prominent artists teach for her over an illustrious career that spanned more than thirty years. Beginning with Tim, who initially guest taught for her from 1974 to 1976 and then again in 1985–86, the roster also included:

Jamey Throumoulos Leverett, now the artistic director of Rochester City Ballet and who taught for Michelle for three seasons while a principal company dancer at Draper Dance Theatre.

Marie Carapezza Welch, Michelle's assistant, who helped launch the careers of several professional dancers, many of whom attended such top-tier colleges as Juilliard, Northwestern, Princeton, and Fordham/Ailey along the way.

Julianne O'Donnell Deming, a founding member and former assistant to the director of Draper Dance Theatre/Rochester City Ballet, a former codirector of the Botsford School of Dance, and a long-term instructor at the Timothy M. Draper Center for Dance Education.

Kara Hulbert, a former Rochester City Ballet star and instructor at the Timothy M. Draper Center for Dance Education.

Pamela Wilkens-White, a former principal of the Mercury Ballet Company and currently a choreographer/mentor to members of the University of Rochester's Ballet Performance Group.

Pamela Scherer Hin, ballet director at Spins Dance Studio.

Brenda Bobby, Pittsford Dance Studio.

Pamela Schickler, a former member of the Draper Dance Theatre/Rochester City Ballet and the founder and director of Nazareth Academy Dance and 25 North Dance Academy.

Marianne Reilly Dalton, a former member of Boston Ballet II, a long-term instructor at the Timothy M. Draper Center for Dance Education, and currently a member of the dance faculty at SUNY Brockport, Fitzsimmons Dance Factory, and Expressions of Dance by Lisa.

Karen Ventura, who had studied at Orcutt-Botsford during the 1970s, had also become a very popular ballet instructor in Rochester by this time. Her studio was located on Canterbury Road in Rochester and had become known as a mecca for both up-and-coming and adult dancers.

Having their friend back in Rochester was by all accounts fabulous. Tim as guest teacher presented a unique set of business challenges, however. Just as his magnetic personality drew students to him in Florida like moths to a flame, so, too, did students in Rochester want to be wherever he was. Michelle was only half teasing when she stated in 1986, after he had been guesting for her for a while and then decided to open up his own studio, "He took half my kids!" The same was true for Karen. Once students had a taste of this charming and enigmatic disciplinarian, who showed up for class in work boots and wool shirts and demanded nothing less than excellence from them, they followed him around as if he were the Pied Piper. Students insisted that their parents drive them wherever necessary so that they could take class from him wherever and whenever he happened to be teaching (something that would change on a fairly regular basis while he was scouting out a permanent location for his school). This was a rather new development in the annals of ballet class lore for preteenagers and young teens in the area. Quite simply, most students attending a recreational dance studio did not automatically live and breathe ballet, despite the best efforts of some school directors to encourage them.

Ballet was tough and unforgiving, required an exceptional memory, and didn't look especially good in the mirror until one became proficient, typically taking years to produce satisfying results. Jazz and tap, on the other hand, for those predisposed with the full panoply of natural gifts (smarts, flexibility, extension, good feet, and rhythm) could be mastered more quickly. Because of the lively music and freedom from dress codes, these genres tended to be far more enjoyable for most. Tim's arrival, however, ushered in a new set of rules. Technique class now meant leotards and skirts, with hair neatly gathered in a bun. It was curious, though, that this was no longer a big deal. The very students who had previously bemoaned their weekly or twice-weekly technique classes were now showing up early with pins neatly in place to face the somewhat scary but very cool ballet teacher.

Of course, not everyone wanted Tim's level of preprofessional training, a regimen that essentially precluded the normal activities of childhood and adolescence. Most teenagers were rather keen on the idea of being able to go to their junior proms without having to tear themselves away from rehearsals or performances with stage makeup still on and doing a quick change in the ladies' room or limo to be presentable. Not all children liked having to give up trick-or-treating, birthday parties, or after-school get-togethers five to six days per week. Indeed, sacrifice was a large component of this singular dedication to their art form, but the rewards, too, were great. For those who dreamed of dancing the roles of the Sugar Plum Fairy or the Snow Queen or the Cavalier in *The Nutcracker*, lessons could not begin quickly enough. Soon the lack of a normal social life was easily replaced with the camaraderie found in the disheveled glory of mismatched sofas, empty Diet Coke cans, bobby pins, hairnets, and foul-smelling *pointe* shoes about three productions past their prime.

To both Michelle and Karen's enormous credit, instead of being furious with the loss of so many talented students to another studio, they never allowed this to stand in the way of their friendship with Tim. Surely it had to be disappointing to see so many of their students leave after investing so much time in them, but they maintained a professionalism that always served them well. Tim was irresistible, and they knew it.

Michelle recalls having issues with her hip during this period and needing to continue dancing. "Tim would come to my studio for hours at a time and give me privates as well as partner me." For years afterward, Tim never failed to provide her with high-quality ballet teachers to ensure that her students had every opportunity to excel. He knew how much she valued ballet as the *sine qua non* that informs all other forms of dance. "You're the only one I'll let my teachers teach for," she recalled him saying on many an occasion. That is how the young and talented Jamey Leverett came to teach and choreograph for Michelle, winning multiple awards of distinction along the way, as well as the impressively pedigreed Marianne Reilly Dalton, who forced her pupils to pay close attention by speaking in a very soft, almost childlike voice, and insisting that her students wear appropriate ballet class attire.

As Tim was settling in once again within his native city and guest teaching—this time, though, as a fully formed artist, teacher, and director—the voice within urging him to start his own school continued to strengthen. His passion for achieving this was further stoked by the encouragement of old and new friends who recognized his enormous talent and encouraged him every step along the way. One of these compatriots was Julianne O'Donnell Deming, an old friend from Harkness House of Ballet Arts in the mid-1970s. Julianne had been teaching dance at the Hochstein School, left for a season to perform with Michael Uthoff at the Hartford Ballet, and then met up with Tim again after she returned to Rochester while both were guest teaching. She recalls that he was intent on securing space, even of a temporary nature, for training the initial small group of very devoted students who were willing to follow him practically anywhere for lessons. Eventually, he learned that an old friend of his from the Olive McCue days, Amy Blaisdell, who had gone on to dance at American Ballet Theatre, had a dance studio in the eclectic Village Gate, a no-frills warehouse cum retail mall that had once been the Stecher Traung Printing Company. Now it housed everything from vintage clothing and record outlets to appliance-repair stores and some of the city's top restaurants. Located in the area of Rochester known now as the Neighborhood of the Arts, across the street from the Memorial Art Gallery on North Goodman Street, it was a well-known, relatively easy-to-reach destination. Even if the buildings at the edges of the neighborhood at the time were somewhat a little the worse for wear, Tim was more than grateful for the use of this studio space, so his very first classes were offered in Village Gate. As word began to spread that he was starting his own studio, however, he and Julianne O'Donnell Deming began a continuing discussion about his establishing a school with a permanent location. From that point on, recalls Deming, "We would drive around everywhere, for hours at a time, looking together for a suitable building." One nonnegotiable item on the list was, of course, obtaining suitable or potentially suitable flooring.

Tim regularly articulated his overarching philosophy for his school and studio to everyone within his sphere, including members of the media. One interview, in particular, stands out:

> I want to establish a good training facility where children get everything they need. If they want to have a professional career in dance, they don't have to leave Rochester at 14 or as young adults. They can stay at home with their families. You know, children leave so early now and I don't think that's necessarily good for their emotional well-being. Tim Draper Studio of Dance is solid training with healthy minds and bodies together in one. I think that's so important today. Too many dancers were trained with the old rigid systems of . . . we beat them into submission and they grow up and we produce some wonderful dancers but they have no self confidence. They don't adjust well to the ballet world. They get out on stage and find that they're really not enjoying it. I think they have to have healthy personalities and minds, so that they can enjoy. Too many dancers now don't enjoy what they're doing.[1]

Also supporting him greatly during this period was a young woman who had performed with the Mercury Ballet Company as a child in *The Nutcracker* and then continued to pursue dance while obtaining a degree in economics from Hamilton College. On graduation, Kathy Ertsgaard returned home to Rochester and took a ballet class with Tim Draper where he was guesting for his old friend Karen Ventura. She recalls vividly,

> I can clearly picture the day . . . when I first met Tim—I showed up for ballet class at Karen Ventura's Studio. I walked by Karen's office and there was this guy standing there wearing a red plaid shirt, khaki pants, and work boots. Karen announced to the class that we had a guest teacher—a friend of hers who had just moved back to Rochester. I remember thinking—that guy in the work boots is going to teach us *ballet?* Yeah, right. Well—it was the best ballet class I had ever had and it turned out that guy had a gift.[2]

Obviously enthralled with Tim's incomparable artistry, passion, and extraordinary skills as a teacher, she followed him "around the city as he taught at other studios, taking class several nights a week." As their acquaintance developed, she, too, actively encouraged him to pursue his dreams, which he expressed to her as a "desire to start a professional ballet company and school to fill the void that he felt existed in the community." In an illuminating Spring 2009 interview with Sarah Lentini, the president and CEO of the Arts & Cultural Council for

Greater Rochester in the organization's publication *Metropolitan*, Kathy recalled how after Tim launched a school, "Draper Studio, in the fall of 1986 and then adding a company, Draper Dance Theatre, in the summer of 1987,' [she] started leading a 'double life,' working full time as assistant curatorial registrar at the Memorial Art Gallery, while simultaneously investing herself completely in the new ballet company and school." In addition to being a founding member and dancer of the company, she held "virtually every possible position" within the company, eventually including that of executive director.[3] Those who knew both Tim and Kathy well recalled that Kathy was Tim's best friend, valued especially for her loyalty and trustworthiness, traits that he considered paramount to lasting friendship.

The primary task for the moment, of course, was finding the proper permanent facility to house this endeavor. In addition to Tim and Julianne's scouting activities, the parents of one of Tim's very promising students, Janelle Cornwell, also got into the act. Janelle recalled wandering through "one warehouse after another" with her folks and Tim in hopes of finding a suitable space.

As it turned out, the best space, both in terms of location, physical structure, and cost happened to be a stone's throw from Amy Blaisdell's studio. The building at 320A North Goodman Street, adjacent to the main Village Gate building and owned by Gary Stern, would be called the Studio of Dance, offering classes in ballet, jazz, modern, tap, and creative movement. This was the place where Tim spent the rest of his life developing artists. For the immediate future, however, learning skills in the construction trades was the highest priority because the studio project, according to those intimately acquainted with it from the start, required EVERYTHING.

Fortunately for Tim, not only did Charlie Cornwell, Janelle's dad, bring with him an acute eye for commercial real estate but he also was a millwright in the Manufacturing Engineering Maintenance Organization at Kodak Park and thus knew a thing or two about construction. Tim simply could not have picked a better general contractor to oversee this massive renovation project. Charlie did superior-quality work and got along with and was able to organize the tasks of everyone else. Also, the price was right (free). He and his wife also brought with them a lovely young daughter, who although not even eleven years of age, showed every sign of star quality.

Also assisting with the renovation effort in a significant way was George Orosz. George, an electrical engineer in the Kodak Research

Laboratories (although he and Charlie had never met), had also found his way to Tim's studio after experiencing a particularly inspiring ballet class while at the Ventura studio. George recalls having first met Tim on January 9, 1986, while Tim was guesting at the studio. Like Kathy Ertsgaard, George was just in awe of his class, so much so that he recorded the date in his journal. Never having been introduced to the arts as a youngster, George did not actually begin dancing until the age of twenty-six. He took to it immediately, however. Having previously tried out some of the various other studios around town, he eventually heard that Karen Ventura had modern and ballet people taking her class, sometimes as many as twenty-five students at a time. He recalls, "When people [from out of town] would visit, they would take class with her. Tim came in to be a regular teacher for her, but his goal was to get his own studio." Chatting after class with Tim about a week later, George recalled,

> [Tim] told me he was interested in starting a regional ballet company. He also told me that he was interested in doing some choreography and asked if I were interested in participating. . . . I had taken a class at Buffalo Ballet Theater one weekend and was offered a position (with hourly pay) by the director, Barry [Leon]. . . . I mentioned this to Tim. I remember that he then said, 'You have to go where you are paid.' Apparently, I did not pay attention to his recommendation.

George further recalled that shortly afterward, Karen had to close her studio, "so it was good that Tim took almost everybody from there."

Construction began, according to George Orosz, on August 23, 1986. "Charlie and Tim may have surveyed work needed a few days earlier, but I believe we all began dismantling the place on that day." In a marvelous foreshadowing of what was to come, George noted,

> The amount of work necessary was much more than I expected. Kathy E. and I were rehearsing our *pas de deux* (I think for "Somewhere") late July through mid-August after class at Karen Ventura's. All classes and rehearsals ceased there in late August. During that time, we focused on weekends, some very late workday evenings, and (for some of us full-time workers), vacation days to get one studio ready for Tim's requested opening on Thursday, September 18, 1986. We did open, but not all of the permanent barres were ready. They were added in the following weeks. I recorded several nights of only three hours of sleep before going to work the next day. We tore out old walls, built new ones . . . removed or fixed old windows . . . built stairs, patched holes in hardwood floors and then sanded and refin-

ished them. Finishing work (patching, painting and trim) continued through that year while classes and rehearsals increased.

George brought to the studio a most unusual and abundantly valuable combination of technical and artistic skills. These played extremely well both behind the scenes and later onstage when he became a dancer. He and Charlie became fast friends as together they "cut holes in the floor, took the old staircase down and built a new one [to the location where people later remembered it] to free up more dancing space on the second level." In the meanwhile, the old guard remembered a temporary ladder that served as the staircase between the first and second floors. "There was also a men's dressing room—for me and Cory English," reminisced the future male principal dancer.

He further recalled how "Charlie was the construction leader and he guided all of what we had to do." The seven additional construction participants included three members of his senior company (Kathy Ertsgaard; Julianne O'Donnell, who did double duty as Tim's assistant director; and Irene Farr); Tim's brother-in-law, Art Hansmann; Tim's partner, Frank Galaska, whom George credited with being a "major contributor to the work effort"; Tim's mom, Hazel, and his sister, Donna Hansmann. "I painted the pipes and helped sand the floors," Mrs. Draper recalled almost to the day, twenty years later. "It was a whole family affair." Donna similarly remembers her mother actually "hanging on a pipe painting a couple of nights before the studio was to open and that she and Art were there sanding the floors. My husband was there a lot helping him. Mark [Tim's older brother] was there helping—he took care of the heating." The studio also obtained the assistance of other parent volunteers who dropped in periodically to assist with various tasks, so moved were they by the commitment and talent of their children's teacher. When the construction was complete and the company was gearing up for its debut performance just weeks away, Charlie and George took out an ad in the program to honor the hard work of the key people involved with this extraordinarily challenging renovation project.

Although Tim was most enthusiastic about the entire renovation process conceptually, his small, faithful coterie quickly became of the collective mindset that Tim might be better off focusing his time and efforts on developing his students' épaulement and *batterie*, rather than attempting to wield a hammer or saw. This is *not* to say that he did not try his best. As Kathy Ertsgaard recalled with great affection in the eulogy she had to deliver seventeen years later,

Starting from scratch—he built his school and company—and I don't just mean figuratively—Tim *literally built* that studio—as I know his mother remembers—many late nights ripping out the old and putting in the new—can you imagine Tim painting the ceiling of the large studio?—standing on a ladder underneath the paint sprayer—getting covered with paint—PINK paint—only to find out that it wasn't water-soluble. He spent the next several mornings in the shower trying to scrub that paint off.

Kathy Joslyn, or "Joslyn!" as Tim called her, recalls that she first met Tim when he was guest teaching for Michelle Buschner. "He told me somewhat later that he was going to be having a company in Rochester and that he wanted to train me. He also told me that he had a school and asked if I might be interested in participating in that." Kathy remembers that she had only just recently come to study with Michelle; previously she was at the Joyce Winters studio and really only knew about Broadway dance. However, Kathy knew intuitively that "Tim was something special" and therefore signed up immediately. "I was part of his very first company," she recalled. "At first, he would teach at different buildings—'Today, we'll have class over here,' he would say, and I would follow him wherever that would lead, along with the small group of other devotees. One class was even held in an odd room in a church! Then he found the Goodman Street building and all of the sudden there was space." She remembered with an amused look on her face, "It was a great thing [the building], but there were some weird things about it. . . . How funny was that bathroom by the downstairs studio?"[4] Kathy looks back wistfully at that first season in which, despite her youth (she was only fifteen years old at the time), she was invited to be a member of the senior company, performing the principal role of Dew Drop in *The Nutcracker* and the lead role in Tim's award-winning *Devenir*, which he restaged on his new company. She danced with George Orosz and was clearly, for a time, Tim's star performer. It was no surprise to anyone who had witnessed her earliest performances for Tim that he wanted her back years later as a member of his faculty. The purity of her line and the quality of her performance as a mere teenager were unmistakable—she looked like a finished product practically from the very start. Michelle herself remembers Kathy Joslyn as a "beautiful dancer." In somewhat bemused fashion, Michelle recalled that Tim eventually took many of her dancers, including Cindy Van Scoter, Stephanie Carpenter, and Janelle Cornwell. "One year he took my entire senior class! I told him, 'Tim—this school is not a pipeline for your studio!'" She knew he was a great teacher, though, and that he could be tough, when he had to be. "He would throw kids right out of class!" she remembered with a smile.

Kathy recalls that Tim's first impression of her, however, provoked one of his famous raised eyebrows. "I was wearing one of those bibs with the shiny material—you know, the parachute pants, the full overalls getup," she recalls. "Mine were purple and I thought I looked perfect. Tim came over to me and said, 'Dear, what are you wearing?' I replied, 'I don't know. . . .' 'Well, can any of this junk come off?' 'Well, all I have is a leotard. . . .'" And then came *the face*, reflecting pure dissatisfaction with what she was wearing, and from that point on, she dressed for class appropriately. In the beginning, there was no uniform requirement as there would be in later years, where the color of the leotard would denote a specific class level, but pink tights were required, accompanied by a leotard of any color. Fairly quickly, class time was ramped up to six days a week. "It is fascinating to think back about that time with Tim . . . what the expectations were of a 16–17 year old, doing a high level of performing in the exact same manner as any other professional in a ballet company would be doing. I spent my entire high school life with Tim," Kathy Joslyn reflected. "He could see what potential I had and what my strengths were—he had that tremendous ability to see people's strengths—by intuition almost—and to build on them." She said that unlike so many other teachers who would only see what was wrong, he would see what was right. "He could home in on what we were good at and build on that." No one would ever see the transformation happening—it would just happen.

It would happen because Tim had the remarkable ability to create analogies on the fly, always memorable and spot-on, that students would eat right up. Whereas other teachers might try to express what they wanted from their charges by words alone, leaving them sometimes wondering afterward exactly what was meant, Tim was more hands on in his approach. As a result, his dancers advanced their artistry at a far more rapid pace.

"Tim was an incredibly gifted and able teacher," recalled his life partner, Randy Stringer.

> I honestly think much of this was innate skill. . . . His time with the Trocks taught him the physicality of women's ballet in addition to what he learned as a male dancer. I think that foundation gave him immense

technical knowledge that he could impart to students of either gender. But his greatest asset was his ability to explain something as esoteric as dance in a way that made sense to the dancer. He found the unique way to teach each student, however they needed to listen to and absorb such information. I think my favorite "lesson" that I saw him teach was about arm/hand movement/positioning. It was in a level 4 or 5 class. He was trying to explain the concept that hand movement had to be technical, effortless, and beautiful. Tim had always thought that the American ballet schools had poor hand/arm training/discipline as compared to the European styles such as what would be found at the Royal Ballet, Royal Danish, et al., and therefore he would try to spend extra time to get it right. The image he created was this: "Imagine that there is a butterfly on the tip of your hand that you are trying to place on the top branch of a tree. The motion should be exact, precise, and flow without disturbing the butterfly throughout the movement." My other favorite lesson I heard him say constantly was 'they should never see the effort of your dance, only the beauty.'

Sometimes, he would literally get down on his knees so that his dancers could see precisely what they needed to do to perfect their craft.

Kathy Joslyn recalls that Tim also had a wonderful way of helping his young dancers connect with the music. "He was wonderful at musicality and phrasing. He would help us to go inside the music and live in it rather than dance on top of it. He would create his exercise so that we felt that we were dancing." She also remembers with fondness many of the images he would create to improve their dancing:

He would say, "when you are *en combre* [an extension of the lower back], don't look like you're sniffing your own armpits. Picture that you have a diamond ring on when you're extending your arm in an arabesque line and looking out over it. . . . The connection between the eyes and the hand . . . you are looking at your diamond ring. I hope you will get a big diamond." In attempting to teach épaulement, he would say, "Picture that you are wearing a beautiful necklace. . . . How you will carry your upper body . . . how you will express yourself is in your sternum?"

Of course, some of his sayings, or "Tim-isms," were memorable just for their delicious sarcasm, particularly among the teenage girls who comprised the majority of his advanced students. Among the favorites were:

"This is not a democracy—it's a dictatorship."
"Stop crying, you'll get dehydrated."

"A pretty face won't get you through everything, my dear."

"It's all about physics. I bet you people failed that course."

"Don't say 'I can't' because you know I'm going to make you do it anyway."

"Anyone can get up on pointe but it takes a true artist to get off."

And then the signature line, used on many generations of his elite dancers: "If you roll your eyes once more, you can roll them downstairs and out the door!"

Then there were the pet names: "Throumoulos!," "Penelope," "Henrietta!," "Ding-Dong," "Anna Nicole Smith," "Goldameier," "Seamore," "The BBs," "The Elsies," "Miss Noodle," "Bambi," "Ginger," "Betty," "Rhoda," "Henry," "Cleo," "Pancake," "Ee-Lanna," "Harley and Heidi," and "Katrina!"

Tim had other memorable analogies that he employed regularly and continually to improve his dancers. Marie Carapezza Welch, the former student who became his lifelong friend and a well-loved assistant to Michelle Buschner, recalls that Tim had a very particular way to remind his students to pull in their *derrières*: "We could have a tea party back there because they are sticking out so much!" Another favorite that he would dispense to help them remember to tuck in their thumbs: "Tuck Johnny into bed." And the most important, of course: "You only improve as fast as you get your corrections."

Of tremendous benefit to Tim during those early years (and illustrative of the social capital he had accrued in the ballet world) were the wisdom and guidance provided by his company's first advisory board:

Nancy Bielski of the David Howard School of Ballet and STEPS in New York City

David Manion, chairman of the Riverside Dance Festival, also in New York City

Judith Newman, director of Miami Dance Theatre, Miami, Florida

Olive McCue, former director of the Mercury Ballet Company, Rochester, New York

Susanne (Sue) Callan-Harris, registered physical therapist, Rochester, New York

As noted earlier, David and Tim became acquainted when David was the director of the Riverside Dance Festival in New York. David recalls, "I was introduced to him by Frank Galaska. The two started attending performances there and sometimes volunteering for the Festival. . . . Tim picked my brain about starting the school and then finally the company. . . . He was new to fundraising and putting a board together, but I tried to assist wherever I could. Tim worked hard to have a world-class ballet school. . . . He would come to New York City on weekends and we would discuss the growth of the school and the company." David Manion remained a dear friend who would rejuvenate him whenever Tim felt the need to return to New York City for inspiration and to catch the performances of his top dancers, who were performing both at American Ballet Theatre (Sari Ostrum, Kristi Boone, and later while in the ABT Studio Company, Sarah Lane) or at New York City Ballet (Aesha Ash). "His legacy lies with the dancers that perform at ABT and elsewhere, and of course the school and company," David later said.

The "soft debut" of Tim's Draper Studio Dance Theatre took place on Sunday, December 14, 1986, billed as a holiday performance at Edison Tech High School, mostly for family and friends. It was a mixed bill featuring artistic direction and choreography by Tim. On the program was *Devenir*, Tim's award-winning work, danced by the senior company, comprising Kathy Ertsgaard, George Orosz, Kathy Joslyn, Cory English, Irene Farr, Julianne O'Donnell, Traci Pino, and Kim Doyle (the latter appearing courtesy of Sandy Stramonine). *Somewhere* was performed by Kathy Ertsgaard and George Orosz. And *Nutcracker* act 2 divertissements were highlighted by Kathy Joslyn in the lead role of Dew Drop, with Irene Farr, Kathy Ertsgaard, Julianne O'Donnell, and Kim Doyle as Flowers; Julianne O'Donnell as Arabian; Cory English as Russian; Irene Farr, Kathy Joslyn, and Traci Pino as Spanish; Sara Silvio, Janelle Cornwell, and Cory English as the Magical Dolls; Kathy Ertsgaard and Dan DeFrank as the Bon Bons; Janelle Cornwell, Sara Silvio, Andora Shek, Aimee Litwiller, Jennifer Rosso, Rachel Hill, and Cindy Van Scoter as Chinese; Libby Kendig as Mother Gignone, with Danielle DePaola, Erin Bull, Jennifer Matties, Cora Kannel, Richard Thompson, Elizabeth Williams, Valerie Taylor, Aimee Senise, and Suzanne Chandler as Clowns; Rachel Hill and Aimee Litwiller as Archangels; and Margaret Joslyn, Elizabeth Joslyn, Danny Mott, Bridget Zakielarz, Meghann Connor, and Kevin Harris as Angels. The guest artist was Carmen San Martin, a principal dancer with the Fort Lauderdale Ballet and a trainee with the Joffrey Ballet under the direction of Robert Joffrey. She danced the role of the Sugar Plum Fairy, partnered by George Orosz as her Cavalier.

Tim demonstrating. Photograph by George Orosz.

That a performance could have come together within just three months of the opening of its official training school is nothing short of remarkable. Although a more cautious artistic director might have been a bit more mindful of the staying power of first impressions and might have thought to wait a bit longer before casting a fledgling company into the public realm for dissection, Tim had confidence in both his company members and the students who were invited to perform with them. He also knew the many residual benefits that would accrue from putting them on the line. The premiere was recorded, revealing both strong performances and those needing work. There is no question that with so many young dancers training daily with such an explosively talented teacher and choreographer, it was only a matter of time before Tim would develop a company with the gravitas of a seasoned regional entity. In reality, however, he would accomplish something far greater.

Notably, the young Cory English of the early seasons would go on to become a wonderfully diverse "triple threat" actor, performing as a Broadway gypsy before studying classical theater at Drama Studio London. After broadening his performance portfolio with such West End credits as *Chicago* and *Guys and Dolls*, he was hired as the headliner in Mel Brooks's hit *The Producers*, playing Max Bialystock at Theatre Royal, Drury Lane, and in the UK national tour. This success led to more roles, such as Igor in the US national Broadway tour of Brooks's *Young Frankenstein*.[5] He then starred on Broadway in *Chicago* as Amos Hart ("Mr. Cellophane") at the Ambassador Theater. And others would follow.

As 1987 unfolded, Tim had much to celebrate, and everything began to jell at a prodigious pace. Plans were made for participation in Rochester's annual Lilac Festival in May, followed by a performance of *Peter and the Wolf* at the Jewish Community Center that featured the principal dancers, Kathy Ertsgaard and George Orosz, and of course, the staging of the company's second *Nutcracker*, considerably more elaborate and well developed than the performance of the previous year but not yet the complete production.

Word-of-mouth accolades were bringing more students into the studio. Despite the studio's warehouselike appearance, it was quite obvious that tutelage of the finest order was taking place within its walls. The Rochester community seemingly had missed having a ballet company-in-residence, and the media were beginning to respond enthusiastically to what was happening in the run-down building next door to Village Gate, particularly with the company's upcoming *Nutcracker* in full rehearsal mode. "You get a good feeling when you walk into Draper's Studio at 320A North Goodman Street," wrote Heidi Lux, a reporter for the *Brighton-Pittsford Post*. In two separate, extensive, back-to-back interviews with Lux and Sebby Wilson Jacobson, a reporter from the *Times-Union*, the excitement and pure delight that Tim was feeling about his new school and company were tangible. "One of the parents built these stairs," said Tim to Ms. Lux as he proudly bounded up the steps to the large pink studio. The reporter, noticing "a side room, surrounded by fabrics and racks of costumes [with] another volunteer worked at the sewing machine," was informed that "most everyone here can sew, so we can buy the fabric and not have to pay anything for the labor. And they can usually make a copy of something I like."[6]

Suggestions as to where Tim was headed were captured in the first few paragraphs of the Lux story, surely emblematic of what his new school and company had already managed to accomplish in short order—the completion of a three-year "plan of progress" in year one. "Draper wants to be more than just another ballet school," explained Ms. Lux.

> That is why he founded Timothy Draper Dance Theatre, a place where dancers from other schools can get a chance to do more performing. "When you go to a company like the Joffrey," explained Tim, "they are naturally going to ask you what performing experience you've had. Being in the *Nutcracker* is good, but they are going to want to know what else you have done. Right now we do two major performances a year, and we're trying to work up to more in the future."

Sebby Wilson Jacobson similarly caught the fervent sense of mission that was taking place within the studio when she visited it prior to the December 19–20, 1987, holiday program, which featured the Snow Scene and act 2 of *The Nutcracker* and *Watercolors*, an original piece that Tim had set to Handel. "Draper has not only trained these dancers six days a week for the past three months; he has choreographed their movements, designed their costumes, and inspired a crew of parents and grandparents to paint scenery, make posters, construct a rickshaw for the second act—anything they can do to make this *Nutcracker* as professional, as magical as possible."[7]

On full display during Jacobson's visit was Tim's use of sarcastic humor to get his teenage dancers to do what he wanted. The Flowers corps de ballet normally comprises the company's strongest female corps, due to the intensity of the six-minute Petipa choreography, which offers almost no respite for the dancers. Tim needled them with, "This has to be sharp, like ice. . . . You have to hold your arms up like there's some life in them. They look like wet laundry."

To his younger Angels, his counsel was provided in more dulcet tones, but the visual imagery would be every bit as useful to his Flowers in training. "Remember, you're supposed to be in the clouds—just skim the floor."

Jacobson's article, in particular, delved deeply into Tim's long-range goals for the nascent company. Because he was mindful of the magic he had experienced himself as a twelve-year-old performing in *The Nutcracker* on the stage of the Eastman Theatre as part of Olive McCue's Mercury Ballet Company, one heartfelt goal he had for his own company was to have them perform *The Nutcracker* where he once had—a wish that at the moment he ceded to the Hartford Ballet, complete with its "300 spectacular costumes" and a budget surely greater than the $4,000 with which Tim had to work. Hartford was then in its fifth year of collaboration with the Rochester Philharmonic Orchestra, and it would be twelve more years of other companies coming into town to perform in this vaunted venue before Tim would finally take his rightful place at the table. "It takes 10 years to make a company," was the observation of the New York City dance critic Doris Herring (who also served as the executive director of the National Association for Regional Ballet), when asked to comment on Tim's chances for success in bringing ballet back to Rochester. "When you're forming your own company, you need to train your own dancers," she noted. "It's not like a symphony orchestra that can import its players. Dancers need roots. . . . The chances of a ballet company succeeding in Rochester are excellent—if they don't push too fast. The first thing you need is an inspired director and then a community structure that will support it economically. But first comes quality." Tim assuredly took Doris Herring's sentiments to heart. Mindful of the keen sense of disappointment the legendary Miss Crofton must have felt after her stunning, ambitious undertaking in Buffalo, so enthusiastically mounted but too soon extinguished as a result of insufficient funding and community support (never mind the catastrophic fire at the end), he was willing to be as patient as he knew how while sensing that true professional quality could be achieved only within the context of an intensive six-days-a-week training program for his dancers. Tim's remaining goals for the company thus included the desire to make Timothy Draper Dance Theatre into a respectable regional company (among the 250 such companies that existed throughout the United States at the time) and perhaps even more importantly, to give his dancers the essential training they would need for professional careers of their own, in Rochester or elsewhere.

The year 1987 also saw the Draper Studio of Dance senior company grow, some ascending into the ranks through organic means, others coming in from the outside. In the latter category was a young dynamo of seventeen, trained by her dance-instructor mother. The teenager leaped onto the scene with a tall, stunning body; stage presence; and a keen sense of dramatic flair that made one take note. Jamey Throumoulos entered Tim's studio with Broadway dreams; within weeks, however, her passion tilted toward ballet. Without question, Tim was immediately taken with the long-limbed teenager who, according to one of the other dancers at the time, "danced in a jazzy way, but so pretty," and who brought a seeming fearlessness to whatever she was asked to do. Another of her fellow dancers, a beautiful performer in her own right, later recalled, "If Tim told Jamey to jump out the studio's second-story window onto the parking lot, she wouldn't question the request; rather, she would ask him in which position he would like her to land." She was also remembered as a "natural turner . . . a very technical dancer with great feet." Without true classical training, however, Tim knew that she would have to push herself extremely hard to take her dancing to the next level and that he would have to work closely with her to develop the classical technique that would allow her to dance such roles as the Sugarplum Fairy and Firebird. With enormous natural talent, boundless enthusiasm, and a strong work ethic, Jamey was more than ready to get to work.

Over the next couple of years, Tim was also pleased to welcome Tresa Randall into the fold and to watch his developing dancers breathe new artistry into both his senior and junior companies. These included Cindy Van Scoter, Jennifer Rosso, Michelle New, Claudia McLaughlin, Tina Brock, Cora Kannel, Rachanna Thomas, Stephanie Carpenter, Heather Matt, Jessica Wilinsky, Jessica Murray, and Aimee Litwiller. In addition, he was completely mesmerized by his twelve-year-old protégée Janelle Cornwell, who would be dancing the role of Clara in his upcoming *Nutcracker* and to whom he had been giving numerous private lessons over the past couple of years while his new studio was being renovated.

By the end of 1987, Tim was feeling very excited about the company's prospects. As Jamey described the company's progress many years later, "By the second year [the company] had polished the choreography, added dancers, built more vibrant costumes, added special effects, and most importantly, elevated the storyline so that it could launch a complete, mouth-watering holiday fare for the entire Rochester community to enjoy."[8]

George Orosz recalls that there were by this time approximately twenty to twenty-five students in the studio, ranging from "adults to teens to early teens to Janelle." George himself was dancing no fewer than twenty-seven hours a week (including two weekend days) while working his full-time job at Kodak. He was always grateful for the care, respect, and encouragement that Tim showed him. He attributes this to the fact that he was already an adult with a different type of relationship with his mentor than that experienced by the younger members of the company and the trainees. He was never really sure if Tim and he were the same age, but he suspected that they were. Not that there weren't the occasional "explosions" that would erupt when something didn't please the master. George remembers (chuckling now, with the considerable passage of time) how in that very first 1986 *Nutcracker*, he was doing a barrel turn during the solo section of the grand *pas de deux* when the music stopped—and so he stopped, too! Tim was not pleased. Of course, not only was this the first time in his entire life that George was performing in a ballet-company production, but he had also been thrust into one of the most vaunted roles in the repertoire— he was the Cavalier! A lesser man surely would have fled, but George was a most definite asset to the growing company and enjoyed critical acclaim over the next few years, both for his solo and partnering work.

Notwithstanding future "corrections" by the artistic director, George and Tim got on well, socializing frequently after class or rehearsals with Frank Galaska and Kathy Ertsgaard, the latter of whom George regarded as "delightful and a wonderfully cooperative partner." Conversation would invariably turn to who was starring in what in New York, which Balanchine was being done, which choreography he did or didn't like—that is, typical ballet "shop talk."

George recalls with a mock shudder how the younger female students in Tim's charge didn't receive quite the same treatment from Tim as he did, particularly the preteen and teenage girls who showed exceptional potential but who didn't always see eye to eye with the director when it came to the discipline required to turn them from competent dancers into artists. "I remember a lot of girls crying and going home crying—the adults and teenagers. Six days per week with one day off."

But there were also many fabulous times, particularly when Tim escorted several of them over a couple of summers to what was surely his favorite place on earth, New York. Due to his many connections, apartments were available, as well. Cindy Van Scoter recalls one summer in particular, where they broke up into two groups in which she, Jamey, and George stayed in one apartment, with Janelle and Jen Rosso staying with Tim in the other. Their routine would be to get bagels when they woke up and then dance all day at Broadway Dance Center and Steps and then be introduced to New York's cultural treasures. Tim loved to expose his troupe to the arts in all of their many forms. Although logistics prevented this in later years (unless the company was performing), these were very special opportunities for Tim's original company members. They would have been hard pressed to find a more erudite connoisseur of all things art than their own ballet teacher. Another summer they went back with the moms, and that was reportedly a lot of fun, as well.

For those who had joined Tim at the beginning, it was impossible not to notice the enormous transformation that had taken place in the short fifteen months of the school's and company's existence. By the end of 1987, the company had enjoyed successful performances at the City of Rochester's historic Lilac Festival, the Waterways Festival in Fairport, Dance Rochester's celebration of International Dance Week. The repertoire included *Peter and the Wolf*, and a wonderfully enhanced *Nutcracker*.

But Tim was always looking ahead. With his company showing promise, 1988 would be the year to honor the special woman who had given him his first taste of company performance experience, Miss Olive McCue. It had been nearly forty years since the Misses McCue and Biracree first restored ballet to Rochester by founding the Mercury Ballet Company. Now in her early eighties, Miss McCue was coming out of retirement to restage one of her works on her student's company. History would be honored, and Eastman's muses would once again smile on Rochester ballet.

Kathy Joslyn, age fifteen, practicing her penché in the Studio of Dance, 320-A North Goodman St. Courtesy of Kathy Joslyn.

KATHY JOSLYN

Tim Draper opened my eyes to the world of professional dance. From the first moment I saw him walk through the studio door as our guest teacher, I knew that there was something very special about him. It was clear that teaching ballet was his passion, his heart, his life. When he asked me to join him in his quest to start a ballet school and company in Rochester, I knew that my life would be changed forever. I completely cherish the years that I was a part of Draper Dance Theatre and have felt tremendously grateful for all the amazing roles I danced. When I left the company after graduating from high school to pursue other academic studies, Tim expressed not only his own tremendous feelings of loss, but also his fear for me that I might have regrets. Of course, with my eighteen-year-old-brain, I thought I knew everything and ignored his pleas. Although I pretended that I was not bothered by my decision and earned various degrees that led me into another profession, I always knew that dance would be back in my life somehow. When Tim offered me a teaching opportunity, I happily accepted because I knew it would be one way of reconnecting with my passion and to give something back. I wanted to do whatever I could to pass on all that I learned from Tim.

Now that I have been a teacher for almost twenty years, I realize quite profoundly that Tim possessed an incredible gift for inspiring excellence in his students and building on their strengths. He was able to see the potential of his students and capitalize on that while simultaneously pushing them to face their own weaknesses. Tim was absolutely a master teacher—that rare breed of teacher whose energy seems to have no limits, who has no tolerance for mediocrity, and who sees where his students can go before they do. Master teachers are not always easy. Tim maintained the absolute highest standards and expectations. He was never one to give false hope or empty praise. Although there were times when his demands seemed harsh, the most pronounced memories I have of Tim are those that involve his sense of humor. He had an incredibly quick wit and a use of imagery that always seemed to get his point across effortlessly in a meaningful and powerful way. I think his humor tempered his demands and added to his overall charm. This charm not only propelled his students to work hard, but also allowed them to trust him. I knew that Tim really believed in me. When he passed away, it was as if the one person in the world who really saw me as a dancer and loved my individual way of moving was gone.

Tim's death was the catalyst for my decision to pursue an MFA in dance, something I had wanted to do for a very long time but was unsure about. My grief over the loss of my mentor cleared the path for me to make some challenging choices in the pursuit of my true passion. Since that decision in 2007, my performance career has been reignited. I have become an accomplished choreographer and now teach dance at the college level. I know that Tim would be very proud of my choice to leave an unfulfilling profession and return to my calling. There are so many times that I wish I could talk to him, ask him about any number of things, but I trust he is with me in spirit. I write this letter in honor of him and his work, although words cannot adequately express how much of an impact he had my life. Thus, the reason I dance!

Kathy Joslyn will forever be remembered in Rochester City Ballet/Draper lore as not only one of Tim Draper's most beautiful dancers but as one whose artistry so matched her master's own that she has been one of a very small group of individuals to carry his legacy forward faithfully, much in the way that Balanchine's disciples have ensured that his star continues to burn brightly into perpetuity. Kathy's extraordinary teaching ability, combined with her ongoing performance and choreographic prowess, ensures that the next generation of dancers are imagining a most brilliant diamond as they gaze down at their hands in *combre* back.

9

WHAT THEY DID FOR LOVE

A lot happened between 1986 and 1988 . . . actually everything happened!" recalls George Orosz with a smile. He was serving the company admirably as a principal dancer, and his engineering and strategic-planning background worked well with Tim's desire to build a strong, multilayered, rich foundation that would enable his school and company to prosper.

The schedule for the 1987–88 season was an ambitious one. As a result, the two met frequently to discuss how to market the company properly and how they might even begin a dialogue with the Rochester Philharmonic Orchestra relative to future collaborations. As early as 1988, in fact, Tim sent a letter to the Rochester Philharmonic Orchestra's conductor, Mark Elder, after they met at a meeting for Arts for Greater Rochester, suggesting in some detail the benefits of collaboration.

Of primary concern, however, was the June 1988 production, which was to be a tribute to Tim's former teacher and the cofounder of the Mercury Ballet, Olive McCue. Miss McCue would not be attending merely as an invited guest, however; Tim had prevailed successfully on this still stylish early octogenarian to come out of a fifteen-year retirement to restage, on his own company, *Emperor's Waltz*, one of the classic works she had choreographed years earlier for an "Opera Under the Stars" performance of the Mercury Ballet with the Rochester Philharmonic Orchestra in Highland Park Bowl. McCue, once considered the "Queen of Rochester Ballet," or at least one of two members of balletic royalty during the 1950s (sharing the tiara with her esteemed colleague of many years, Thelma Biracree), was a "glamorous, dramatically dressed woman . . . whose graceful movements lit up the ballet world of Rochester—and left a lasting legacy."[1] The company was excited about the production, which was a mixed bill.

"She taught me how to perform from my heart. She let me know it was OK to let some of myself out," enthused Tim in a preperformance interview with the *Times-Union* reporter Sebby Wilson Jacobson. "It's my way of saying 'thank you.' I owe my career to her; she started me on my way." Tim studied with her for only two years, but "those two years were seminal . . . exposing me to the real world of ballet—discipline, partnering, rehearsals, working with an orchestra, performing in the Eastman Theatre. She made me love it so much. I wanted more and more."[2]

Rehearsals for this performance took place in the original, smaller downstairs studio because it would have been impossible for McCue to negotiate her way to the large pink studio upstairs. She walked with a cane but took on the project with gusto, considering the fact that in her own words "she was coming out of the woods again" after fifteen years. According to Sebby Wilson Jacobson, Russell L. "Peter" Clarke, Miss McCue's husband of forty-six years, was happy to chauffeur her back and forth to 320-A North Goodman Street, despite the fact that he was in ill health. "I am blessed with a husband who loves ballet," Miss McCue confided.

It was obviously a heady experience for the once larger-than-life teacher to collaborate with the then larger-than-life student cum artistic director, even though he would forever remain her pupil. "Watching Miss McCue working with [my] troupe has been enlightening. . . . She brings out so much detail. She'll say 'Listen,' and you start hearing notes in the music you didn't hear before."

Among those dancing in the revival were Kathy Ertsgaard and George Orosz. For Kathy, the tribute was also a reunion, because she had studied with Miss McCue as a child. Also joining the production were two former students of Miss McCue's, Basil Megna and Sonia Koch Wendt. Basil, who had partnered Jackie Fulreader Ostrum when both starred in the 1973 Mercury Ballet production of *The Nutcracker* as the Snow Queen and King, reprised the role in *Emperor's Waltz* that he had last danced in the 1970s. Sonia, who had performed with the Mercury Ballet for twenty years, would now be assisting her former mentor in recalling the steps and movement "through muscle memory and music memory." One of the most memorable moments of the collaboration took place, however, when Miss McCue furnished her own impromptu personal prescription for what it takes to be a dancer. When describing to Ms. Jacobson how her own background took her on the path to dance, she stated, "Once I was in it, I definitely knew this was for me. Dancers are strange people, believe me. They have to be 'fey' which according to Miss McCue's definition, was 'an Irish word, meaning part sprite.'"

In his very first review of the relatively new company—"Draper Dancers off on Right Foot with Premiere"—Robert V. Palmer, the dance critic for Rochester's *Democrat and Chronicle*, was mildly favorable. "The flicker of a glowing ember has appeared on what seemed a cold hearth of ballet in Rochester," Palmer begins. Notwithstanding the "wretched rented sound system and a tape that failed to function," the performance "hinted at bigger and better things to come." Although he expressed reservations over the choreography of *Sheeps Meadow* by the guest choreographer Christine DiMario, he very much liked the dancers, led by Kathy Joslyn, who "carried it off with a fair measure of panache." In addition, he paid tribute to the Draper-choreographed middle section, which consisted of *Patterns* and *Concerto*. He was also smitten with Draper Dance Theatre's principal dancer. "Dancer Jamey Throumoulos, whose facial expressions were as comfortably dramatic as her long-limbed extensions, drew the audience onto the stage throughout the concert." Concluding with a reminder that "creating a viable company is a long-haul operation," he ended on a positive note. "But a good start is a good start and that, Draper has made."[3]

More than anyone else, Tim himself knew that building a quality company was a process. Not only did he need to train his dancers to an exceptional standard but he also knew the importance of nurturing and cultivating relationships within the community. George Orosz clearly shared this view. They therefore took every opportunity to build audiences by performing wherever and whenever possible, developing a strong rapport with influential individuals and organizations throughout Monroe County and engaging the print and broadcast media with luscious visuals and access to the organization. Not that it was always easy. Prior to the 1988 *Nutcracker* production, for example, a very poised Jamey and George danced the entire Snow *pas de deux* in the News 10 WHEC studios as guests of the very welcoming and encouraging news anchor at the time, Maggie Brooks, just after the very serious-looking artistic director in uncharacteristic suit and tie tried hard to explain to Ms. Brooks what made his production special. Tim's normally unflappable and supremely capable board chair, Susanne Callan-Harris, meanwhile, presumably brought along to steady *his* nerves, began scowling and motioning frantically to the dancers just as they were about to begin their *pas de deux* by trying to get them to move into a more favorable viewing position—all of which, unfortunately, was caught live on camera. The dancers did quite save the moment, however, and undoubtedly spurred many viewers to purchase tickets to the production that took place shortly thereafter at Monroe Community College. Throughout his career, it is probably reasonable to suggest that Tim never did feel 100 percent comfortable with media interviews, but over time he did become more adroit at managing them. To his credit, he was always willing to do whatever was necessary to promote his company.

One aspect of the growing venture that was much more instinctive to him was the idea of building something from scratch. In his rare spare time, Tim was an avid gardener. He knew the importance of investing in the soil to produce beautiful blooms all season long. Always a big-picture thinker, he understood that the quality of the onstage product was paramount and that the dancers would need to be of the finest caliber if this undertaking were to succeed. At the same time, however, he would need to mount simultaneous efforts to ensure that such crucial behind-the-scenes deliverables as staffing, business development, finance, operations, marketing and advertising, public relations, and community outreach would meaningfully support all that was happening onstage.

In the previous two years, Tim had already proven that he could train his dancers to a professional level, that he could stir volunteers into working around the clock on his behalf, that he could engage the media to promote his various endeavors, and that he could tap into the community's substantial roster of events to showcase his budding troupe. Now it was time for him to engage the services of other high quality teachers and to establish a local board of directors that would both design and implement a strategic plan for moving forward. He needed to procure the kind of serious funding that would enable him to produce the quality of product he envisioned so as to bring his company to the next level. His advisory committee had served him admirably, primarily by impressing upon him the importance of installing a local board of directors that would enable him to accomplish all that he needed to do. As evidenced by the financial statement of January 8, 1988, we can see that at this point the company was not only operating as a labor of love but was doing so in grand fashion.

That Tim was actually succeeding at developing a high-caliber ballet company (and an unpaid one at that) speaks volumes about what he was contributing as a teacher and artistic director. The company dancers did not consider themselves to be students when they were performing; they were rather principals, soloists, and members of the corps de ballet of a company that rehearsed no less (and assuredly much more) than organizations twice its size. As the consummate artist, Tim knew that the proverbial devil was in the details and that the discipline and etiquette he was instilling, along with heavy doses of technique and élan, were qualities not lost on the company's growing audience.

Supporting the artistic side of the enterprise was a mostly volunteer staff. By this time, the culture of operating on a shoestring was fully embraced. Costumes were for the most part constructed by mothers of the dancers and other supporters; set construction fell to the fathers, male performers, and family; and fund-raising (at least in the beginning) came from advertisements in the program and some small grants, including one that had provided for Olive McCue's restaging of *Emperor's Waltz.*

With the 1988 *Nutcracker*, however, Tim wanted to pull out all the stops. This one was going to be a historic move forward for Draper Dance Theatre, because it would be their very first offering of a full-length version. In fact, Rochester was getting ready to usher in the 1988 holiday season with three such offerings. "Three Nutcrackers in Town?!" was the headline that greeted *Times-Union* readers on the afternoon of December 1, 1988. "Here in Rochester," wrote Sebby Wilson Jacobson, "three cultural institutions—the RPO, Draper Dance Theatre, and the Orcutt-Botsford School of Dance—have hitched their wagons to the *Nutcracker's* irresistible star." The *Times-Union* even supplied a consumer guide that spelled out all the various features and benefits from size of cast to cost to the kinds of special effects. It was clear that Rochesterians could have their *Nutcracker* treat one way or another. As RPO's president and CEO, Dean Corey, so astutely noted when discussing the production's mass appeal, "People will go to see *Nutcracker* who don't even like ballet." Tim's enthusiasm for this production was in full overflow mode as he treated a *City Newspaper* reporter, Isobel Neuberger, to the controlled mayhem taking place in his studio workshop. Praising his newly formed Ballet Guild for their assistance in supporting this production, whose costs fell somewhere within the $25,000 range, he was clearly excited to be staging his first full *Nutcracker*, which would include an ever-improved troupe of his own dancers to perform most soloist and principal roles. In addition, he was bringing in Katrina Killian and Michael Byars from New York City Ballet to dance the roles of the Sugar Plum Fairy and the Cavalier.

Tim's 1988 pre-*Nutcracker* interview with the *Times-Union* went
very well, particularly when he referred to the nuances of his own
choreography after Petipa and the long-range investment he was
making, not just in this production but in his troupe's future as a
professional company.

> At this point, says Draper of the Draper Dance Theatre, we proba-
> bly don't make money on *Nutcracker* because we put any money we
> make into more costumes and scenery. . . . This isn't just about *Nut-
> cracker*. This is about us as a company being able to survive and grow
> and eventually foster other things for the community besides *Nut-
> cracker*. . . . But if you're going to get people to see you, they're more
> likely to go if your performance is *Nutcracker*.[4]

The performance itself was widely praised. "Draper Delights," by
Karen Flynn, a freelance reporter, led off a review that boded well for
the company.

> Saturday evening, December 10, was the Draper Dance Theatre's pre-
> miere performance of the full-length version of the *Nutcracker* Bal-
> let at Monroe Community College. It looked to be a sell-out show,
> despite two additional performances scheduled for the following two
> Sundays—an accurate barometer of a growing interest in local dance,
> one hopes. All around professionalism and polish was apparent
> throughout the entire production, but a few performances deserve
> special mention. Kathy Joslyn danced the roles of the Dew Drop Fairy
> and Spanish Chocolate with an impressive technical strength and
> spirit matched only by two professional guest artists from the New
> York City Ballet; they were Katrina Killian and Michael Byars, danc-
> ing the Sugar Plum Fairy and Cavalier roles. Jamey Throumoulos and
> George Orosz gave impressive performances as the Snow Queen and
> King, and Janelle Cornwell danced the role of young Clara enchant-
> ingly. The Draper Dance Theatre is a company to keep a watch on.

And they did watch. Most significant was the fact that the young
dancers (the future of any company) were being trained to the same
high standard from the ground floor. Among the Party Children listed
in the program's first act, for example, was Aesha Ash, whom Julianne
O'Donnell brought to the studio when she was five and who, along
with Tim, trained her and helped develop her into a world-class ballerina. Aesha would one day be selected to join the prestigious School
of American Ballet and later, the New York City Ballet. Another young
dancer of note was Rebekah von Rathonyi, already another of Tim's

precocious stars who would garner much acclaim throughout her impressive career.

The school and company continued to grow both in number and in stature, and by 1989, Tim needed an expanded faculty. He was also becoming more adept at forging connections wherever he went. One critical priority for him, in addition to taking his dancers to the highest artistic level, was providing them with new performance opportunities and exposure to other faculty members who would broaden their perspectives and their knowledge of other styles. He knew that the professional dance world wanted dancers with a diverse skill set, and so he set about to make this happen. As Heidi Lux confirmed, "Since its opening, the Studio has grown at such a rate that it has become necessary for Draper to find qualified teachers to take over the classes. Reliable people like Sally Atkins Stepnes of Pittsford, who teaches his advanced class, allow him the luxury of worrying about administration and choreography. Jo Helfer [formerly of the Orcutt-Botsford School of Dance] now handles the business of public relations."[5] Tim had already procured the services of teachers for the young children in tap, jazz, and modern. With Sally now in place to train the advanced students, he would be able to continue to focus on the big picture.

Sally was a crucial hire who brought far more than reliability, however. Simply put, Sally Atkins Stepnes was a treasure for the emerging studio and company. She had performed as a principal dancer and a soloist with numerous professional ballet companies, including Alicia Alonso's legendary Ballet Nacional de Cuba (from the ages of sixteen to eighteen), Ballets de San Juan, the Brooklyn Civic Ballet, Ballet 70, Ballet Teatnal, and Teatro de Danza Jose Paus. A highly experienced teacher at all levels of ballet in Puerto Rico, New York, and Indiana, she had more recently codirected her own ballet school in Rochester, Ballet Arts Center, and had been at the Orcutt-Botsford School of Dance. She brought to the studio the full measure of the classical ballet tradition. Hearing that she was in town and aware of her pedigree, Tim was thrilled to have her join him. By 1989 he gave her the title of assistant to the director and later assistant director. She brought something else to the Studio of Dance—true empathy for children. "Tim and I complemented each other," she recalled. "He was very stern about everything—so mine would be the shoulder they would cry on. It was really a love-hate relationship with his students because he demanded perfection and because he had no children of his own, he didn't have the compassion to know when the kids needed a break. I was often the one who stepped in and smoothed things over."[6] She worked for Tim through 1997, leaving to move to England for a year and then periodically teaching at Indiana University and Butler University.

"I was there to fix everyone's arms and posture," she recalled, noting that "Tim could do male arms but not female arms." After developing Jamey's talent in this area, she then turned to the younger students. Her talents most certainly contributed to the rich artistry of Sari Ostrum, Kristi Boone, Sarah Lane, Rebekah von Rathonyi, Meredith Seeley, and many others whom she "fixed" during this period. As a coach, she was similarly superb. Rebekah von Rathonyi recalls that Sally was invaluable to her as she prepared later on for her role as the Sugar Plum. Even after Sally moved to Florida, Rebekah trained with her in preparation for the International Ballet Competition Luxembourg, to which Sally accompanied her. Fiona Fairrie soon furthered this tradition within the studio, most notably as one of the inspiring summer teachers and coaches when she began teaching there in the late 1990s.

On May 6, 1989, Tim unveiled his latest work to be added to his growing repertoire with the premiere of Stravinksy's *Firebird*, earning significant kudos from Herbert M. Simpson of the *Democrat and Chronicle*.[7] Simpson, a critic's critic who performed double duty as the Upstate New York correspondent for *Dance Magazine*, had high praise for the company in his May 8, 1989, review. Most gratifying for Tim was the fact that Simpson clearly appreciated the strides the company had made in such a short period of time, referring to this concert as a "significant event in Rochester's dance history." He also was pleased that Simpson appreciated his choreographic break with tradition in the finale, in which Tim brought back the title character in an exhilarating, stunning blaze of rapid-fire *châiné* turns that perfectly matched Stravinsky's dramatic final chords, rather than continuing the wedding processional, as is usually done. An interesting note concerns how the principal dancer, Jamey Throumoulos, performed the role of the Firebird with a bad injury to her foot throughout the performance, to the extent that another piece on the program had to be pulled so as not to completely derail its centerpiece. Although the exact nature of the injury was not discussed in the review, years later Jamey's own students would hear about Jamey's bloody foot being tended to in the wings between onstage appearances, an event that would become as much a part of company lore as the bloody sock of the Boston Red Sox pitcher Curt Schilling, when he took his team to victory in the 2004 World Series. Mindful of that first fateful *Firebird* performance, students of the stoic star years later would do their utmost to "manage" their injuries with a stiff upper lip, whenever possible.

Heidi Lux of *Wolfe Magazine* had similar high praise for the premiere performance, calling it "nothing less than a fairy tale come true. . . . It was hard to remember that Jamey Throumoulos was not a mythical creature. She flitted across the stage with the grace of a fragile bird."

In a review for the *Times-Union*, Karen Flynn remarked on the extraordinary potential to be found in the "young and raw" company, being brought out by a master teacher capable of creating artists. "*Firebird* was a showcase for the company's rising stars. Janelle Cornwell is one. Somewhat anonymous under her black hooded 'creature' costume, the young ballerina breathed much of the fire into *Firebird*. A member of Draper's Junior Company, Cornwell has been with Draper the longest of all his students. As testimony to the quality of Draper's training, she also splendidly danced the role of Clara in the company's *Nutcracker* Ballet this past December."[8]

Besides presenting other special performances throughout the year, including *Peter and the Wolf*, the company finished out 1988 with *The Nutcracker*. "Draper Dance Theatre took another big step forward toward becoming Rochester's long-awaited regional ballet company with the opening of *The Nutcracker* last night. Timothy M. Draper's full-length version belies its modest means, looking sure-footed and downright lavish," declared Herb Simpson. Not only did he give high marks to the Draper troupe but he also took the opportunity to make comparisons with organizations of lesser stature. "There's a disreputable, long-established, well-financed Buffalo ballet company that tours a *Nutcracker* hereabouts. It's a mark of how fast the Draper company is progressing that theirs is already superior in every way."

The troupe's dedication to Tim had a great deal to do with it. As *Wolfe Magazine*'s Heidi Lux reported earlier, "a bit of normal teenage grumbling would be understandable, even justified [with respect to the amount of rehearsal time required]. But that isn't what you hear when this group gets together. Sitting on an old sofa, surrounded by dance bags and coats and *pointe* shoes, conversation revolves around the price of a bus ticket to New York City, who ate the most nutritious dinner, and stretching each other's insteps before class. The Cosby Show is a great favorite among the advanced class because it falls on Thursday nights, their only free evening." This doesn't mean, however, that there was never any squawking about the schoolwork that was due ("And how is

The Draper Studio of Dance at 320-A North Goodman, or better known to many dancers as "the home away from home." Photography by Rebekah von Rathonyi.

that supposed to happen?") or "Wouldn't it be nice to be able to really sleep in on a Saturday or a Sunday?" But in the end, these adolescents were hugely talented and had to feel more than a little pride in what they were accomplishing. For all of the superficial complaints, they adored the man who was committed to turning them into artists. When all was said and done, they knew that they were a part of something important and would not trade that for all (or at least most) of the more conventional activities their nondancing friends were able to do.

"Tim was a phenomenal teacher and everything I learned in dance, I learned from him," said Cindy Van Scoter, who came to the Studio of Dance when she was thirteen years old. She had met him while a student at the Michelle Buschner School of Dance and he was teaching the class the Chinese divertissement from *The Nutcracker* as their recital piece. She thought this was pretty amusing for a "jazz and tap studio." When Tim told the class that they had to wear black leotards and pink tights, they all went crazy. But she followed him a year later to his new studio and never looked back. "He taught me how to wear technique shoes and how to tie my shoes and how to cut the top of the satin off so you weren't slipping all over the place. "I really latched onto dance and I took it to the next level—to the tenth power as a bunhead," she recalled. "I was very technical and when I went on pointe—that was the absolute end—I could enjoy it so much more." Heidi Lux's December 1989 article quoted Tim as saying, "Cindy Van Scoter, particularly, has just blossomed this year. You can teach someone to portray certain emotions, but the more they experience life the more they can express in dance. Life, love, heartache—everything just comes together when they know what they are doing." Cindy, like Jamey Throumoulos, Kathy Joslyn, and Janelle Cornwell, became another one of the company stars, dancing the premier roles of Dew Drop and Snow Queen in *The Nutcracker*, and having many featured roles in Tim's other choreographed works. Cindy would go on to dance with BalletMet Columbus after winning the highly coveted Arts Alive! Scholarship, created to commemorate the work of Raymond R. Delaney. Delaney was the superintendent of schools in the Rush-Henrietta School District from 1971 to 1990; many remember him as a great champion of the arts across New York State.

It is easy to appreciate the tremendous underlying affection that four of Tim's advanced teenage students felt for him during those early years. An amusingly scripted "Day in the Life" sendup gives the best possible sense of what class and rehearsal time were like at that time. Prepared, executed, and presented to Tim by his four stars, Jamey, Cindy, Jennifer Rosso, and Michelle New, it reveals how they felt they could take some "playful liberties" with their young master during the time when the school and company were small and growing.

When the jokes subsided, Tim was a true father figure to all of his special dancers. He was strict or hard on them to help them become all that they were capable of becoming. "There was lots of drama, lots of tempers, lots of egos, lots of feelings, lots of emotion, and that is what came out in the dance," recalled Cindy Van Scoter.

For all of the corrections, remonstrations, and flares of temper that would sometimes show themselves in pursuit of the ultimate goal, however, Tim was absolutely in a class by himself when it came to teaching, motivating, and mentoring his students. For those who went on to have a professional career, it was invaluable preparation. Even with the tears and disappointments, his was the approval they most sought. He encouraged them to reach for the stars and motivate them in a way that no one else ever had. And so they kept coming back. To this day, a decade after his death, several can barely think about him (much less speak) without choking up.

The question has been raised over time, from a pedagogical perspective, as to whether or not dancers can reach the very highest levels of classical dance without the accompanying histrionics. In a University of Michigan study published in the fall of 2002 edition of the *American Educational Research Journal*, a contributor related just how important the tantrums and the melodramas might have been, at least as part of a cultural normative expectation for the time. He tells the story of how one of his English students, who was training for a professional career in ballet, came into class one night very dejected because her ballet teacher did not yell at her the night before:

> She came into the period where she was my aide . . . and she seemed very down. And I said to her, "Well, what's the matter." And she said, "Well, last night at ballet,"—this girl was really quite a fine dancer—in fact, is a professional dancer in New York right now—"well last night at ballet, the teacher didn't yell at me." And I said, "well, wouldn't that be more an occasion to rejoice rather than to be sad?" And she said, "well no, not really, because he only yells at the dancers he thinks really have talent and that could get better. The kids that he knows, you know, they're just there, he doesn't yell at them, he doesn't give them a hard time, 'cause he knows they're sort of doing their best and sort of passes it off, and he usually yells at me, and he didn't last night, and I'm worried." And I said, "well, maybe he will yell at you tonight." So the next day she came back and was her usual effervescent self. And in fact, he had yelled at her, and everything was okay again. And she went on to do a lot of solo dancing and chorus line dancing and major Broadway productions and continues as a professional dancer.[9]

Rebekah von Rathonyi, or "Becky" as she was known to most everyone throughout the Draper community, became another one of Tim's stars from the moment she hugged her first Nutcracker onstage in the Party Scene. Like Kathy Joslyn, she remembered Tim's exceptional ability and intuition to build on an individual dancer's strength.

The dancers also knew that Tim would go to any length to ingrain a particular concept or movement into a developing dancer. Unlike the heads of most recreational dance studios, who devote a significant portion of each year to perfecting routines for recital and competition performances, Tim was more concerned about developing his students' technique, performance quality, breadth of styles, and appreciation for their art form. Regarding the last, he assuredly would have shared the sentiments of the Ballets Russes de Monte Carlo dancer, teacher, and ballet master Howard Sayette. In a July 2003 interview five months after Tim passed away, Sayette stated, "It's a shame that a lot of the young dancers of today are so driven by technique that they have little curiosity about the past and the important figures from the history of ballet. Some of them have barely heard of Margot Fonteyn."[10] It was not unusual for Tim to walk into class, turn on the haunting first strains of the oboe from Tchaikovsky's famous Swan's Theme, stop the music, and then put each of his students to the test. "What ballet is this from?" he would ask, challenging each dancer around the room to come up with the correct answer. The one who could come up with *Swan Lake* was rewarded richly with maybe only the smallest hint of a smile and a comment such as, "Well, at least someone in here knows a little something about the classics" before Tim turned back to his cassette player. This, however, was currency of inestimable value.

Nineteen eighty-nine had been another banner year for the company. As the decade was coming to a close with the company's artistic infrastructure now essentially in place, it was time for the company to prove to the community that it was truly worthy of its full support. Just as the Mercury Ballet's concert programs featured page after page of benefactors from Rochester's most prominent families, so too did Draper Dance Theatre require a concerted effort to obtain the resources that would enable it to thrive, tour, and grow into the best-in-class operation it was showing every sign of becoming. Those who had been involved from the beginning—a mere three years earlier—could look with enormous pride on what they had accomplished. From the start, Tim had insisted that his become a company of more far-reaching repertoire than the annual *Nutcracker*, and his choices had been bold ones. He also recognized that within one of his stars, the principal dancer Jamey Throumoulos, there burned something more than an indefatigable work ethic that allowed her continually to perfect her technique and roles, as impressive as that was. She was also becoming passionate about creating her own works, and he did not hold her back. Years later, she would recall how Tim fully supported her desire to choreograph for the company. She explained how she then went about the process of setting a work on the company that would make him proud. When all was done and she showed it to him, he told her that although what she had done was very nice, it wasn't unique. He thus challenged her to go back and do something that would be singularly hers. From that point on, neither of them looked back. Jamey became indispensable to Tim in everything that was choreographed. According to several of their students in later years, Tim was a great choreographer—but Jamey was an even better one.

Aesha Ash and Rebekah von Rathonyi as Tree Presents in *The Nutcracker*. Courtesy of Rebekah von Rathonyi.

Cindy Van Scoter as Rochester City Ballet's first flying Christmas Spirit in *The Nutcracker*, 1993. Courtesy of Cindy Van Scoter Chamot.

CINDY VAN SCOTER

I met Tim Draper around the age of thirteen at Michelle Buschner School of dance. What I didn't know then is that he would change my life by introducing me to the world of ballet. I will never forget when Tim told us that we had to wear pink tights & solid colored leotards. I wondered what would make me stand out? I realized that the bland uniform was a blank canvas for us to paint with our movement.

When I met Tim, I was a mess. I couldn't point my feet, stretch my legs and was certainly not on pointe. Tim would say, "Dear, point your feet" and I would cry because it would hurt so much. There were a lot of tears and complaining, but I could not get enough of dance.

Tim opened the school at 320-A North Goodman Street, which became my home away from home. I felt like I lived there. The weather did not matter, if it were rain, shine, snow storm or blizzard, you'd better be dead if you missed a class. One summer night we had a sleepover at the studio. We had a blast—with all the movies and popcorn we could eat. I slept, ate, and breathed ballet. The other students became my family. The rigorous hours in the studio, avoiding the poles in the middle of the floor, climbing the ladder to the main studio, and using the window sills as ballet barres were some of the best times of my life.

We all worked so hard, and yes, sometimes Tim said it was not enough, but I do remember more of the good than the bad. I recall a particular performance when I sprayed my hands with hairspray holding glitter in my fists and when I flew across the stage as Christmas Spirit I sprinkled the glitter like star dust in the air. When I got off stage all I could think of was that Tim was going to kill me because my idea was not rehearsed. When he came onto the stage he looked at me with one eye brow up and one eye brow down and said, "What a great idea—you should do that again in the next performance."

I grew up at that ballet school, leaving to dance with BalletMet, returning and leaving again to dance with the Buffalo Ballet. The last time I returned, I stayed, planning the next stage of my life. I was introduced to a whole new world when I discovered dance, and loved every crazy minute of it!

After an illustrious career with Draper Dance Theatre in which she performed many principal roles, Cindy danced for John McFall of BalletMet Columbus, performing in *Cinderella*, *The Nutcracker*, and *Coppélia*. After dancing for the Buffalo Ballet and returning to guest for Tim, she later taught ballet to deaf and hearing students at National Technical Institute for the Deaf for Michael Thomas, who had danced with San Francisco Ballet. On receiving permission from Tim to stage on RCB and NTID her very favorite of his ballets, *Devenir*, Cindy hired Kathy Joslyn and Sarah Lane for the principal roles, the latter performing in her very first *pas de deux*. Following Michael Thomas's passing, Cindy worked with Thomas Warfield, serving as dance captain for National Technical Institute for the Deaf's memorable production of *West Side Story*. The last time she saw Tim was when she returned in February of 2002 to the place where she had grown up, the old studio at 320-A North Goodman, to introduce him to her baby, Parker. Tim could not have been happier.

MOMENTUM

With singularity of purpose and attack, Tim Draper entered the new decade of the 1990s with unabated fervor, proud of the transformation that was taking place within the Studio of Dance and Draper Dance Theatre but wanting more—much more. Juggling a complicated schedule that included developing the next generation of artists, managing the company and a feeder school that was now training hundreds of students, teaching dance at SUNY College at Brockport, forming important collaborations within the arts community, building the company's repertoire, locking down venues for performances, managing media and donor relationships, ensuring the taste level of the company in its every nuance from costume fabric to the choice of gels used in the lighting to keeping up with his personal relationships, it was a daunting task. Much of the day-to-day details of the operation fell to his trusted friend, Kathy Ertsgaard, a self-described perfectionist who eventually maintained two full-time jobs, serving as both the managing director of Rochester City Ballet and assistant curatorial registrar at the Memorial Art Gallery. She would leave one job at five o'clock and then travel the (fortunately) short distance to the second, arriving for the night shift, as it were. Additional staff handled front-office operations—tuition and attendance records, a growing database of supporters, and related administrative matters. Although 12- to 14-hour days often were the norm for the principals involved, Michelle Buschner knew that Tim would do whatever it took to give Rochester back its ballet. "He had a dream and nothing was going to stop him," she explained many years later. Somehow within this frenetic life, Tim still managed to carve out time for family, especially at Christmastime. To this day, his beloved sisters, Donna and Jaye, still remember how he ran around and played with the young ones in the group. "He would lie down on the floor playing Mousetrap with them. One day he was at [his niece] Melanie's house making Christmas cookies with the kids. In the middle of frosting them, he jumped up on the countertop, making believe that he was afraid of a nonexistent mouse. The young nieces and nephews ate it up. They all did. Home was where he could 'just be Timmy.'"

But once the holidays were over, it would be back to work. Indicative of the pace that Tim was establishing at this time, Friday, January 12, 1990, saw the troupe head out early in the morning to Smith Opera House in Geneva, New York to perform Prokofiev's *Peter and the Wolf* for a few thousand children at 10:00 a.m. At 8:00 p.m. that evening, they performed an evening of ballet for the general public.[1] The latter was a mixed bill of *Consultation*, "a new ballet based on Puccini arias and choreographed by Draper"; *Bailey's Espanole*, and the Snow Scene and "Waltz of the Flowers" from the company's *Nutcracker* production. The guest artist Ron Stewart of Montreal's Ballet Classique also appeared with the company. Cindy Van Scoter, not yet eighteen, had emerged as one of the leading stars of the company. An elegant technician, she enjoyed local media coverage for the multiple roles she performed that day. Overall, the engagement was significant for several reasons. First, it revealed the growing esteem in which the troupe was held. Smith Opera House had received funding from the New York State Council on the Arts as part of its Arts-in-Education series, "Schooltime Performances." Geneva had chosen "Rochester's only ballet company" to bring an outstanding cultural experience to the community. This was very meaningful for Tim, who always loved to have his company perform for children. In addition, the January date, according to Tim, was "particularly significant since almost fifty years ago to the day, January 13, 1940, Ballet Theater of New York City offered the first American performance of the beloved *Peter and the Wolf*." In fact, this production would long be a staple in the Draper Dance Theatre/Rochester City Ballet repertoire, regaling thousands and thousands of children over the years with a well-loved, well-paced 45-minute production. To this day, it is considered by many educators and parents to be the very best way to introduce music to young children.

The company then set its sights on readying its summer performance, a mixed bill, reprising the critically acclaimed *Firebird*, with Jamey Throumoulos again in the title role; a new ballet entitled *Classical Whimsy*, choreographed by Sally Stepnes to music by Vivaldi; *Hungarische Tänze*, choreographed by the late Patricia Olaide; and an important new work, born of a collaboration between a young emerging choreographer, Leslie Tillotson, whom Tim had met at SUNY Brockport, and the composer Andrew Waggoner. Tillotson, who had received her master's degree in dance from Brockport and who had won the National Dance Association's Outstanding Graduate Student Award, wanted to choreograph a piece for Tim's company, having long admired it. Waggoner was an assistant professor of composition, theory, and music history at Syracuse University. After earning degrees at the Eastman School of Music and Cornell University, he had collaborated with her frequently. Tim was thrilled with the prospect. "It will be great for the dancers to work with a new choreographer, new music, and live musicians. The ballet is abstract and is about limitations and discoveries. There's a lot of tension in the music, and in the dance a soft flow that contrasts with angular movements." Featured in the program, in addition to Jamey and the guest artist Ron Stewart, were Jennifer Rosso, Tina Brock, Claudia McLaughlin, Cindy Van Scoter, Michelle New, Stephanie Carpenter, Janelle Cornwell, Heather Matt, Claudia McLaughlin, Jessica Wolinsky, Aimee Litwiller, and Jessica Murray.

The season ended with what was now becoming a highly acclaimed production of *Nutcracker*, headlined by Jamey Throumoulos and Miguel Campafuera as the Sugar Plum Fairy and the Cavalier, Cindy Van Scoter and Miguel Campafuera as the Snow Queen and Snow King, Rebekah von Rathonyi and Aesha Ash alternating as the Claras, Rachanna Thomas and Nicole Axelrod alternating as the Fritzes, Victor Trevino appearing courtesy of Les Ballets Trockadero de Monte Carlo as the Nutcracker Prince, "Nina Enimenimynimovi," and English/Toffee and Tina Brock as the Dew Drop Fairy and Harlequin. The names of three little girls jump off the pages of the 1990 program for their precocious charm and the loveliness with which they would grace Draper stages in later years to come—Sari Ostrum and Natalia Malley-Masten, both of whom were Party Children; and Annaliese Pipech, a Page. Again reflecting Tim's commitment to the community, the first show was a benefit performance to support Community Health Network, Inc.

The 1990s came to be a period of significant growth for the company, with the artistic side of the enterprise still light-years ahead of the business side. However, in fairness to those working tirelessly to raise money—which always at the end of the fiscal year seemed to be a few zeros short—the Upstate New York region was in the throes of the infamous 1990–91 recession, slow in being named but one of the most debilitating in modern times. Unlike previous recessions, however, this one didn't seem to want to quit, being attributed to the "public's gloomy outlook." If this wasn't the ideal time to be asking for funding for dance, neither was it the worst, recalling Thelma Biracree. Biracree had achieved some of her very best work in the 1930s, right in the throes of the Great Depression. Tim refused to let anything slow him down, recession or no recession. In the program notes for the 1991 *Classical Whimsy*, in fact, the company projects a fairly robust outlook relative to its financials. "Support from the State of New York via the New York State Council on the Arts, corporations and businesses, as well as individual contributors has enabled the Company to sustain a measured growth as well as foster the growth of individual dancers." In addition, "The Company provides a vehicle for bringing talented artists to Rochester. This talent includes teachers, choreographers, and dancers with diverse backgrounds and expertise who enrich the dance experience for both the Company and the community."

The exciting mixed bill, the 1991 Spring Performance, was captured mostly favorably by the *Democrat and Chronicle*'s dance critic, Robert V. Palmer. "Grieg, Vivaldi Meet Pink Floyd: Introductions by Draper Dance" particularly paid homage to the work of the dancers. "For starters, Draper's troupe is ever more disciplined. . . . Almost without exception, individual dancers shone in Draper's neoclassic choreography. Heads were held steadfastly erect, facial expressions attended to, arm gestures detailed to the last finger joint."[2]

The 1991 class schedule told the story, in which there were no fewer than thirty-five classes per week, from creative movement though level 6, the professional division. Noted next to the professional division entry was "Minimum of six years of ballet required. Students aspiring to a professional career must take all classes offered." It would interest dancers of later years to learn that tap had once been offered at the studio and that the adult dancer had many options available in which to pursue their passion, including "Adult Beginning Ballet," "Adult Int./Adv. Ballet," "Adult Pointe," "Adult Intermediate Jazz," and "Adult Intermediate Tap."[3]

Over the next few years, ambitious programming continued at a fast clip, with a new level of technical sophistication imbuing each production. The 1991–92 season included participation in the annual Lilac Festival, *Peter and the Wolf, Carnival of the Animals, Paquita, The*

Nutcracker, and *Swan Lake,* act 2. As Palmer noted in his "Grieg" review, "Production qualities were professional. . . . House lights should have come up during pauses. But stage lighting was effective; costumes pleased without distracting."

Advance press for the 1991 *Nutcracker,* this time being staged at the National Technical Institute for the Deaf's Robert F. Panara Theatre on the Rochester Institute of Technology campus, could not have been more favorable.

> Tim Draper has filled a couple of voids in the local dance scene over the past five years. His company, founded in 1986 at 320A N. Goodman St., is the only professional ballet company in Rochester. And the school that houses it has a professional program for those wishing to pursue a career in dance. "It's our professional programs, which have the dancers in the studio 20 to 30 hours a week, that really set us apart from everyone else (in town)," he says. . . . "We don't push the (professional) program. We let the students decide if they can do it. We try to be honest."[4]

Behind the scenes, work continued unabated, with scores of talented and dedicated volunteers putting in untold hours of work both in-studio, backstage, and at home to give Tim what he wanted. When the stress of his inner world did not completely overwhelm him, his enormous talent, brains, charm, and a hundred other positive attributes inspired legions of volunteers to support him in all that he was trying to accomplish. One extraordinary volunteer, Jackie Ostrum, captured this very well. "He was a professional at collecting powerful people, people with influence and money, and was able to put them all to work for his cause. He was actually able to get anyone to work in his behalf. He could be very charming and magnetic and his words flowed effortlessly with elegance. He was so well spoken that he could be a bit intimidating but always embracing with his impressiveness. This was the Tim everyone fell in love with and the Tim everyone hoped to please. However, his moods were volatile, and his behavior was not consistent. Many times this led to ill feelings and a permanent parting of the ways. Randy Stringer, Tim's partner, explained it this way. "Tim truly had the artist's temperament. A mixture of genius, brilliance, and constant self-doubt pushed him to be an exceptional teacher/artistic director. But the temperament was rough on those who knew (and loved) him. We can all remember how acidic his tongue could be if he got angry or upset, which was often at times."

When the demons showed themselves, some volunteers would bite their tongues, take his displeasure in stride and try harder to please him the next time around. Others would walk out of the studio, never to be heard from again. Still others would make mental notes about the cost of furthering such a noble cause and become more selective about when and where to help. It was particularly hard on the mothers and fathers, who always wanted to be as supportive as possible for their children. The mood at the studio, with so much hanging in the balance—being on the cusp of greatness while not yet enjoying recognition as a major Rochester cultural institution—could at times feel downright unpleasant for the volunteers, who often set aside a significant number of hours of their own valuable time to be of help. Particularly peculiar to the surroundings at the time was how some "senior volunteers" (usually mothers who had been around for quite some time and knew the drill) took it on themselves to berate junior members, who would be absolutely bewildered to find themselves being castigated when all they were trying to do was give of their valuable time. In hindsight, it was the clash of Tim's drive for excellence in a race against the clock with a temper flowing downstream that caused the problems and thwarted, or at least slowed down, the very thing Tim most coveted—the company's move toward greatness.

"I can't really remember how it began," recalls Jackie.

> But somehow he initiated that I start sewing and designing costumes. I consider myself a hard worker and I can say without reservation that I have never worked harder for anyone in my life! And I'm not alone! I told him that before his passing. Unfortunately, Tim had a way of making me and everyone else feel we never did enough for him, which in turn kept us all going at an extremely difficult and unrealistic pace trying to please. He would forget or possibly not care that most everyone carrying heavy workloads were volunteers! It took me a year, and a half a dozen trips to the garment district in New York City, to design and have costumes made for his first full-length ballet of *Cinderella* in 2000. I think that was one of my biggest accomplishments in life. Like everything artistic, you can't go home at night and forget about it until the following day. It's an all-consuming job where you find yourself working and creating even in your dreams. On occasion, he was complimentary. It didn't matter if you were a dancer or working for him in some capacity, you lived for those few moments of praise. However, if he didn't like something, he was unforgiving and bitter even if you had the best of intentions. . . . There were a number of triggers that would set off this anger in Tim which when surfaced, resembled a bomb! The most obvious was criticism. If Tim

ever caught you verbalizing a critical word or heard about something you had said concerning him in a disapproving manner, you could consider your relationship with him severed—permanently! I think everyone that spent time at the studio witnessed that behavior. . . . It was hard for him to let go, to forgive and forget.

When the criticism was delivered in a playful fashion, however, it would mostly motivate the volunteer to attempt to do better the next time around. One volunteer had worked tirelessly all week long to get a little coverage for one of his upcoming productions and was thrilled when even a small publicity photo did make it onto the cover of the *Democrat and Chronicle*'s Living pages. While the good news was that it did make the phone ring, Tim's assessment, "But it's only the size of a postage stamp!" did check her pride a bit and prompt her to work harder the next time around to produce something a little more impressive!

The dancers were continuing to make such enormous strides, however, that Tim oftentimes did not take legitimate concerns such as these to heart. As a result, he lost several excellent people along the way. New volunteers continued to come forward, however, but it would sometimes only be a matter of time before they, too, would become disenchanted and leave. Colleagues, vendors, collaborators, employees, parents, and others might also experience Tim's irascibility; the next time around, they were less inclined to be of service. Nevertheless, his nearest and dearest usually forgave him these outbursts as a consequence of his artistic temperament, and his reputation continued to grow both locally and in New York, as well, where he had already enjoyed many positive associations and close friendships within that incomparable universe. When he needed top-tier dancers for his Sugar Plum and Cavalier, for example, he could procure the services of a Michael Byars or a Wendy Whelan, who performed the role of Sugar Plum Fairy for Tim as a guest artist from New York City Ballet in 1992. His one ongoing disappointment, however, was not being able to collaborate with the Rochester Philharmonic Orchestra for *The Nutcracker*. Instead, he was continually being thrown into competition with them, because they engaged out-of-town organizations season after season. When he recalled his many years of dancing *Nutcracker* at Eastman when the production was a completely home-grown affair with Olive McCue directing the Mercury Ballet and either Sam Jones or Paul White in the pit, it didn't seem right, particularly when his company was earning kudos right and left.

In keeping with the tradition of regional touring established by his early mentor, Olive McCue, Tim actively sought to develop new audiences in various venues throughout the area. In May 1993, for example, his troupe, now boasting fifteen ballerinas, performed at SUNY Brockport's Hartwell Dance Theater in four ballets. Although he had brought in two guest choreographers, it was nevertheless Tim's own *Adieu* that had the most appeal.

In a May 10, 1993, *Democrat and Chronicle* review, Sharon McDaniel stated, "Despite Manhattan and Miami imports, Rochester choreography raised the most ruckus. Artistic Director Timothy Draper set his new *Adieu* on Aesha Ash, revealing the dancer's technical and artistic strengths: an elegant sense of line, intense musicality, and bird-like delicacy." Others cited in the review included Tina Brock ("the corps sustained fluid lines but it remained for soloist Tina Brock to infuse real emotional intensity into the dance. . . . the dancing inspired. Brock again engaged the audience with a delightful mix of mischief and aplomb"); Jamey Throumoulos ("Jamey Throumoulos tapped directly into the music's vitality, recharging the work"); and Jessica Murray ("Soloist Jessica Murray drew viewers so deeply into Sorrow, that Elation, the finale which followed literally on her heels [danced with MTV sharpness] came as a shock"). Jamey was also credited as the choreographer of *Triptych* where she "fearlessly mixed the last three decades of pop dance styles with modern ballet traditions. In dance terms, she paralleled the music she chose: three excerpts from *Watermark* by the New Age vocalist Enya and her instrumental ensemble. Jamey's ability to choreograph well for both corps and soloists doubled the work's impact: She kept the panoramic overview of each emotion steady while still focusing on individual responses."

Jamey was also assuming additional teaching and choreographic responsibilities during this time as a guest teacher for Michelle Buschner, in keeping with Tim's promise to Michelle of providing her with excellent teachers. "He always protected my need to keep ballet a major force at my dance studio. He always gave me his best teachers. He always reminded me that if I saw a student with potential that I should forward them to his studio. Which I did!" recalled Buschner. Jamey not only emerged as an outstanding teacher in her own right but also took numerous dancers to competitions. She herself earned the Outstanding Teacher of the Year award at the prestigious 1993 Rochester Invitational.

Although commonplace to most of the studios in the Rochester area at the time, dance competitions were generally not something Tim favored. These regional and national competitions—typically glitzy, high-energy Vegas-like affairs—would come to a city for the weekend with an M.C. and judges of high merit to adjudicate the entrants, who participated in combinations of all sizes and shapes, from solo numbers to large group ensembles, and across all genres, from ballet to hip hop. With most studios, they required an enormous amount of rehearsal time on the part of teacher and student, elaborate costumes, entry fees, coaching fees, meals. Studios that enjoyed out-of-town travel also added all of the associated expenses of being away for a weekend. But the kids loved the competitions. The savvy competitions knew to offer enough categories so that no one school would dominate, regardless of its merits. The students adored the camaraderie, the excitement, the drama, and the chance to push themselves to be their best.

Jamey knew that the visibility from these events, coupled with the exceptional technique that Draper students brought from hours and hours of being at the barre each week, could be of great benefit to Tim. She began working on him to give competitions a try. She knew that they both would be unwilling to concede any time away from class or company rehearsals for this purpose, but if he would agree to participate even once or twice a year, it would have a good effect all the way around. She knew that the competitions would be of particular value to the students, since it gave them fine performance experience (which they loved), and nice bonding opportunities as well, where they could enjoy each other's company even more outside the normal studio routine.

Thus, a new type of visibility was established, and along with it, the "Draper Brand." Tim was naturally very proud of his students and enjoyed seeing them perform. However, the moment they were done with their pieces, he typically bolted from the auditorium—his patience extended only so far!

Also new for the company in 1993 was a joint *Nutcracker* in collaboration with the Buffalo City Ballet, established in 1988, involving the sharing of dancers, scenery, sets, resources, and ideas. The joint production was performed in both cities. The artistic directors said the goal was to develop stronger audiences, "[where] they can plant themselves more firmly in their respective communities while carrying the city names onto out-of-town stages." Having had their own dancers guest for one another's companies the year before, they felt that this arrangement could work. Tim was of the opinion that a regional *Nut-cracker* would provide the credibility that both companies needed in order to survive long term. He also was concerned about the benefit to the community. Although he did not possess the resources of a George Eastman, his passion for Rochester's schoolchildren was equally strong, and he felt that, with the money earned from such collabora-tion, donations could be made to the schools. "I just read an article in *Newsweek* that said that *Nutcracker* accounts for 80 percent of dance-company budgets. If we establish a *Nutcracker* in this region, the money earned can return to the community, like into the public schools, to make up for education cuts."

Other new twists for this *Nutcracker* season included the creation of a "Christmas Spirit" character to fly above the dancers, spreading magic, and cameo appearances by several community dignitaries as Party Parents in act 1. These included Mayor-elect William Johnson; the choreographer and artistic director, Garth Fagan; the city council members Tim Mains and Gary Muldoon; and a council member-elect, Michael Fernandez. This was a masterstroke of good-will and good politics rolled into one. Bringing Garth Fagan in at this point also indi-cated Tim's growing confidence as an artistic director.

But the most momentous aspect of the 1993 *Nutcracker* was the company's name change. "Just as the main characters are transformed in the ballet story, so is the whole company. For its seventh [*sic*] *Nut-cracker*, it sheds its former name of Draper Dance Theatre and emerges officially as Rochester City Ballet."[5]

In many respects, with the company maturing and expanding in so many different ways, some felt that the "fly by the seat of one's pants" mentality that had worked so well for the organization throughout its launch and heady early years needed to evolve into something more formal.

Penny Warenko, along with her husband, Norbert, served on Rochester City Ballet's Board of Directors from 1993 to 2000. She had met Tim when her granddaughter began studying ballet at the Studio of Dance and was so impressed with what he was doing that she wanted to help him in any way possible. "Tim wanted to bring classical bal-let to Rochester. That was his goal." Penny gave generously of herself out of great affection and admiration for Tim, particularly due to "the tremendous discipline he instilled in his dancers." She recalled with humor the time when someone who didn't recognize him asked him if he were involved with the organization. "INVOLVED? I AM the Rochester City Ballet!"

The chair of the board at the time was Dr. Allan O'Grady Cuseo. Board members included Kathy Ertsgaard, Penny and Norbert Warenko, Diane Chevron, John LoVecchio, Elizabeth Skender, Michael Snyder, Debbie Tretter, and Paula Zahniser. Their focus was on building and managing the brand, expanding audiences, encouraging business development, expanding community outreach, and achieving organizational sustainability. As is characteristic of brilliant artists, Tim knew precisely what he wanted and when he wanted it. Executing the artistic director's vision was never an easy task, but nothing was ever as rewarding, either. It helped that Allan O'Grady Cuseo and Diane Chevron, gifted actors and directors well known in theater circles, understood the métier.

Nineteen ninety-three also was the first year that the school offered a summer program, running from 9:00 a.m. until 8:15 p.m., Monday through Friday, with a Saturday Adult Intermediate/Advanced Class offered at 10:00 a.m. The faculty included Jamey Throumoulos, who in addition to her appointment as principal dancer with Draper Dance Theatre/Rochester City Ballet was emerging as a trusted confidante of Tim's; Sally Atkins Stepnes, who was also at the time pursuing an MA in Dance; and Kathy Erstgaard, the managing director of the company. The guest faculty included Miguel Campaneria, a native of Cuba who won the prestigious silver medal at the Varna International Ballet Competition when he was sixteen and went on to dance with the American Ballet Theatre and the Pittsburgh Ballet Theatre; Michael Thomas, previously of ABT, Stuttgart, Les Grands Ballet Canadiens, Dutch National Ballet, and San Francisco Ballet and who became an assistant professor of performing arts at Rochester Institute of Technology/ National Technical Institute for the Deaf; Mary Wilson, who trained at Botsford, danced with ABT from 1983 to 1989, and was entering her senior year at Yale University; Nina Pinkus, who had recently arrived from Eastern Europe after touring with the Belarusian State Philharmonic's Khoroshki folk troupe; Colleen Hendrick of Rochester, who performed her choreography extensively throughout New York State; and Carol Domenico, a former student of Tim's who danced with the Park Avenue Dance Company and earned a BFA and masters of science in teaching (MST) in art education from RIT.

A typical day for advanced dancers would be

Ballet from 9:00 to 11:00
Pointe/Variations from 11:15 to 12:15
Lunch from 12:15 to 1:00
Character/Modern/Jazz from 1:00 to 2:00
Break from 2:00 to 2:30
Workshop from 2:30 to 4:30.

In terms of curriculum, little changed over the next twenty years, with the exception of a second technique class added to the daily curriculum and the addition of Fiona Fairrie to the guest faculty roster. Fairrie brought with her some of the most famous names in the world of classical ballet. The summer intensive, as tough as its name implies, helped serious students of dance improve immeasurably from year to year. Without having to contend with homework and the myriad other activities that make up a normal school-year routine, dancers could concentrate solely on what they were doing in class and enjoy exposure to many varied forms of dance with an outstanding international and in-house faculty.

Innovations continued to take place within the school and company, not the least of which was Rochester City Ballet's participation with Dance Rochester! This twenty-six-member organization represented over five thousand dancers in the area. On April 23, 1994, RCB was proud to present two guest artists, the legendary Leslie Browne of ABT and *The Turning Point* fame and Eldar Aliev, in the *Corsaire pas de deux* with Rochester City Ballet company members performing on the same program in two separate performances at the Auditorium Theatre.

In July, it was announced in the *Democrat and Chronicle* that "Timothy Draper, founder and artistic director of Rochester City Ballet (formerly Draper Dance Theatre) is in Japan for three months as ballet master for Les Ballets Trockadero de Monte Carlo. He also worked with the company this spring for its tour of Russia." The article continued to explain that the summer program would be managed by the acting director, Katherine Ertsgaard, and the assistant director, Sally Stepnes, with a fully expanded guest faculty from the previous summer, including the former Rochesterian Beth Bartholomew of the Dutch company Scapino Rotterdam. Beth had enjoyed a stellar career with earlier appointments at the Joffrey and Washington Ballets. Eventually she was named ballet mistress of the Rochester City Ballet, with her husband, Fidel Orrillo Puga, as ballet master.

Rejoining the Trocks after being away for over ten years had to prove irresistible to the now forty-year-old Tim Draper. The kimonos that long graced the west wall of the large studio on North Goodman Street were souvenirs of these tours to Japan, where the fans absolutely adored the Trocks and accorded them true celebrity status.

One of the best aspects of taking on the role of Trocks ballet master was that Tim would be connecting professionally once again with his old friend from South Florida, Victor Trevino. Although Victor would conclude his tenure with Trockadero in 1994, both were on the Russian tour. Victor recalls with tremendous fondness Tim's new role with the troupe, particularly one experience they shared in Lithuania. They had been at the Opera House, and Victor was doing a *pas de deux* in rehearsal. Tim kept having Victor do *fouettés* over and over prior to the performance that night. Victor recalls that he and Tim argued a lot because Tim was "trying to train us the way he trained his kids. I'd tell him, 'You can't train us that way because we aren't kids and we are on tour—we are thirty-year-old guys in shoes!'" Victor always appreciated Tim's passion for excellence, however, and for trying hard to raise the standards, even if not everyone in the troupe was in agreement. Reiterating this was Tim's friend Brian Norris, who first met Tim through the Trocks. Brian dedicated his 2008 memoir, *The Hardest-Working Ballerina*, to Tim. Brian recalled that the idea of meeting Tim was a little nerve wracking because there were rumors about "this horrible ballet master" they had just hired. Brian had joined Trockadero in 1994 but wasn't yet a full member, so he did not make the Russian tour. When he did finally meet Tim prior to the trip to Japan a couple of months later, he was rehearsing a ballet and there stood Tim, arms crossed, watching him carefully with that special look that he had when paying careful attention to someone whose work he respected. At the end, Tim said it was a nice job and Brian didn't think him a tyrant after all. However, within short order, Brian saw him "fly off the handle as he would do, even getting into an argument over spacing." Apparently, he could not understand why after telling the dancers to look across to see what the others were doing, after he showed them how to do this, they weren't doing what he had asked. After some pushback, he exploded with, "Who do you think you are talking to? I could get you fired!" It probably did not help the situation that Tim also was more than happy to tell the troupe that he had sixteen-year-old dancers back home who could "dance circles around them." However, Brian, a dancer for ten years, recognized immediately the quality that Tim brought to the class-room where he "learned more in the first couple of weeks than the entire time previously." Toward the end of the tour, he asked Tim if they could have a meeting, at which time he told him how much he had learned from him and asked if he could study with him in Rochester, "thinking that Rochester was an hour or so from New York City." Tim thought that was a great idea. In the winter of 1994–95, six hours of travel later, Brian came to do *The Nutcracker* with another friend from the Trocks, Gary David Shaw. The arrangement was for Shaw to teach class while Brian studied with Tim, preparing for his role as the Nutcracker Prince, while Shaw performed as the Snow King. Brian recalls how extremely generous Tim was, to the extent that he even let him drive his car. At that time, Tim was teaching at Brockport during the day and at the studio at night. In January 1995, Brian returned to New York. Tim returned as the Trocks' ballet mas-ter from 1994 to 1998, doing Japanese and US tours and a couple of European tours. Brian periodically came back to Rochester to per-form. Brian recalled a memorable 1995 Spring Show, in which he set the *Corsaire* Odalisques *pas de trois* on Meredith Seeley, Kara Hulbert, and Becky von Rathonyi. In 1996, he set *Don Quixote* on Heather Fer-ranti, a soloist with Rochester City Ballet who had trained earlier at the Botsford School of Dance and Pittsburgh Ballet Theatre School.

Throughout this entire period in the mid-1990s, Brian had a chance to see Tim in a very different light, much in the way that Tim's family did. During 1996, Brian occasionally substituted for Tim, when between his heart and diabetes issues Tim needed time off. Hearing from his doctors about how he had perhaps two months to live—"You should not be alive now"—Tim made the decision to join Bally's Gym and work out there every day. The quiet courage that Brian saw was not seen by most. Whereas at the studio "he was very stern and sarcastic but he tried to make you laugh—he'd do this a lot—there was also the side of him where he'd talk and let his guard down and he was just Tim."

Even in the studio, however, Tim would be extraordinary.

> Many people don't know this, but he knew about art and music and he would bring that into the studio. He would teach class and disci-pline the kids, but he'd also teach them about the arts, asking them, "What is the difference between the two kimonos? Look at the details of them." He would also ask them, "What is this music and where is it from?" He would take the time to do this so that they would be

Ballet artist Brian Norris is proof positive that a beautiful elongee can be found anytime, anywhere. Author's collection.

exposed to it. When he came home, he would talk about ballet. He would sit down and let it go—he didn't want to yell at anybody so he would become more of a "softy." There were times when we would sit back and contemplate why people would act this way or that—why they would be mean to others or why they would be parents. The parents were difficult, and he wondered why they would be that way. But instead of being angry about it, he'd just wonder why things were the way they were. . . . He also seemed to have plans for people within his inner sphere. . . . He had an inherent sense of their value. . . . When I quit the Trocks in 2000 [for example], Tim said "Come teach for me!" He always had a plan.

Brian remembers how Tim often talked about choreography not being his strong suit.

He was a classicist, and when he choreographed, anger came into the studio. He knew that it wasn't the best, and he would get frustrated over the kids not doing what he wanted, and the kids would get frustrated because it was always "not right." He didn't know how to get it out of them. There would be ongoing friction, and then Jamey would tell him, "I'm going to rechoreograph the battle scene," and he would say, "Okay." She was really young at that point—a teenager—

but he didn't want to do it. When he choreographed, it had a more classical or lyrical look, and when Jamey did it, it was always more contemporary but there was a nice balance to it.

During this time, Tim decided Victor Trevino also needed to be in Rochester. Tim saw in his old friend much more than a dancer. He thought Victor had the potential to be a great choreographer and so invited him to choreograph a piece on his dancers. Victor remembers working with Aesha Ash during this period and how gratifying it was to choreograph. Just as Victor had encouraged Tim to begin his own school and company, Tim was again seeing continued greatness in Victor and continually pushed him to do more. Beyond dance, however, the two shared a special connection with regard to Tim's progressively deteriorating heart. Victor was able to see firsthand how disciplined Tim was in doing everything possible to tend to his health needs, while at the same time giving 100 percent to his students. Tim was a very good confidante, and the two truly enjoyed a special connection. To this day, Victor credits Tim with encouraging him to reach for the stars. Ultimately, Victor founded and directed Ballet Grandiva and Ballet LOL.

In early 1995, Tim was very enthusiastic about the upcoming year. "Founder Sees Big Steps Ahead," was the lead dance story by Isobel Neuberger in the *Democrat and Chronicle* of January 28. Tim was in negotiations with RPO's president, Nan Harman, to have his company finally get the chance to collaborate in the annual November *Nutcracker*. The RPO was considering RCB along with one other company, the Kirov. In addition, RCB was in the process of planning a fund-raiser for the following month. Tim said, "I'd like to expand to do more in-school programs and to give people in Rochester a taste of what's happening in the dance world." He also spoke of his desire to have a company of sixteen permanent dancers, paid thirty weeks of the year. "With a larger, established company . . . he could bring in guest dancers and choreographers whose work is not generally seen in this city. New ballets could also be created for his company." It is interesting to contemplate how Tim might have been remembered if he had received the funds necessary to launch this type of company at this time (something that did come to fruition on Jamey Throumoulos' watch ten years later). The largest part of his legacy was that he succeeded in creating artists to assume their roles on the world's most famous stages. If he had kept those dancers in house and paid them, even if he did first introduce them to the global ballet community through international competition or the occasional tour, one has to wonder if his reputation would have been at the same exalted level at the time of his death.

Following a Trockadero review from 1995, "The Trocks Toe the Line between Art and Camp Dance: The All-Male Les Ballets Trockadero de Monte Carlo Parodies the Classics with Technical and Dramatic Skill," one is left to contemplate just how instrumental Tim was on improving the technical capabilities of his former company.[6] In his new role of ballet master, it would be almost unthinkable that he could enter a studio of any kind, after what he had established back home in Rochester, and not demand complete adherence to his every direction. This was borne out in the same review, which stated:

> One post-performance conversation between audience members . . . seemed to indicate that technically, at least, the Trocks were on track, said McDougle, who has been with the 15-member company since its 1974 inception. "One day, two well-dressed elderly ladies were walking out (of the theater) and I overheard one say, 'Well, they weren't bad dancers, but those were the ugliest girls I've ever seen.'"[7]

This was also a time when Tim's elite dancers back home were getting ready for a larger stage. Aesha Ash was a prime example as a young dancer of unlimited promise. At the age of thirteen, she had auditioned for and was accepted into the School of American Ballet. She went on to join the New York City Ballet, becoming one of the company's most celebrated dancers before moving on to Béjart Ballet Lausanne and Alonzo King's LINES Ballet. Her star rose particularly after being the dance double for the Zoe Saldana character of Eva in the 2000 feature film, *Center Stage*. Tim remained bitter, however, over the fact that Aesha would never be promoted beyond corps at City Ballet and the sense of alienation she felt due to her skin color. Years later, Gia Kourlas, in a 2007 New York Times article, "Where Are All the Black Swans?" would raise the same question. "Ms. Ash, an enormously gifted dancer who performed many prominent parts, never progressed past the corps de ballet. After her father died, she said that she asked Peter Martins, the company's ballet master in chief, for a short leave of absence. 'He actually encouraged me to leave the company, because, in so many words, he told me that he didn't see me really doing any more than what I was doing at City Ballet, period. It was very difficult. I fought my way through the school, and I felt like I continued fighting through the company—fighting with the image that I had of myself.'"[8]

Shortly after Aesha left Rochester in 1995, a *Democrat and Chronicle* article appeared entitled "Dancers in Flight," which announced "Our 'Firebird' has flown the coop. Ballerina Tina Brock, who danced *Firebird* with the Rochester City Ballet, now has a new nest in Chicago, as part of Hubbard Street Dance. And Heather Ferranti, another company member, has joined the Colorado Ballet. Rumor has it that a third ballerina is being courted by the Shanghai Ballet."[9] Another article stated that "Tim Draper has big plans for the little company. Nine members will dance at 1 p.m. today and tomorrow on the steps of the Memorial Art Gallery. . . . Then Draper starts his new season with a production of *The Nutcracker*. It will tour in November to Smith Opera House in Geneva and to the Canandaigua Academy, both in Ontario County. Home in Rochester, *The Nutcracker* performances are at 2 and 8 p.m., December 16 at the Auditorium Center."[10]

Despite this eagerly anticipated *Nutcracker*, previous optimism dissolved into intense disappointment with the RPO once again opting to bring in an outside troupe—this time The Kirov Ballet and the Kirov Academy of Ballet. In previous years, the rivals were Pittsburgh and Hartford. "I was in heaven when I thought I had a chance to work with the RPO," Tim said wistfully about what eventually came to him—but just not that year. Sharon McDaniel of the *Democrat and Chronicle* noted with a little irony that while Draper can't seem to break into the big time locally, some of his dancers have made it internationally. "An impressive list of larger companies has confirmed the quality of Draper company members. Hubbard Street Dance Chicago hired Tina Brock, the Colorado Ballet coaxed Heather Ferranti away, and the Shanghai Ballet snapped up Claudia McLaughlin. Aesha Ash, currently attending Manhattan's School of American Ballet, is dancing Nutcracker this season with New York City Ballet. And current Draper dancers—like Sari Ostrum, who alternates in the role of Clara on Saturday—have studied on scholarship with companies nationwide."[11]

This production had lasting significance because it introduced a group of young dancers who later defined Tim at the very pinnacle of his success. Tara Lally shared the role of Clara with Sari Ostrum; the Party Children were Laura Fernandez, Sarah Knerr, Cynthia LaForte, Sarah Lane, Elana Katz Mink, Jillian Nealon, Elizabeth Owerbach, Erica Ratkovicz, Erika Snyder, Jessica Tretter, Melissa Wyble, and Laura Ziegler; the Mice were Ashley Anzalone, Amy Bonner, Kristi Boone, Tracy Hosenfeld, Jenna Kosowski, Erin Lemcke, Jill Marlow, and Diana Vreeland; the Soldiers were Sylvia Bluhm, Rachel Carson, Kristi

Chechak, Maria Fox, Lisa Hunt, Alexandra Johnson, Jessica Latacki, and Jessica Odasz; the Spanish corps included Cathy Baker, Kara Hulbert, Laura Kenney, and Rachel Westlake. Katie Lally was the Lead Angel, Jordan Drew was a Sprite, and Brittany Monachino was a Page. Principals and soloists included Rebekah von Rathonyi as the Sugar Plum Fairy and Snow Queen. Cindy Van Scoter was the Dew Drop and English Toffee. Jamey Throumoulos was the Christmas Spirit and Russian Trepak. Elizabeth Reisinger and Charles Thompson danced as the Magical Dolls. Meredith Seeley was the Harlequin; Rachel Westlake, the Mouse Queen; Jason Jacobs, the Nutcracker Prince. Rachanna Thomas and Samantha DiPaola shared the role of Spanish Chocolate; Cora Kannel and Charles Thompson danced Italian Ice. Kerry Shea, Michelle Szlewski, Tiffanie DeValve, Meredith Seeley, and Elizabeth Reisinger were the French Mints; Camila Papini and Rob Schickler were Arabian Coffee; and Carrie Jones and Sara McCoubrey were Chinese Tea. The production manager that year was Tammy Brackett, the stage manager was Timothy Cawley, and lighting design was handled by Derek Madonia. Board executives for the 1995–96 season included Dr. Allan O'Grady Cuseo, president; Leslie Senglaub, vice president; Pat Cummings, treasurer; Paula Zahniser, secretary; and Timothy M. Draper, artistic director.

Although several of Tim's dancers had "flown the coop" by 1995, he was thrilled to see them excel on a larger stage. In a few more years, with several of his students dancing in New York, he would behave like a proud papa, practically bursting his buttons with dramatic explanations as to who was doing what. He also had more than enough to keep himself busy between the continuous up-and-coming talent needing his attention and the general state of the company in the mid 1990s."[12] Ultimately, Tim wasn't overly discouraged about the Kirov casting—this was just a little setback. Despite the disappointments, he also thought about how far along the company had come. "'Comparing Saturday's resources—dancers, sets, and costumes—to the debut *Nutcracker* nine years ago, Draper laughs. 'The school opened about 10 years ago, but I don't count the first *Nutcracker* we did! There's no secure place in the arts . . . but we're in a good place.'"[13]

Hayley Meier. Photograph by Ed Flores, www.edflores.com.

HAYLEY MEIER

Many years ago, my mom pulled up into the parking lot of my new dance studio. The dilapidated building looked like it was in serious need of repair. I remember thinking, "What are we doing? This doesn't look like a dance studio. It's more like a warehouse." My mom said, "You can't judge a book by its cover." I was eleven years old then, and I wondered what the heck she was talking about. As we creaked up the stairs to the studio, I wasn't comfortable with the idea of going to a new school. After all, I loved my dance teacher and couldn't help thinking that no one could take her place. I loved all of my friends, and even though I was only eleven, we had done so much together and traveled to a lot of dance conventions and competitions. I was so anxious about making this switch, but I knew in my heart that I wanted to take my dance ability to the next level, and that this school was a way for me to pursue that. It's true. You can't judge a book by its cover, because inside this run-down building was a hidden jewel and something I will always treasure throughout my life.

The Timothy M. Draper Center for Dance Education was named for its founder. He built the school up from just a handful of students into a successful studio. Taking class with Tim was tough. Not only did he insist on pushing to get the very best out of everyone but he did it in a way that commanded respect and dedication. Whenever he wanted to explain what the correct form was or the right way to hold your arms, he would always paint a picture in your mind and draw analogies. He gave everything a feeling. His goal for every class and rehearsal was to tap into your own greatness. He would never let you settle for mediocrity. He set high standards for himself and expected everyone around him to follow suit. His students both feared and loved him at the same time. He was such a precious gift to the dance world, and he was taken from us at the age of forty-nine.

Looking at Tim, you didn't envision him as a dancer with sleek, long lines, but rather a body-builder. Every muscle was developed to its fullest. He was an example of how to keep your body in tip-top shape. He lectured us about the right way to eat, sleep, work, dance, and live. That's why when we were all brought into the studio to be told that he had passed away from a heart attack, we were in such shock. How could that be possible? Tim was so strong and so healthy—at least that's how he appeared to be on the outside. "You can't judge a book by its cover." I remember thinking about that and I knew exactly what it meant now. The truth was he was very sick indeed, and his heart was not able to carry on. He had been a diabetic for many years, and the disease finally took its toll. He never once complained. He worked so very hard to help us all achieve our greatest potential.

Oftentimes, when I'm working at the barre, I still imagine him there. His words play over and over in my mind. I know he is still watching over all of us. I always wish I had the chance to tell him how much my fellow students and I loved him. We miss him dearly. I hope we continue to make him proud as he lives on through all of us dancing and performing. When you have someone who gives you inspiration and fuels your desire to be the very best that you can be, you consider yourself very fortunate. I have been very lucky that I knew Tim for six years before he passed away. I will always treasure what I found in that run-down building and studio. Thank you, Tim.

Hayley Meier presently performs with River North Dance Chicago. After dancing numerous principal roles in the Rochester City Ballet repertoire (including title roles in *Cinderella* and *Firebird*) and performing by invitation at the fourteenth annual International Festival of Ballet in Peru, Hayley received a BFA in dance at the University of Arizona on full scholarship. After graduating in 2009, she returned to RCB for two seasons to dance under the direction of Jamey Leverett, performing in numerous works including George Balanchine's *Serenade*, Gerald Arpino's *Valentine*, and Patrick Corbin's premiere work, *Shady III*. She originated the role of Anna in Jamey Leverett's *Blood Countess*.

11

AN EMBARRASSMENT OF RICHES

One can look to three very significant advances that took place within the school and company during the mid- to late 1990s, which led, in turn, to many more fortuitous developments. One was the transition of Jamey Throumoulos, now Jamey Leverett, from company principal dancer into teacher, choreographer, and associate artistic director. One was the addition of Susannah Newman to the faculty to oversee the modern dance curriculum. One was the explosive growth of the studio's summer intensive program, to which several legendary names in the world of ballet came summer after summer for the opportunity to work with Tim and Jamey's exceptionally well-trained students.

With Jamey's ascension to the role of her teacher's most trusted advisor, Tim was now given two precious gifts—the gift of time (of which he knew he had very little) and the gift of partnership. With regard to the first, he could now take on those assignments that were most gratifying to him. He had the luxury of being able to look at the big picture, concentrate on what it would take to get to the next level, explore new collaborations, and engage with the right people to help him achieve his dreams. As for the second, and perhaps even more important, he would no longer have to plan strategy on his own—he would now have a true artistic partner by his side to help him train the current and next generation of artists to the highest standard in the same manner as she herself had been trained. Together, they could brainstorm, sort out the tough decisions (artistic and otherwise), create and clean choreography, develop programming, be spokespersons at the myriad public events in which the organization participated, and manage the hundreds of other projects large and small that consumed the life of an artistic leadership team. Kathy Ertsgaard would continue to manage the administrative end of the company, bringing to the organization strong process orientation; meticulous record keeping;

institutional knowledge as a founding member of the company; and the steady, loyal friendship that defined the two friends.

Susannah Newman, a long-time friend and colleague of Tim's at SUNY Brockport, brought to the studio the essential modern dance training that was beginning to become increasingly important in a professional ballet dancer's toolbox. Susannah, then associate professor of dance, graduate program director, universitywide artist, and cofounder of the resident dance company, toured solo work during her performance career with Viola Farber, Anna Sokolow, and Lynn Dally.

A generous and inspiring teacher, Susannah encouraged the dancers to find their own artistic voices and develop their own choreography, and then provide them with the vehicle to showcase it. Several of the top studio dancers over the years chose to pursue a BFA in dance after their training with Tim and Jamey, where the modern idiom was a key element within the curriculum. They found their training with Susannah to be of tremendous value in this regard. It was far sighted of Tim to bring her on board because not all of those training for a professional career with him were necessarily predisposed to work in a classical ballet company. With their extraordinary technique, they would be in the enviable position of being able to join several of the prestigious modern troupes or contemporary ballet companies.

The summer program, which began in 1993, grew dramatically when Georgina Parkinson taught for Tim in 1995 and Fiona Fairrie arrived the following summer. Miss Parkinson, a personal friend of Tim's, had been a star of Britain's Royal Ballet in the 1960s. After a magnificent career that included coaching by Bronislava Nijinska for her critically acclaimed role in *Les Biches*, she was invited to teach company class at American Ballet Theatre, which is where Tim met her.

Fiona Fairrie, another extraordinary dancer from across the Pond, had a sumptuous Royal Ballet and Stuttgart Ballet pedigree. A former ballet professor at the University of South Florida and a teacher at American Ballet Theatre's Studio Company, the Cleveland Ballet, the Atlanta Ballet, Houston Ballet, and the Central Pennsylvania Youth Ballet, Fiona was certified by examination in Cecchetti but educated herself in many different styles, as did Tim. She brought to the studio not only exquisite classical technique and a deep reverence for the nineteenth-century classics but also an exceptional knowledge of the art form and the artists who brought it to life. For her White Lodge graduation performance with the Royal Ballet, for instance, one of her teachers, the legendary Ninette de Valois, honored Fiona with the opportunity to perform in Sir Frederick Ashton's *Patineurs*. The chore-ographer himself later told her personally that she did a beautiful job in the *pas de deux*, which he had originally choreographed for Dame Margot Fonteyn and Michael Soames.

As a former student of Fiona's in Florida, Tim knew firsthand the true weight of her talent. He had enormous regard for her, and she felt the same way about him. Students of hers were highly respectful and a little intimidated as well, particularly in the early years when training with their slim, glamorous instructor with the throaty British accent. The highest compliment a young dancer could receive from Fiona was if she remembered his or her name the following summer when she returned, something they actually discussed among themselves in advance of each summer season. Although they had to work very hard for her in class, this is what they were used to and loved.

Fairrie's esteem for the students, likewise, was bottomless. In the December 13, 1997, review of *The Nutcracker* dress rehearsal, per-formed before 2,500 Rochester city schoolchildren, the *Democrat and Chronicle*'s Sharon McDaniel contacted Fiona in Florida to get her take on what made this company so exceptional.

> "They're truly extraordinary," says Fiona Fairrie, former Royal Ballet (London) and Stuttgart (Germany) Ballet soloist, by phone from her home in Florida. "I don't think I've seen a private school in this coun-try with so many well-trained dancers," adds the British-born teacher who coached the *Nutcracker* here last month. She also praised Artistic Director Timothy Draper and his assistant, Jamey Throumoulos Lev-erett. She points to a bevy of exceptional ballerinas, ages 14–16, who "don't look it because they look really professional—especially Sari Ostrum who danced the *Nutcracker*'s Russian solo."[1]

Not only was Fiona a key member of the Draper faculty mix over the years, but the breadth of her contacts in the dance world mean that she could bring in other internationally renowned faculty, includ-ing Eva Evdokimova, one of the ballet world's most celebrated interna-tional stars and Rudolf Nureyev's favorite partner later in his career; Sasha Ypparov (Bolshoi Theater); Clara Cravey (Harkness Ballet); Les-lie Peck (New York City Ballet); Alla Nikitina (State Academic Ensem-ble of Dance, Russia); Susanna Hanke (Stuttgart Ballet); and Sandra Robinson (North Carolina Dance Theatre and Pennsylvania Ballet). Other greats who have served on the summer faculty include Geor-gina Parkinson (Royal Ballet); John Meehan (Australian Ballet and

American Ballet Theatre); Ivonne Lemus (Ballet Nacional de Cuba);
Dawn Scannell (Houston Ballet); Joseph Kerwin (Finnish National
Ballet); Edward Ellison (San Francisco Ballet); Parker Esse (Broadway);, and Andrew Parker (Southern Methodist University). In addition, Fiona always was a most helpful advocate when it came to her
students' futures. It was not unusual for her to pick up the phone and
call an old friend who happened to be the artistic director of a high-
quality company and recommend a promising dancer.

The 1997 *Nutcracker* symbolized, perhaps more than at any other
time in the company's history, its rich depth. Each of the twenty-six
company members cited in the review is remembered today by name,
both inside and outside the company, for exquisite artistry and stage
presence. Most were not yet eighteen years old. Tim was fully aware of
the extraordinary talent that defined his company, and he could not
have been more proud. "Draper agrees he has an embarrassment of
riches in the 26-member company," noted Sharon McDaniel.[2]

Earning special recognition for their performances (in addition
to the aforementioned Ostrum) were Kristi Boone as the Dew Drop,
Rebekah von Raythoni as the Mouse Queen and the Sugar Plum
Fairy, Alexandra (Allie) Johnson as Clara, Elizabeth Reisinger as the
flying Christmas Spirit, Jill Marlow as English Toffee, Meredith Seeley
as the Snow Queen and Italian Ice, and her partner in both roles,
Jimmy Rodriguez.

Rebekah von Raythoni's unique story illustrates the extraordinary training she received after coming to Draper from Botsford
when she was nine. Rebekah's mother had danced with Tim in the
Mercury Ballet, so when she heard that he had opened up his own
school, there was no question as to where her daughter would study.
Rebekah initially took lessons with Julianne O'Donnell Deming and
Sally Stepnes. After making rapid progress, she began training with
Tim, twice dancing the role of Clara as a ten- and an eleven-year-old
in 1989 and 1990.

Rebekah's reputation within the studio grew quickly. By then the
school already had a supply of precocious talent. When she was fourteen, her family moved to Mexico City. Due to the fact that her training
with Tim had been of such a very high caliber, she was asked to join the
Compañia Nacional de Danza, whose artistic director was Fernando
Alonso, the ex-husband of the famed Alicia Alonso of Ballet Nacional de Cuba. Although it was extremely difficult for Rebekah to leave
Rochester, she felt prepared. "I knew that Tim had given me the tools

to make it in the outside world," she recalled. "Not only did he give me what I needed technically but also artistically. He taught me how to 'wow them artistically.' He has always carried me through, and there is not a day that goes by that Tim is not in my heart." Tim told her that when she returned, she would always have a home at Rochester City Ballet. The family did move back to the United States, but Rebekah had been offered a position with the Pennsylvania Ballet. Fifteen years old at the time, she danced with them and then returned to Tim when she was seventeen. She remembers getting in touch with him regarding the stress she was under and wondering whether a career in ballet was truly her calling. His response was exactly what she needed to hear. "Rebekah, you have a wonderful gift, you always have. There is no doubt in my mind whatsoever, you will make it as a dancer." Rebekah wrote in her journal, "Tim doesn't say things like that often and not to many people. He was sincere and really meant it, he was more sure of it than me!"

Rebekah performed most of the coveted roles in the Rochester City Ballet repertoire over the years that followed, throughout all kinds of life events, including pregnancy. (Tim was always ready to overlook the little details of weight gain—"Becky, it doesn't matter what you look like physically—it's how you dance it and how you make the audience feel.") He was a true mentor in every sense of the word.

Her repertoire with the company included *Gâité Parisienne*, Kitri from *Don Quixote*, many Sugar Plum Fairies, the *pas de trois des odalisques* from *Le Corsaire* with Meredith Seeley and Elizabeth Reisinger, and several of Tim's own choreographed works, which she absolutely loved, especially *Moments*. In 1997, Tim recommended that Rebekah audition for the International Ballet Luxembourg competition. She was accepted into this august body of competitors, no small feat considering that this was the same competition won in later years by American Ballet Theatre's principal dancers, Natalia Osipova and Daniil Simkin. As it turned out, Tim had a scheduling conflict with the Trocks that prevented his rehearsing and traveling with Rebekah to the competition. Rebekah's former teacher, Sally Stepnes (who by this time had moved to Florida) took over this role. It was an exhilarating experience and an honor, because this was the first time in the school's history that anyone had been accepted into such a prestigious international competition.

Much excitement greeted the 1998 season. The spring production starred Rebekah as Kitri in *Don Quixote*. In the mixed bill that preceded it, fourteen-year-old Sari Ostrum was paired with Jimmy Rodriguez Jimenez in Jamey Leverett's *Gershwin in the Park*. Sari was also a featured dancer in Tim's *Reflections*, along with Kristi Boone, Jamey, Rebekah, Jimmy, Kara Hulbert, Allie Johnson, Jenna Kosowski, Jill Marlow, and Elizabeth Reisinger; and in *Forest Walk*, which also included Courtney Barker, Kristi, Rachel Carson, Lisa Hunt, Laura Kenney, Jenna, Cristin Loeffler, Melissa Preston, Stacey Tyler, and Laura Zygo.

The 1998 *Nutcracker* was no less spectacular than the one that had preceded it. The dance critic Herbert Simpson commented not only on the quality of the production and the ballerinas but also on the superior quality of the studio itself.

> I can't really say "It don't get no better than this!" like those yokels in the commercials, because—even ignoring the nasty grammar—there are a handful of major ballet companies in this country that are better. But I do insist that Rochester City Ballet's *Nutcracker* is much better danced than any of those I've had to look at recently except National Ballet of Canada's. And NBC is the third-ranked ballet company on this continent, huge, internationally known, and therefore, an unfair comparison. The level of our local dancers' work is astonishing.
>
> There have been a few regional outfits in recent years that were admired for turning out a number of slightly freaky child-prodigy ballerinas. I saw several from Pennsylvania who could whip off triple pirouettes on pointe before puberty. But Rochester City Ballet's young dancers are remarkably balanced in their musicality and unaffected, gracious stage manner, as well as precocious technique. I sat next to an actress and teacher of acting during this year's *Nutcracker*, and she was astounded at the young dancers' stage presence. "They're not just doing steps," she said. "They're really dancing." Exactly. The kids from Artistic Director Tim Draper's school move on to major companies, but keep getting replaced by other top-notch students who also don't dance like students. So we can rerun my 1997 review of RCB's Nutcracker, perhaps changing a few names. But the production does improve subtly in its overall polish. The sets are still mostly tacky, and some of the annually upgraded costumes still don't look like much. That's all a matter of money. Draper seems to hone [*sic*] in on the little dramatic touches each year, so that this merely acceptably choreographed *Nutcracker* now plays smoothly as fairly decent entertainment.
>
> But what is really at work is the dancing, which is now so uniformly well rehearsed and presented that it carries the ballet on its own, without elaborate performance values as much as execution of movement, this dancing is exquisite enough to enrapture the audience.

Again, local adjunct talents contributed valuable assistance. Actress Diane Chevron pantomimed the funny Maid, and elegant modern dancer, Clyde Morgan, Jr. lent great panache to the mysterious connecting role of Herr Drosselmeyer. Jimmy Rodriguez, now working in modern dance in New York, returned to bring his high-flying fancy footwork to the role of the Mouse King and to rejoin his perfectly matched, bravura partner Meredith Seeley in their exciting Italian Ice duet. And little children, and even littler children, and finally children who looked too tiny to entrust with walking onstage and off alone, all performed with adorable spirit and amazing assurance.

Guest artists Alexi Zuberia—still handsome and a generous, noble partner as the Snow King—and Pierre Francoise Vilanoba—now with San Francisco Ballet, but clearly showing the soigné fluency of his Paris Opera Ballet training in the Grand Pas de Deux—gave strong male support to their ballerinas. So did muscular Todd Speranza in the Arabian dance.

But the ballerinas are the story here. Alexandra Johnson was super-flexible in the Arabian Dance. Natalia Malley-Masten was suavely in technical control as the Harlequin doll. Laura Kenney showed especially impressive extensions in the Spanish dance. Lisa Hunt won applause with terrific jumps and turns in the "English Toffee" solo. Tara Lally looked dazzling executing mostly male-steps in the Russian Trepak. Elizabeth Reisinger flew up and down on wire and danced beautifully as the Christmas Spirit and also the Chinese Dance soloist. She and the radiant "Waltz of the Flowers" soloist, Jill Marlow, topped this line of succession for leading ballerina roles in the future and the current leading ballerinas also keep getting better. Sari Ostrum [who had just turned fifteen] as the Snow Queen . . . negotiated the taxing choreography with no problems and though she will gain in strength with maturity, Kristi Boone is already a true ballerina with very distinctive arms. Her Sugar Plum Fairy had the sweet quality of movement that one associates with a leading ballerina's Aurora in *The Sleeping Beauty*. And my big enthusiasm this time went to Sarah Lane, just turned 14 (!), charming in the role of the young girl, Clara. Lane is physically very beautiful with stunning extensions and absolutely gorgeous feet. Where does Draper keep finding these starlets? I have no doubt that backstage these accomplished beauties will look like little adolescent girls. But in this entirely pleasing *Nutcracker*, they are dancers performing at a competitive standard that is a little hard to believe.[3]

It is thus not surprising, and more than a little prescient on Simpson's part, that the last three dancers mentioned, Sari Ostrum, Kristi Boone, and Sarah Lane all went on to dance at the American Ballet Theatre.

And the riches kept pouring in. Tim and Jamey's dancers were being recognized at the national level. Not surprisingly, this began to create a bigger buzz among local audiences. The mood was high at 320-A North Goodman. With the exception of a crazed, gun-toting woman entering the studio one night (bravely held off by Tim while all of his dancers were ushered to safety outside), everything was beginning to gel. Productions were garnering critical acclaim, dancers were continuing to win coveted positions at larger companies as well as gaining admission into prestigious collegiate programs for BFAs in dance, summer scholarships at top-tier companies and universities were arriving in quantity, donations were up, and the elusive "top of mind awareness" was finally beginning to come to the fore, reflecting the outstanding training offered in Rochester.

New for ushering in the 1998–99 season was a lovely multicolored subscription trifold in hues of pink and burgundy, no less impressive in style (if not in size) than those sent out in advance of the upcoming seasons for New York City Ballet and American Ballet Theatre. In addition to the superb photos of the dancers, snapshots of past and upcoming repertoire, and information concerning both its history and commitment to its involvement with Young Audiences of Rochester, the back cover listed an opportunity to join the Rochester City Ballet Guild, with a suggested donor level of $50 for individual sponsorships and ascending $5,000 or more at the Corporate Diamond level. "Contributions enable us to grow and expand our repertoire of dance experience, which we in turn share with our audiences," was the pitch. By becoming a member, subscribers would receive the following benefits (depending on the level of contribution):

- US Airways dividend miles (up to 2,000 miles)
- Invitations to special events, including a backstage tour following rehearsal
- Priority seating
- A subscription to the company newsletter, "To The Pointe"

With the exception of the minor glitch in announcing somewhat prematurely the upcoming year's performance of *Cinderella* (which wouldn't happen until the spring of 2000), this promotional piece was outstanding, reflecting that the administrative arm of the operation, at least in terms of external presentation appeared to be finally catching up with its long acclaimed artistic counterpart.

Nineteen ninety-nine was shaping up to be the company's best year yet. But the long-sought key to Eastman's kingdom had not yet been conferred. North Carolina Dance Theatre had been the latest thorn in the local company's Land of the Sweets. Although there was no question that Draper Dance Theatre could dance rings around most if not all other companies, this was the prize that mattered most. The board had its marching orders.

Tim flanked by Brittany Monachino and Jim Nowakowski at the Rochester Airport upon returning with Jim from the Ukraine in October of 2002. Photograph by Charles Monachino.

BRITTANY MONACHINO

"There is something in the student teacher exchange that is ancient, simple, and powerful."

—Alonzo King

I remember fondly the day I found out I had reached the professional division, the highest division in our school. It was after our end-of-year demonstration, and my family and I decided to go out for dinner to celebrate the performance. I literally screamed for joy when I read my assigned class for the following year, probably alarming many in the restaurant! I would be studying with Tim that fall! I never wanted to study with a teacher more. Now at least my mother would get a break from driving me to ballet nearly two hours early before my class. I insisted on doing so at such a young age, so that I could watch Tim's classes and rehearsals, remembering everything so that I could practice in my kitchen at home. We were all so happy because it was my dream to study with him since I began at Draper. He would come into the studio to teach wearing a form-fitted tank top baring his sculpted muscles, dark jeans, and jazz shoes. Tim loved teaching, and his students loved taking his class. From the beginning, I felt that he was one of the few teachers that really understood me. He often knew how I felt without my ever saying a word and with just one smile I knew he was pleased. A teacher knows when and how to motivate, when to challenge beyond comfort lines, and when to simply wait for the concepts to settle in; Tim possessed this discernment. He saw where I was at the moment, and spoke confidently to where I was destined to go.

There were pictures all around the studio, but there was one in particular of Paloma Herrera on the streets of NYC doing a beautiful back attitude. He turned to me with a smile, "Can you do that?" He was always pushing me beyond the limits of what someone at my age of eleven was supposed to do and beyond what I could conceive possible; he believed in me. I'll never forget how he would call me Chiquita Banana, Blueberry, and the many coffee-influenced variations of my last name. "The BBs" was a name he had for me and my friend Brittany Shinay.

It was *Nutcracker* season, and we were in the middle of our dress rehearsal, with me performing the role of Clara. I remember Jamey was giving me some corrections over the microphone when I heard Tim take over. "Monachino, how many fingers am I holding up?" I strained my eyes, attempting to see through bright stage lights and a pitch black theater, all while completing my solo. I couldn't see anything and he knew it. "Two," he yelled with a laugh. He was a man with fierce attention to detail, as well as a very playful side. On that day, he taught me to be courageous and bold, giving myself fully to the dance, leaving nothing off limits. Tim wanted us to be unafraid of honesty in our dancing. He trained us to trust our artistic intuition and to follow through with integrity. I will forever remember this man and the huge part he had in developing me into a woman who is persistent and steadfast in pursuit of her dreams. I thank God for the time I was able to spend with Tim and for his legacy that lives on through me and all of his dancers. I can confidently say that my life is forever touched.

Brittany Monachino studied at the Purchase Conservatory of Dance and earned a BFA in dance from SUNY College at Brockport. She danced on scholarship at the Chautauqua School of Dance, Central Pennsylvania Youth Ballet, Washington School of Ballet, EMIA, LINES Ballet, and Cedar Lake Contemporary Ballet. Brittany was the recipient of the 2008 Dr. Martin Luther King Jr. Award for academic excellence, character, and community service, and for making a difference in children's lives by exposing them to the world of the arts throughout Rochester and Western New York. She has competed in the Youth American Grand Prix with honors and performed with the Washington Ballet. Brittany has worked with the choreographer Dianne McIntyre in her rendition of Ntozake Shange's choreopoem *why i had to dance* and is a member of PHILADANCO! The Philadelphia Dance Company.

12

FINALLY

W e hope this translates into a wonderful hometown *Nutcracker* that brings together the whole community." With these words, uttered by Richard Nowlin, RPO's chief executive officer, Tim finally was going to the show. He would at long last be able to bring his beloved Rochester City Ballet home to where he had danced as a boy with the Mercury Ballet—on the historic stage of Rochester's magnificent Eastman Theatre. For the first time in its remarkable history, the company would be dancing to Tchaikovsky's glorious score, performed live by the world-renowned Rochester Philharmonic Orchestra. Tim could not have been more thrilled.

Laboring tirelessly to build his company from the ground floor into a world-class powerhouse, Tim surely had faced and conquered many obstacles along the way. Nothing, however, could have prepared him for the extraordinary wait—twelve years—before the resident orchestra would take a good look at the out-of-town talent they'd been importing ever since Rochester's Mercury Ballet Company had closed its doors and compare it with what the press and public were raving about down the street at the Auditorium Theatre—Rochester City Ballet's lively, mesmerizing, and exquisitely danced *Nutcracker*. Each organization initially posited slightly different reasons for joining forces, with Nowlin saying that as part of the orchestra's community outreach effort, "it just made sense to produce an all-Rochester *Nutcracker*" and Tim maintaining that "joint productions are the norm for most cities because they don't want to compete over this major moneymaker. Generally, the local orchestra does not use anyone else but the local ballet company." But now that the deal was done, artfully crafted by the leadership teams for both sides, there was a great feeling of excitement, pride, and determination to make this production as memorable and as magical as possible.

For those who knew, loved, and respected Tim, it meant mostly one thing—that his work was finally being validated at a level it had long deserved. His young company continually had been garnering critical acclaim from many of the most internationally prominent names in the ballet world. Thus it was fitting and appropriate that his hometown would recognize these achievements by inviting him to take a seat at the table of Rochester's legendary cultural institution, the Rochester Philharmonic Orchestra. This exciting collaboration promised to usher in a new era for the community, and most assuredly, to take this annual holiday confection to new heights.

It should not have been a surprise to anyone who had followed the career of this extraordinarily gifted artist, particularly because his pedigree included performance time years earlier in the very Eastman Theatre complex whose marquee now bore his name. It seemed to confer an added source of legitimacy that he would now choreograph and direct his *Nutcracker* on the Eastman Theatre stage in a manner that those who had previously been imported to do the job over the past several years simply never could.

Of course, the *Nutcracker* that was coming to the Eastman Theatre in 1999 had long been ready for prime time. "When we entered into a collaboration with the RPO," says Leverett, "*The Nutcracker* was already an exceptional production."[1]

And in the time it took Katie Lally's Fritz to thoroughly confound Diane Chevron's Maid into provoking a good old-fashioned *batterie*-filled spanking with beats hardly possible for an eleven-year-old, it was all over. Children roared, parents settled in for a cherished two hours of R&R, and both organizations knew immediately that they had a hit on their hands. The next day's rave reviews confirmed the stunning success. "It's a magical mixture: appealing dancers, creative choreography, the Rochester Philharmonic Orchestra and Tchaikovsky's *Nutcracker*," effused Sharon McDaniel of the *Democrat and Chronicle*. "To the onstage excitement, add a huge, attentive audience of friends, family, and *Nutcracker* fans, and the Eastman Theatre was abuzz for hours."

John Russo, who conducted the RPO for the perforamce, earned kudos for his "upbeat, magnetic" tempo as did the percussion section "that sparkled even more than usual." But the story that holiday weekend was the extraordinary, inspired dancing accompanied by a world-class orchestra. The highest praise went to Tim's reigning star, Snow Queen Sari Ostrum, and her partner, Eric Otto of American Ballet Theatre. "Snow King Eric Otto of American Ballet Theatre danced as if he enjoyed his partner, City Ballet's Sari Ostrum, as much as the viewers did. The pair's lifts were gorgeous, accented by Ostrum's endearing elegance. Their moving performance to close Act I was a show-stopper."[2] Other performances that stood out included those of Elizabeth Reisinger ("a poised, ever-graceful Christmas Spirit"), Hayley Meier ("you could rarely take your eyes off [her] as the infectiously joyous, naturally outgoing Clara"), and "of the many memorable character dancers and actors, Tara Lally's 'Russian Trepak' and Alexandra Johnson's 'Arabian' ranked at the top." High praise also was accorded the youngest members of the cast, who trained rigorously for weeks with buns always expertly in place. "If Mother Gigogne's baker's dozen of acrobatic clowns was a joy, so were the littlest dancers: the baby angels and tiny, trumpet-tooting pages." Along with Rochester City Ballet's sixteen company members, it was reported that "a dozen character actors and a hundred children joined the cast from the Draper Studio of Dance, along with children from five other local studios." Vocal accompaniment for the Snow Scene was provided by the Churchville-Chili Women's Chorus.

Apparent to everyone connected in some way with the production was that the behind-the-scenes operation resembled a well-oiled machine. Parents who were being exposed to Rochester City Ballet for the first time were astonished at its high degree of professionalism, which in some ways resembled government advance work. Nothing was left to chance. Parents were expected to attend meetings and sign myriad forms and releases to ensure that they were familiar with everything from tight security measures to their duties as volunteers. A few parents could be overhead grumbling that "once was enough," due the rigors of participation, but the other 99 percent were thrilled with the opportunity to have their children be a part of something so special. They were willing to turn over the next eight to ten years of their lives to chauffeur, support, put up hair, and do whatever else might be needed if their children, did in fact, get the "bug."

The end of the decade was bringing other changes, as well. The board of directors, an individually and collectively talented and dedicated organization on whom Tim had relied as his "nearest and dearest" for developing the company into the best ballet company in Western New York, had to expand significantly to achieve all of the ambitious plans needed to bring Rochester City Ballet to an even higher level. In addition, a five-year strategic plan was being called for, a project that would be placed firmly in the capable hands of Elizabeth

Skender, the chair emerita. Along with the board president, Michael Snyder, she had brokered the deal with the RPO.

The dynamo Kate Lipsky, who had been appearing as Frau Stahlbaum in the RCB production of *The Nutcracker* for several years and had been asked to join the board in the late nineties, was very excited at the continued critical acclaim the company was receiving and shared fully in Tim's dreams for the future. A true cultural arts rainmaker in Rochester, with vision, infectious enthusiasm, and a strong head on her shoulders, Kate was passionate about broadening the scope of the city's only ballet company. Working in close concert with other prominent, forward-thinking movers and shakers such as Susanne Kennedy of Naples, she soon clarified the idea for an advisory board comprising ballet lovers from the Canandaigua area. Led by Susanne, the new group included Pamela Burger, Michelle Carson, Sue Dickens, Lauren Dixon, Sue Evans, Zoe Fackleman, Margaret Farnsworth, Leslie Kennedy, Barbara Koelling, Pat Regester, Stency Wegman, and Prudy Whitehead. It hosted an extraordinarily successful fund-raiser that not only established a new development mindset within the organization but also accorded it the talents and advice of some of the area's most influential arts lovers who were very impressed with Tim and what he was doing to provide the region with outstanding ballet.

Kate worked indefatigably over the next several years on behalf of the company, serving as board member and sitting on several subcommittees to ensure that work progressed in a timely manner. She was particularly adept at bringing new blood to the organization and tapping community leaders and her many friends (usually one and the same) to assist her in this worthiest of causes. She also understood the importance of bringing in not only arts aficionados but also strategic-thinking executives who could promote growth within the organization, even if they didn't know a *plié* from a *ronde de jambe*. She was very successful in this regard, and many of the corporate sponsors' names appear in the preperformance announcements today as a direct result of her tenacity in bringing in the right kind of support to help bring Tim's dreams to fruition.

Tim naturally adored and trusted Kate, frequently telling others that he wished he had "ten of her." He listened when she advocated the staging of an audience-grabbing *Dracula* over the more traditional *Coppélia* for the greater pizzazz potential at the box office and always appreciated being introduced to her many friends who were eager to attend performances of the company's now glorious and expansive repertoire.

Kate played a critical role in helping provide the leadership to bring on a development professional to launch an annual fund, a capital campaign, and personally to run an upscale boutique to complement the onstage productions (replete with original, visually stunning Nancy Sands photographs, hand-crafted tutus, tiaras, Cinderella wands, jewelry, dolls, retired shoes donated by company members, and logo-inspired attire of all kinds that would rival the inventory of any boutique of any major ballet company in the country). Much like the irrepressible title character of *Mame*, Kate during this period was a catalyst for taking the company forward, bringing in the right partners with her energy and optimism to achieve ambitious but realistic goals.

In addition to this exciting behind-the-scenes activity, another dancer was getting ready to "fly the coop" to another world-class organization. Kristi Boone had begun training with Tim as a thirteen-year-old. Sharon McDaniel reported in the *Democrat and Chronicle*, "[Kristi] had recently won one of the few, highly competitive openings in the world-famous American Ballet Theatre, based in Manhattan. Boone, while still attending Fairport High School, earned top awards at national dance competitions. Before graduating in 1999, she performed the title role in *Firebird*, and was a soloist in *Cinderella* and *Nutcracker* productions."[3]

At the same time, there was more good news. Aesha Ash, who had been training at the School of American Ballet for five years, had just been offered a position with New York City Ballet. Tim was absolutely thrilled at these two back-to-back announcements. Those in the studio at the time could not help but notice just a little more bounce in his step and a grin that wouldn't quit, particularly anytime anyone mentioned his Kristi or Aesha.

On the home front, however, sometimes he was engaged in a battle of wills with his teenage dancers, who occasionally had something other than dance on their minds. "The teenage years," recalled one mother who knew the situation intimately,

> were also difficult for Tim as many of the girls all of a sudden had boyfriends and were interested in dating. This was a great distraction in his eyes, lest the intense focus he demanded of them be threatened with this new diversion. There was also that one dancer who was tardy or didn't show up for class. If he hadn't heard that the student was in the hospital, the consequence was a humiliating scolding in front of classmates upon their return with an angry phone call home in between. There was also usually an added punishment of a

Several Members of Tim's beloved professional division in the late 1990s. *In front left to right:* Natalia Malley-Masten, Lisa Hunt, and Jenna Kosowski. *In back:* Kristi Boone, Sari Ostrum, Tara Lally, and Jill Marlow, rehearsing for Jamey Leverett's *White Rabbit.* Courtesy of Rebekah von Rathonyi.

demotion in class levels. The unfortunate student would have to take classes regularly beneath his or her level until Tim felt they [*sic*] had paid their dues.

As with previous generations of his dancers, the placement of professional responsibilities on the shoulders of high school students, who understandably wanted to experience all that life had to offer, brought with it inevitable conflict. Tim had succeeded in developing a program capable of creating young artist after artist at a level and rate that was unprecedented. Ultimately, it would be up to each dancer to determine if the sacrifices were worth it.

The Cinderella Court, Season Fairies (*clockwise from top*): Natalia Malley-Masten as the Summer Fairy, Meredith Seeley as the Winter Fairy, Alexandra Johnson as the Autumn Fairy, and Jenna Kosowski as the Spring Fairy. Tara Lally (*center*) is shown as the Fairy Godmother. Photograph by Nancy Sands. Costumes by Jacquelyn Ostrum.

NATALIA MALLEY-MASTEN

Tim Draper wore many hats for us. Teacher, choreographer, mentor, friend and even foe. Looking back, Tim was tough on all of us. But would we have wanted it any other way? Yes, there were times when fewer tears would have felt better, but those tears prepared us for the road to come.

When I was fifteen years old, the tendonitis in my hips was so bad that my mother had to dress me in the morning, but I would not stop taking class. Tim suspended me from the company, which made me so upset. Years later he told my mother that suspending me was the only way I would heal and if I was angry with him for a little while, he was okay with that. Our health and growth were his concern, not giving us a free pass.

For me, Tim was like a father. He was well aware of the very difficult relationship I had with my own father, and he stepped up to the plate without having to be asked. He protected me when mine fell short. The strength and courage Tim gave my mother and me during those trying times will never be forgotten.

One memory that stands out was during my first season with a ballet company in Hartford. It was the fall before Tim passed, and I was often complimented on my technique and artistry. I owed these compliments to Tim. Since I had never really thanked him for what he had done for me since I was six years old, I wrote him a letter. I thanked him for the praise I had received and for all the years of guidance. After he passed, I remember Jamey telling me how much that letter meant to him. And while we still remember some tears, we remember the strength he gave us more.

We love you, Tim.

Natalia began dancing professionally at the age of fourteen with the Rochester City Ballet, performing many leading roles in *The Nutcracker*, *Cinderella*, *Don Quixote*, *Firebird*, *Gaîté Parisienne*, *Sleeping Beauty*, and numerous original works created for the company. More recently, she has performed with Albano Ballet in Hartford in a repertoire of original works choreographed by Joseph Albano, and with MergeDance Theatre.

When Natalia was twelve years old, Tim chose her to be his Clara. Anyone who used to stop by the Rochester City Ballet table at the Corn Hill Festivals during the earliest years of the new millennium will remember a beautiful young ballerina in a sea of yellow. That was Natalia as the Summer Fairy in RCB's *Cinderella*.

13

GOING TO THE BALL

O f the many dancers Tim developed into artists of the finest caliber over the years (and there were scores of them, many of whose names fill these pages), one dancer truly was his muse. That was Sari Ostrum, an exquisite blonde, blue-eyed beauty who came to Tim as a five-year old with a work ethic and technique so extraordinary in a young dancer that even American Ballet Theatre's Kevin McKenzie told her after she had joined American Ballet Theatre, "When you are onstage, I cannot take my eyes off you." It is generally considered a part of Draper Studio lore that not only did Sari race through the levels in unprecedented fashion but that she also possessed every single gift that could possibly be bestowed on a ballet dancer (perhaps symbolically not a little unlike the gifts the good fairies bestowed at the infant Aurora's christening in *The Sleeping Beauty*). From the moment the young daughter of Jacquelyn (Jackie) Fulreader Ostrum, Tim's old friend from Mercury Ballet days, came to the studio, Tim, Jamey, Sally Stepnes, Julianne Deming, and the rest of the faculty knew that they had someone special in their midst. Years later, when Tim wanted the company's publicity apparatus do some community outreach at Rochester's legendary summer festivals, the volunteers would turn to a large, color poster of Sari to craft a display that placed an inspired image of her *développé a la seconde* front and center.

Jamey, in particular, took Sari under her wing to mentor her. Eventually, the two became very close friends.

Sari was only in her mid-teens when she had already danced solo and principal roles in RCB's *The Nutcracker, Gaîté Parisienne, Firebird, Gershwin in the Park,* and *Inner Voices.* She was regularly selected to attend summer programs on scholarship. These programs included the Chautauqua Institute, the School of American Ballet, and American Ballet Theatre, where she was named the Coca-Cola Scholar of the

Year and an American Ballet Theatre National Training Scholar for the years 1997–99.

Sari was a standout among standouts, performing most major roles in the company's repertoire, with several set on her, including the title role of *Cinderella* in 2000 and Jamey Leverett's tribute to Tim after his death, *Pedestal*, in which Sari portrayed Jamey. The younger dancers coming up in the Draper studio would watch her rehearse and look on her with unabashed awe; her graciousness to them made them want to try all the harder. It is no surprise that she developed into a well-loved teacher, both within the Draper studio and at other studios. In the summer of 2012, she invited one hundred of her dancers to perform at her fairy-tale wedding, which took place on the lush grounds of her childhood home.

The expectations for such a gifted individual had to be enormous, not only from Tim and his staff but the media. Most 14–15 year olds are not referred to in the press as "current principal dancers" but Sari projected such an aura about her that chronological age simply did not signify.

Sari was such a stunning performer that toward the end of the 1990s, Tim began to think about taking her to compete in the fabled Prix de Lausanne International Ballet Competition. In the spring, he also set the title role of *Cinderella* on her. Much ado surrounded both events. The international competition required meticulous preparation with magnificent costumes to match. Simultaneously, the entire studio committed itself in "all hands on deck" fashion to manage all of the necessary preparations involved in mounting a new ballet. Thus the year 2000 began with Tim, Jamey, and Sari flying to Lausanne after Sari was selected from a pool of the greatest young dancers in the world, following a DVD submission.

Sari made an excellent impression on the panel of international judges, offered scholarships to the prestigious Vienna State Opera and the Stuttgart Ballet Schools. Along with the American Ballet Theatre's own interest in her as a future member of their company, as evidenced by her selection as a National Training Scholar, no further affirmation was needed to show that she was headed toward a most prominent professional career in dance.

With *Cinderella* next up, RCB's publicity committee of the board of directors, chaired by Tim's partner, Randy Stringer (a finance executive who was also a skilled marketer avocationally), went into high gear to build excitement for the new ballet, which was to have its premiere

Sari Ostrum rehearses with her partner as a young teen in the ABT Studios where she trained summers on full scholarship as a recipient of the Coca Cola Scholarship. Courtesy of Jacquelyn Ostrum.

in May. In addition to the affable Randy, the committee consisted entirely of dancers' mothers—not a bad plan, considering that there has yet to be found a constituency more passionate about advancing their children's interests. The primary task at hand was to create a high visibility "Slipper Search," a citywide scavenger hunt to mirror Cinderella's own search. The Slipper Search took place throughout the months leading up to the production. *City Newspaper* readers would be given periodic clues to help them find their own metaphorical glass slipper. The winner would receive a package of princely proportions for his or her efforts, including orchestra tickets to the Auditorium Center and an overnight at a bed and breakfast, appropriately located on Rochester's Prince Street. With no shortage of creativity, business development savvy, or networking talent within the committee, the clues were inspired, and the assembled package of goods that had been procured strictly by volunteers was worth thousands of dollars.

In tandem with the contest, the board was preparing for a glorious Cinderella Ball to take place at the venerable Oak Hill Country Club. Without question, this production indicated the level of confidence the community now had in its resident ballet company and the degree

Tim rehearsing principal dancers, Sari Ostrum and Jason Kittelberger for
Cinderella. Photograph by Nancy Sands.

to which Tim had created an absolutely astonishing number of artists.
Inspiring Tim and Jamey on the production from start to finish was
National Technical Institute for the Deaf Artist in Residence, the late
gifted choreographer Michael Thomas, on whose choreography and
staging the Rochester City Ballet production was based. He was a good
friend and an exceptional artist. The program, a marvelous triumph
for all, was dedicated posthumously to him.

The dance critic Herbert Simpson had high praise for the production, referring to it as "good enough to tour" with Sari Ostrum as a
"charming Cinderella" and Jason Kittelberger partnering "her solidly,
looking entranced with his beautiful princess." Simpson went on to say
that Thomas Baird and Brian Norris were scene-stealing Ugly Stepsis-
ters in the English tradition (more than the Russian original).

Norris plays his Stepsister with more feminine glamour than usual in the role, but his impeccably timed slapstick [well honed by his years with Les Ballets Trockadero de Monte Carlo] was very funny. Jamey Leverett's authoritative Stepmother got all the necessary comedy without any of the overacting that other Cinderella ballets usually offer in this role. The company's showy *demi-caractère* dancer, Jimmy Rodriguez-Jimenez, provided highlights as the Dance Master and Jester. And of the more than 20 gifted company members and another two dozen students, all performing well, a few should be singled out. Tara Lally as the Fairy Godmother, Jenna Kosowski, Alexandra Johnson, Jill Marlow, and especially Natalia Malley-Masten danced solos and ensemble-work that any regional ballet company would be proud of. The refinement of their bearing and technique is dazzling in dancers so young.[1]

Sari joined American Ballet Theatre's Studio Company in 2000 and performed in the corps de ballet from 2001 to 2002, dancing in such signature ballets as *Swan Lake, Giselle, Eugene Onegin, La Bayadère, Don Quixote*, Balanchine's *Symphony in C*, and *The Nutcracker*. In 2006, she choreographed *Romance by Mozart* and variations with the organist Hans Davidsson in Goteborg, Sweden, and performed it for Princess Désirée of Sweden.

Throughout the summer of 2000, wanting to capitalize on the momentum that had been generated by *Cinderella* and wanting the company to continue being a visible part of the community at all times, the publicity committee first set its sights on the Corn Hill Arts Festival, followed by the Clothesline Arts Festival at the Memorial Art Gallery. Frank Hyland, the grandfather of principal dancer Hayley Meier, constructed a magnificent traveling backdrop for use at these events. Along with his artistic wife, Anne, his daughter Janet Meier, myself, and many other volunteers did their upmost to promote the company at every turn.

That October, Tim's reputation took a leap onto the national stage with a cover story, "The Curtain Rises on The Draper School," in the October 2000 issue of *DanceTeacher* magazine, written by Jeanne Palmer-Fornarola. In an article augmented by glorious photography furnished by Timothy Leverett—including photos of Kristi Boone, who had just joined American Ballet Theatre's corps de ballet two months earlier, Tara Lally, Sari Ostrum, Laura Kenney, Jill Marlow, and Alanna Lipsky—Tim was profiled in high form, explaining his philosophy as well as giving direction to his dancers.

"At this February's North American Ballet Festival in Boston, one school swept the top five scoring places," began the article. "This studio's dancers were technically impeccable, self-assured and professional in their demeanor. They cavorted through difficult choreography as if it were easy: their turns were multiple with clean finishes and their extensions sky-high. The dancers had the sleekness and agility of students in a rigorous pre-professional program, yet they didn't come from a major urban center. They were instead the advanced students of the Draper School of Dance in Rochester, NY." Sarah Lane was awarded first place and the Capezio Class Excellence Award.

The reporter went on to describe how Tim had returned to find his hometown community badly in need of a professional school and how he had founded his studio in 1986 to meet that need. She particularly homed in on his past training with the Trocks as a key to his success. "Draper's experience dancing with Ballet Trockadero, an all-male comedy ballet company, gave him a personal understanding of pointe-work that is rare in a male teacher. 'I also gained a sense of humor working with Ballet Trockadero,' he says. 'If you can't laugh at your art form, I think you are taking it too seriously.'"

However, his seriousness of pursuit was on full display as he discussed the school philosophy and the standards that he had set for himself, his staff, and his students.

> I wanted a school of the highest level of classical ballet and dance that also taught the virtues of life. . . . Fifty percent of our students go on to pursue careers as professional dancers, but no matter what their career path, what they learn here will help them in the future. . . . Children today want instant gratification. We teach that the more you put into something, the more you get out of it. Time management, memory skills, commitment, and focus are all old-fashioned values that I'm trying to re-instill. Whether you are going to dance professionally or for a hobby, these are the ingredients for a successful human being.

Fornarola was additionally impressed by the quality of professional companies that had hired Draper graduates to that point. In addition to Rochester City Ballet, they were dancing with New York City Ballet, Joffrey Ballet of Chicago, Milwaukee Ballet, Pittsburgh Ballet, Pennsylvania Ballet, American Ballet Theatre, Hubbard Street Dance Chicago, Garth Fagan Dance, and River North. "Success begets success," she said in conclusion, "and the Draper Studio continues to grow and develop as a premier training ground for dancers as well as an up-and-coming regional ballet company."

With rehearsals well underway for *Nutcracker*, after a previous highly successful appearance at the Clothesline Arts Festival sponsored by the Rochester Memorial Art Gallery, the studio was thriving. Notwithstanding his own personal health demons, Tim was at the top of his game. Just as the previous season witnessed a most magnificent collaboration with the RPO, the 2000 *Nutcracker* reviews continued to be as yummy as the bon-bons that graced the scenery. It had been a most satisfying year. For the 2000–2001 season, several new faces had been added to the board, equally committed to bringing ballet of the highest order to the region as the members who had preceded them. In addition to the Canandaigua Guild, they included Lynn Barber, Fran Gersbach, Laurie Ganon, Dr. Nancy (Nana) Bennett, Dr. Roberto Baun Corales, Lauren Gerber, Anne Harvey, Earl Kage, Fayga Press, and Nancy Sands. Dr. Allan O'Grady Cuseo had agreed to continue to serve as president emeritus and Elizabeth Skender would remain on as chair emerita.

And as the season was put to bed, possibly this time with visions of sugar plums firmly in place, no one could have sensed that the carpet was about to be yanked out from underneath them all.

Tim Draper "fixing" one of his beloved professional-division dancers, Erin Bellis. Courtesy of Dona Bellis.

ERIN BELLIS

Tim was a strong figure in my life. Growing up, I was definitely intimidated by him, but this helped me to grow stronger. He expected perfection from us. I would get so frustrated sometimes because I didn't think I could deliver what he wanted all the time. What I soon came to realize is that he believed in and wanted the best for me. I am so grateful he gave me the opportunity to work with him. His influence helped me become the person I am today. As a child, I was afraid of everything. His tenacity helped me get beyond my fears and focus on doing my best. It wasn't just with dancing, but in my everyday life. I was better able to focus and do well in school, which had always been a challenge for me. I loved that he was such a strong figure but that there was also a softer side. One thing he was known to do was give all of us nicknames. He said mine out of nowhere one day and called me Ding Dong. At first, we all looked at him confused and didn't understand why he called me that. He then said, "Well, her last name is Bellis. So Bells. . . . bells go ding dong. Get it?" Of course we all laughed and that nickname stuck throughout the rest of my time there. It always made me smile when I heard him say this. I will also never forget the two kimonos hanging up in the main studio of the old building. He would always ask us what the difference was between the two. Of course we would say the obvious; the colors were different. He would get mad because we were not looking at the closer details. He would soon explain to us the fine details on each kimono that made them different and unique. A lesson like this helped me look at the finer details in life and to not settle for simple answers. Tim passed in the middle of my senior year. There were things I never had the opportunity to thank him for. If I were to write him a letter this is what I would want to say.

Dear Tim,

You made such an impact on my life, and I want to thank you for everything you did for me. You never ceased to surprise me. This was the great and unique quality about you. I was too old by one month to dance at the Prix de Lausanne. I thought you were crazy when you suggested that I forge my birth certificate. You were so determined to have me in the competition. Of course this could not be possible (my mom did not want to see us both land in jail), but I was so excited you were even considering me. I thank you for that.

There was always something new I could learn from you. At first, I didn't understand what you wanted out of me, but as I got older I saw that you loved us and wanted the best for us. I will always remember the day you pulled me into the office to have a meeting while training in the 1997 summer program. I was sure I was in trouble. The last thing I expected was to receive a scholarship to join the school full time. I was shocked and honored to be able to receive the best possible training from you. I knew you would help perfect my technique, but you did more. Your discipline helped me become a strong, disciplined, resilient person. I learned to think independently and be confident in whatever I set my sights on. I've carried this throughout my everyday life. I remember the lessons you taught us. I keep them with me for whatever life throws my way. I always want to do my best and deliver the best product. I try to stay on an even keel and leave my baggage at the door—one quality that has helped me manage a business. You allowed and even encouraged us to speak our minds and not hold back. I am definitely one to say what's on my mind and am grateful to you for developing this confidence. You will always mean so much to me. I miss you, even ten years after your passing. You were taken from this life far too soon. I am so honored to have known you and to have been one of your students.

Love, Bellis

Erin Bellis was such a memorable dancer with RCB that when people approached her after a performance to inquire about how old she was and the reply turned out to be only fifteen, a large sigh of relief could be heard. Her fans knew that they would be able to catch her performances for at least a few more years.

14

A NEW HOME FOR A NEW DECADE

"Ballet Troupe on Slippery Ground"

No one was prepared for the *Democrat and Chronicle* headline of February 14, 2001. The veteran reporter Stuart Low reported that "The Rochester City Ballet, western New York's leading professional dance company, is scrambling to find a new home as its studio faces possible demolition. The troupe's rented headquarters at 320A N. Goodman St. was recently sold to the adjacent Village Gate Square. The popular mall will take possession on June 1 and might raze all or part of the building to create parking space, says owner Gary Stern."[1]

This was hardly the valentine the school and the company needed, particularly because despite its warehouse appearance, for over fourteen years the studio had been a beloved second home to everyone connected with the organization, housing rich memories, tradition, costumes, beautiful old floors, photos, and irreplaceable paraphernalia, much of which would be lost, as is the case when any type of move takes place.

It was ironic that the news came directly on the heels of four studio triumphs: Sarah Lane repeating her performance as the first-place winner of the North American Ballet Festival and Capezio Class Excellence Award; Katie Lally taking the fourth-place high score overall for her division with others performing at a predictably very high level; special performances of *Peter and The Wolf* being staged on February 3, with a second performance scheduled for March 10 in Geneva's Smith Opera House; and Jamey Leverett being selected by New Choreographers on Point: Ballet Builders as one of the top emerging choreographers working in the United States. Leverett was invited to showcase her work in New York City's French Institute Alliance Française. She brought eight professional-division dancers along with her lighting designer, Gordon Estey, for a well-received performance of *Overtones,* featuring Erin Bellis, Alexandra Johnson, Yoshi Kobayashi, Sarah Lane, Natalia Malley-Masten, Jill Marlow, Jillian Nealon, and Jessica Tretter.

With regard to the building crisis, Tim's overwhelming concern at the moment was the thought that everything might be lost if a suitable new building was not found or could not be financed. As he told Stuart Low, "We're in a desperate mode. I've spent 13 years building this company's reputation, and now it could all go down. I can't even find interim space to use while we search for a permanent home." Even the dancers were worried. Said Sarah Lane, who had emerged as Tim's latest star and who would be dancing the title role of *Cinderella* in the upcoming performance three months later, "I would be very sorry to see it close," said Sarah, who hoped to become a professional dancer. "You receive very good technical training here, and I need to continue that." Losing that momentum would assuredly be catastrophic for her and her young colleagues, who depended on the studio as their way of life. Particularly difficult about finding space for the school and company (which, according to the article, had "gained prestige in the past two years for its *Nutcracker* performances with the Rochester Philharmonic Orchestra . . . [and] its feeder school, the Draper Center for Dance Education, [which] now trains 250 students and [an] international summer workshop for about 100 dancers"), was the fact that dancers have special physical requirements that inform all decision making. "They can't rehearse in spaces with posts or other structural supports that could turn a pirouette into a fractured leg. And because children take evening lessons at the studio, it would require ample parking and well-lighted streets. The cost of building a new facility would be exorbitant," Tim told Low.

As bad as the news was, however, it became a rallying cry to the troops. The board jumped in headfirst with calls for a capital campaign, an expanded annual fund, and with a spirit of exigency surrounding the organization, which at the exact same time was distinguishing itself with one exceptional artistic accolade after another. Everyone felt the need to contribute in any manner possible. And Tim did his part in keeping up his own spirits by reminding himself that his first purpose was to continue to bring out everyone's personal best, both in his own studio and at SUNY Brockport's dance department. To that end, Tim asked one of his most promising eleven-year-old dancers, Brittany Shinay, if she might attend the master class he was planning to teach at Brockport "so that I can show all those college students what real technique looks like." Positively thrilled to be invited, Brittany asked if she could bring along a friend or two. Permission was granted and Brittany, Sarah Hillmon, and Katie Rose Owerbach remained on Cloud 9 for the rest of that year.

One very profound but underutilized gift that Tim had in his artistic arsenal at this time was his old friend from the Crofton years, Donna Ross, whom he had brought back to Rochester a few years earlier to both teach and serve as his ballet mistress. After a stellar performance career with the Joffrey, Donna had turned to teaching with very fine results. Along the way, she had obtained a BA in Italian from Columbia University, which enabled her to provide the students with the essential back story of their art form, much in the manner of Tim and Fiona Fairrie. Donna also had a plethora of good ideas to garner both expanded funding and exposure for RCB. She was interviewed by the local affiliate of National Public Radio and proved to be a superb on-air personality and did much to engage the listenership on behalf of the company.

It was at this time that an individual with tremendous vision and strong ties to the organization as its most gracious and dedicated company photographer offered to take on an expanded role to help the company. A dancer who had studied at American Ballet Theatre years earlier, Nancy Sands was a natural as a dance photographer. She spent entire weekends during each *Nutcracker* season in her own photography studio, taking shot after shot of hundreds of dancers, from the smallest students selected to perform with the company to company principals, both in individual poses and in groups. Tireless in her enthusiasm and a highly skilled professional, as well, she quickly became a beloved member of the Draper/Rochester City Ballet community. Her photos were extraordinary because not only was she able to suggest poses that were attractive and consistent with the choreography (which she had previously observed during rehearsal) but she also was able to capture the movement at the perfect moment to show off the dancers' technique, an ability quite rare in a photographer.

Not surprisingly, the marketing arm of the organization quickly came to the realization that Nancy's exceptional gifts could also be a wonderful visibility tool for promoting the dancers in their schools and the community, which the dancers enjoyed because the rigorous nature of their lives usually precluded involvement in school-based extracurricular activities. They were excited to have their schoolmates see them in promotional pieces regarding their various upcoming company productions. The increased exposure also helped to sell tickets.

Nancy was naturally also very concerned about the fate of the school and company. As the need for space became more pressing, she and her husband, Rob, made a magnanimous decision to help out Tim and his company with a financial gift that was truly unprecedented for the organization. Overnight, it transformed the entire dialogue concerning the survival of the company, galvanizing everyone into doing their part to bring the new building to reality.

Along with many others, I, too, wanted to help Tim, and after mentioning the building plight one day to Bob O'Leary, my best friend from our earlier days as aides at the New York State Assembly, he reminded me of one of the great marvels of New York State government, the Supplemental Budget! After I explained to Tim that state monies might be available to solve the building issue, our job was to make the case that Rochester City Ballet was worthy of receiving this type of funding. A meeting was convened at the offices of Assemblyman Joseph Morelle, a budding superstar in the Assembly. He had already earned an excellent reputation as one of the key drivers behind New York State's revitalization through his role as chair of the Assembly's Committee on Tourism, Arts, and Sports Development. In attendance were Tim Draper, Nancy Sands, Rob Sands, and myself. After we explained our plight, we made a formal request to secure state funding. Between Assemblyman Morelle's excellent efforts and his suggestion that the state senate might also help out (which it ultimately did, thanks to the hard work of State Senator James Alesi), the company was able to obtain a building. For the remainder of that year and into the next, Nancy and I sought out commercial real estate. In concert with the board (on which Nancy sat), we procured corporate donors and did everything possible to help find the troupe a new home. Although Tim never saw his goal of moving into a new home realized, he did have the satisfaction of knowing that monies would be available and that his life's efforts would not be for naught.

While these building issues were taking place, preparations were underway for a reprise of *Cinderella*, to be staged at the Auditorium Theatre as Rochester City Ballet's Spring 2001 production. This time, the ballet would feature Sarah Lane in the title role with swan-song performances by the company's stable of stars. Eight of them were due to graduate a month later and move on to either their first professional engagements or to BFA dance programs at prestigious colleges across the United States.

Again, the production was hailed as an artistic masterpiece. The WHAM 1180 arts critic, Bill Klein, or "the Klein" as he was affectionately known, was unequivocal in his praise: "With 10 being excellent, this is an 11." Mindful of the level of talent gracing the stage and behind the scenes, the company also thought it an ideal opportunity to use the production as a marketing and advancement vehicle. Although many community leaders were aware of Rochester City Ballet through its annual *Nutcracker*, particularly after the collaborations with the RPO began, they had not yet been introduced to another full-story ballet by the company. *Cinderella* could not have been a better choice. Many dignitaries did choose to come downtown to see "what all the fuss was about" and walked away very satisfied and committed to helping out the company in any way that they could. A small team also spearheaded a successful group sales effort. For the first time, discounted rates were offered by e-mail to corporations and institutions throughout the community, aided in huge measure by the glorious Sands photos that were arriving in mailboxes throughout town. The program was also made available to the company's most faithful constituency, its parents. Now this loyal group could buy tickets in bulk at attractive rates in advance, thereby insuring a strong presale and saving the company from having to depend so much on same-day purchases at the door.

At this time, one of the region's most prominent advertising agencies, Dixon Schwabl Associates, became involved with the organization as its pro bono PR and marketing agency of record, thereby providing Tim and members of his leadership team with the full measure of their expertise. Included in their offerings were strategic planning, the development of high-impact collateral, a new logo, and other visuals that would draw the community in. In addition, the agency was responsible for the creation of a gorgeous development folder whose cover featured a radiant Jill Marlow as the Dew Drop, and on the inside, another lovely photo of dancer Jillian Nealon, with a collage of articles, laudatory letters, and even a letter written in longhand by Sarah Lane, asking for company support. The folder went a long way toward facilitating the donation effort.

Cinderella was once again an exquisite production. It more than lived up to its stunning preview coverage by the *Democrat and Chronicle*, and the reviews were very favorable. With a big sigh of relief that such a costly production had ultimately done no discernible damage to the books, thoughts became centered on the bittersweet end-of-year

June demonstration. Tim, Jamey, and Kathy bade farewell to several of the finest artists the studio had ever nurtured, then turned their attention to the widely attended summer intensive, which spanned July and August.

On Saturday and Sunday, September 8 and 9, 2001, at 1:00 p.m., the Rochester City Ballet performed at the Clothesline Arts Festival. as it had for many years. to packed outdoor audiences in front of the magnificent old main entryway to the Memorial Arts Gallery. The performances were very successful, and feelings ran high. No one could imagine the evil that would follow only two days later.

The horrific tragedy of 9/11 hit everyone at the studio personally. When news of the calamity was announced, Tim, knowing how many of his loved ones lived in the city, began making frantic phone calls to ascertain everyone's whereabouts and safety. He was devastated to learn, as was the rest of the studio that one of his most diligent professional division dancers and company members, Kelsey Buchanan, had lost a beloved brother that day. Kelsey would most bravely soldier on with extraordinary inner strength and grace, taking class after class and performing with every fiber of her being as she always had, but now bearing a cross that no one should ever have to bear.

The company performed *The Nutcracker* with its usual panache in 2001, but this time with a very heavy heart.

Jill Marlow as the Dew Drop in Rochester City Ballet's inaugural 1999 year at the Eastman Theatre in performance with the Rochester Philharmonic Orchestra. Photograph by Nancy Sands.

JILL MARLOW

I often wish that I could pick up the phone and ask Tim questions. I often fantasize about a conversation between the two of us over a cup of coffee or a glass of wine. I am often reminded of his voice in my head before I take off for a pirouette (especially when nothing else will help me get on my leg). When it feels right, I dedicate a show to him in the wings before I make my first entrance. I'm constantly reminded of his once huge involvement and presence in my life. It's impossible to ignore and, more important, impossible to forget, the impact he has on my dancing, and me as a whole person.

Tim would often tell us, "If you can handle this, then you can handle anything!" His plan was to make us strong and resilient, because he knew very well that life wouldn't always be a bowl full of cherries. Even though it took me time (okay, years) to initiate a truer understanding of his motives, I always knew that he loved and intended the best for us.

Personally, I think Tim was proud of me when I stood up for myself. He knew that in uncomfortable or difficult situations, I would naturally want to hide in my shyness, and so he made sure that didn't happen or become too habitual to stop me from excelling. Even if he knew I would roll my eyes, he would be that teacher anyway. (Once he said to me, "If you roll those eyes one more time, Jill, than you can roll them down those stairs and out that door.") He didn't back down on the days when I wished that he would. He knew I would get over it, learn quickly from it and in the end, and love him more for it. He was absolutely, with no hesitation, right on!

One moment between Tim and me repeatedly flashes through my mind. It during was my final year of high school, after a run of Arabian in the large studio at the Goodman Street studio space. He choked up and told me I had come so far, and that he was proud of me. To this day, I can't help but think that he knew that I would make it, with or without him. His face couldn't deny it. Mine said back, "You will always be with me, Tim."

Jill Marlow Krutzkamp is presently a company member of Kansas City Ballet. After a highly distinguished career with Rochester City Ballet and additional training with American Ballet Theatre and the Boston Ballet and at Indiana University, Jill danced professionally with Pittsburgh Ballet Theatre and Cincinnati Ballet. Some of her most notable roles have included Juliet in *Romeo and Juliet*'s balcony *pas de deux*, the Lilac Fairy in *Sleeping Beauty*, the Fairy Godmother in *Cinderella*, Titania in *A Midsummer Night's Dream*, Stomper in Twyla Tharp's *In the Upper Room*, Waltz Girl in *Serenade*, and Marie in Val Caniparoli's *Nutcracker*. She holds a BS in health promotion and education from the University of Cincinnati. A most beautiful and reliable Dew Drop for Tim and Jamey during RCB's seminal *Nutcracker* season with the RPO, she showed the true meaning of grace under pressure when she was requested to learn brand new choreography just moments before the dress rehearsal—all of which was accomplished effortlessly with a wink and a smile.

15

LIVING THE DREAM

DANCE REVIEW

Promising Young Talent on Display, With or Without Music
By Jack Anderson, *New York Times*, May 15, 2002

Dance students shared the stage with experienced professionals
when Youth America Grand Prix held its 2002 gala and awards ceremony last Monday night at Alice Tully Hall. The competition, for
classical and contemporary ballet students 8 to 19, was founded
in 1999 by Larissa and Gennadi Saveliev, former dancers with the
Bolshoi Ballet of Moscow. Mr. Saveliev is now with America Ballet
Theatre. An unusual feature of the competition is that it provides
some of the students with scholarships to American and European
ballet schools.

A panel of teachers and company directors awarded the Grand
Prix to Matthew Golding, a 16-year-old Canadian who has studied at
the Kirov Academy of Washington. Mr. Golding is to receive a contract with the ABT Studio Company, American Ballet Theatre's second company.

There were three special awards: to the Kirov Academy as outstanding school; to Tim Draper as Outstanding Teacher; and
Barry Hughson, outstanding choreographer. The gala featured
performances of classical and contemporary ballet snippets by
some of the students and Maria Kowroski of the New York City Ballet, Marcelo Gomes, Ethan Stiefel, Xiomara Reyes, and Mr. Saveliev of American Ballet Theatre; Desmond Richardson, a founder
of the company called Complexions; members of Momix, a contemporary troupe; and the ABT Studio Company. Students from
the Washington School of Ballet, last year's outstanding school,
danced Lynn Cote's "McYoYo." Roayn Kelly of City Ballet was honored as an emerging choreographer with a performance of his
gamelike "Times Three."

The evening, for which the actress and dancer Liliane Monte-
vecchi was the effusive host, put a lot of talent on display. But it

was not always displayed well. The program, which lasted almost four hours, started 30 minutes late, and a faulty sound system sabotaged taped accompaniment for several pieces, sometimes forcing performers to continue dancing in silence. They all deserved awards of A: for aplomb.

Thank goodness for the faulty sound system, because in addition to Tim Draper's being honored as outstanding teacher that magical night at Lincoln Center, another star was born: his Sarah Lane, who was awarded the bronze medal in the competition's senior division. It was she of whom Anderson spoke—the dancer who made the split-second decision to continue to dance her variation after the music had stopped! That she was able to execute it so flawlessly reflected not only her assured technique but also her superior musicality. The result was a rousing standing ovation by ballet's illuminati at the conclusion of her tacet variation as well as the admiration of Kevin McKenzie of American Ballet Theatre, who ultimately offered her a contract to join his Studio Company. What the review also failed to mention was the extreme level of competition, featuring exceptional teachers and their students from ballet schools the world over. The students previously had excelled at the regional level before moving on to the New York City finals. The adjudicators were true household names in the ballet universe. It is interesting to note that Youth America Grand Prix became an overnight sensation at its launch as an international competition, a "must do" competition for two compelling reasons: Larissa Saveliev and Gennadi Saveliev. Not only did the couple bring to their undertaking the impeccable personal credentials of the Bolshoi but also a true passion for helping elite students make the transition to professional status by providing them first with a showcase for their talent and then introducing them to the world's worthiest adjudicators and ballet company directors. The Savelievs' passion came through in a variety of ways. After the competition, Larissa sometimes continued to provide ongoing performance opportunities for or networked on behalf of exceptional students who might not have medaled on a particular night but whose talent, she felt, deserved company placement. Or Gennadi worked personally just minutes before the start of the Gala to find SRO space for mothers of dancers who hadn't realized that they were supposed to purchase tickets in advance to this traditional sold-out affair, so they could watch their progeny perform in a once-in-a-lifetime event at Alice Tully Hall. Although no one enjoys technical mishaps, if the worst that happened in 2002 was a rare glitch in the logistics department, it was more than compensated for by the enormous benefit of bringing together two key constituencies—those looking for jobs and those offering company contracts or scholarships to their feeder schools for the future of ballet and schools within its orbit. Today, much of the world not even connected with ballet knows about this storied competition through the 2012 movie *First Position.* Youth America Grand Prix has been hailed by the critics worldwide, stars in their own right who simply cannot get enough of this event, from *Dance Europe Magazine*'s Emma Manning ("Gala of Galas!") to *Dance Magazine*'s Wendy Perron's ("It's hard to pick highlights . . . the level started high and stayed high") to Clive Barnes of the *New York Post* ("The highlight of the New York dance season!) to the *Moscow Times*'s Jocelyn Noveck ("A truly impressive parade of artists").

For Sarah Lane, in particular, the competition was a chance for the world to see what everyone at the Draper Studio had known for years—that she was a star of huge potential destined to dance on the great stages of the world.

There is ample evidence that Tim deserved his award as Outstanding Teacher. In addition to Sarah, who won the bronze, four other of his dancers were honored at the highest levels. Thirteen-year-old Jim Nowakowski won the Junior Grand Prix award to such comments as "a dancer like that comes along once only every 40 years."[1] Jordan Drew, an eleven-year-old, won the Hope Award, the highest award in the precompetitive division. Two other exceptional dancers from the studio acquitted themselves in most marvelous fashion, with a Top 12 Award going to Tara Lally in the senior division's final round and a Top 12 Award going to Hayley Meier for the junior division. In addition, Jamey Leverett's new piece, *Push and Pull,* had been sent to the regionals to very high acclaim, with the result that all members of the ensemble were invited to the finals to present it before that august body of adjudicators and a New York audience.

The competition set the pace for the rest the year. Tim continued to collect accolade after accolade. If it didn't occur to most of the people that this was a race against the clock for the artistic genius, it assuredly did to his nearest and dearest, who were well aware of the fact that with his very bad heart, he was living on borrowed time. To everyone else, however, he projected the epitome of excellent health, working out regularly and continually enthusing about his next ballet or next project, what was going on in the dance world generally, and his next up-and-coming dancer. The Lifetime Achievement Award by the Arts and Cultural Council for Greater Rochester, conferred on Tim posthumously in 2004, was fitting recognition for what he had managed to achieve in such a short period of time.

Immediately on the heels of the triumphant Youth America Grand Prix came preparations for a significant regional competition in which over forty students from the studio danced, followed by the spring show. The show consisted of an act 1 mixed bill featuring Jamey's *Push and Pull* and Fiona Fairrie's *Fête de Printemps*. Act 2 was *Don Quixote*, starring Sarah Lane as Kitri. Particularly poignant about act 2 was that this was the last time for a while that local audiences could see Sarah perform. She had been selected to compete the following month in the prestigious USA International Ballet Competition in Jackson, Mississippi. Every four years, the crème de la crème of the ballet world descends on Jackson in true Olympic style. Students compete for prizes and company contracts before a host of legendary judges in what the *New York Times* hailed as "the most fiercely contested of them all."[2] It was a tremendous honor for Sarah to be accepted and recognition of the highest order for her outstanding teachers, as well. Tim and Jamey accompanied Sarah to Jackson. Prior to the two-week event, Sarah trained with her longtime friend and coach, Fiona Fairrie. Multiple variations needed to be prepared and costumes to be made. Jamey was busy choreographing Sarah's contemporary piece.

What made this extraordinary event even more exhilarating was the fact that Sarah had previously been named a Level 1 Winner for Dance in the National Foundation for the Advancement of the Arts (NFAA) Young Arts Dance Competition as well as a Presidential Scholar in the Arts. One of the special rewards of being a Presidential Scholar is participating in a performance before the president of the United States at the Kennedy Center in Washington, DC. That year's performance happened to fall right in the middle of the USA IBC at Jackson. Respectful of all that had been bestowed on her, Sarah made a whirlwind trip to Washington, where she performed for Vice President Richard M. Cheney (President Bush was out of town), met with US Senator Hillary Clinton, and then flew back to Jackson. The pace was nothing short of grueling, and she began to develop flu-like symptoms. Undaunted, she performed in true bravura fashion and was the silver medalist that year, the highest medal bestowed in the junior division. It was

Sarah Lane's exquisite performance wins her the highest medal bestowed at the prestigious USAIBC Jackson, June 2002. Here she is shown in the Paquita Variation, round 1 of the competition. Photograph by Richard Finkelstein.

only later that a diagnosis of mononucleosis was confirmed. The young champion had more than proved her mettle. Sarah soon left for New York to begin her career with American Ballet Theatre's Studio Company, where she would go on to take the dance world by storm.

And neither Tim's activity level nor his proclivity for bringing his best to world stages abated. Tim had been asked to bring his young male protégé Jim Nowakowski to Ukraine, where Jim thrilled audiences at the World Ballet Stars international festival in the early fall. This prestigious event had been launched in 1994 and was made famous by the appearance of the renowned Georgian dancer Nina Ananiashvili, as well as by top dancers from other world-class companies. The trip would always hold special meaning to the young star, who was off to see a part of the world he had never before been and where he would spend priceless one-on-one time with the mentor he adored like a second father. Tim was similarly ebullient about the trip, both going and coming. Notwithstanding the dramatic retelling of some thorny visa issues at the conclusion of the trip, he was aglow on his return.

Additional reminders that Tim and his Rochester City Ballet had finally reached prominence in the cultural community were the plethora of A-list invitations that were arriving: one from Garth Fagan requesting that Tim's dancers perform at St. Bonaventure University for an arts award honoring Fagan and another requesting a collaboration between his troupe and the Memorial Art Gallery for its celebrated Degas Exhibit. Jamey had also done the company proud once again with the creation of an electrifying medley entitled *Respect,* honoring the work of Aretha Franklin.

Meanwhile, back in the studio, the much-anticipated *Nutcracker* casting had been posted, with two twelve-year-olds, Brittany Monachino and Brittany Shinay, thoroughly overjoyed to learn that they had been cast in the role of Clara. The "BBs," as Tim liked to call them, were very good friends both inside and outside of the studio. They always cherished the fact that one time after a long rehearsal, Tim had called them "his next Sarah Lanes," promising them that he would take them to Jackson and then all over the world.

In 2002, the *Nutcracker* was in its fourth year of collaboration with the RPO—and for Tim, his last. It is particularly fitting that the production was reviewed by the critic Tim respected more than any other, the intellectual Herbert Simpson, who now was the theater and dance critic for *City Newspaper.*

A Sparkling Gift from Rochester Artists
by Herbert M. Simpson

Snow was gathering outside Eastman Theatre and onstage as the Rochester Philharmonic Orchestra and Rochester City Ballet gave us an early Christmas gift last weekend. Saturday night, I saw another extraordinary performance of the *Nutcracker* ballet. It was rewarding to a degree far beyond any appreciation born of boosterism or local pride. I've said that any major ballet company would be happy to have such young talent emerge as RCB artistic director Timothy Draper trains and regularly turns out. In fact, our nation's top companies have already hired a number of RCB alumni and lined up several current dancers for the future.

Guest artists this year included Company alumni Kristi Boone (now with American Ballet Theatre), Sarah Lane (of American Ballet Theatre's Studio Company), and Meredith Seeley (formerly of the St. Louis Ballet, recently moved to Chicago). I missed Boone and her partner, Isaac Stappas (also of ABT), but saw Lane partnered with ABT dancer Jared Matthews.

I can't overestimate the contribution of local guest artists The Bach Children's Chorus, whose singing punctuated the Snow Scene's Act I finale with a lovely counterpoint. Their director, Karla Krogstad, demonstrates sensitive rapport with the music and the balletic moment.

Unfortunately, gifted young conductor Michael Butterman wasn't given enough rehearsal time with the principal dancers, and evidently doesn't have much experience accompanying dancers. Butterman made Tschaikovsky's beautiful score swell thrillingly in the magical transformation scene, and brilliantly flit in and out of the sparkling Snowflake scene. But his tempi were out of synch with the rhythms and pace of several solo dancers, and erratic enough to cause them some trouble. It's a tough assignment, of course, to do justice to the music and also make it fit the complex stage action, which includes not only dancing, but pieces of scenery moving in and out and a Christmas "Spirit" who literally flies all over the stage.

Company principal Jessica Tretter danced (and flew) that role with appropriate magic. Other principal dancers included Timothy Lawler, who showed great stretch as the handsome male doll; Adam Kittleberger as both the Mouse King and danseur in the Italian Ice trio; and Derek Stratton as the virile, muscular partner of rubber-limbed principal Erin Bellis in the Arabian Dance. Alexandra Johnson, once RCB's pretty, young Clara, now studies and dances in SUNY–Purchase's professional dance program, and led the Spanish Dance with glamorous authority. Jimmy Rodriguez-Jimenez returned to bring the house down with his flashy Russian Trepak. Elegant Hayley Meier was assured beyond her years in the English Toffee solo. Ditto Katie Lally's Harlequin dance; with precocious physical strength, she is clearly a young dancer to watch.

So is Saturday night's charming little Clara, Brittany Shinay. Jonathan Davidsson was her adorable Nutcracker Prince. The Snow Queen and King—Meredith Seeley and her strong, attentive partner, Jason Kittleberger—performed their Act I *pas de deux* with polished zest.

Amazingly, leading the dancers who are beyond "up and coming," little 13-year-old Jim Nowakowski continues to astound me with his beautiful feet and legs and refined technique. This year, he also astounded an international audience that included some leading dancers from the great companies of France, Russia, and Germany when he was invited to an Eastern European gala performance. Tara Lally, reported to be headed to the touring Cirque du Soleil, took bravura charge of the Dew Drop role. Ballet dancers notoriously look younger than they really are; but in Draper's company, they're all so well trained and gracious in manner that you won't believe how young they are.

Except for some problems with accompaniment (perhaps leading to their awkward exit from the *Grand Pas de Deux*), Sarah Lane and Jared Matthews capped the evening dancing the Sugar Plum Fairy and her Cavalier. I don't know where their exotic costumes came from (not from this ballet!), but they looked attractive. In the few months since she graduated from high school and the Draper Center for Dance Education here, won the Youth America Grand Prix and the silver medal at the USA International Ballet Competition, and joined ABT's Studio Company, Ms. Lane has gained grandeur in her line and deportment and dances almost flawlessly. Matthews has a big jump and very fast, pretty pirouettes, and partners solicitously. Onstage in classical ballets, ballerinas and danseurs ideally should look more perfectly beautiful in movement than normal human beings can hope to be. Except for their obvious youth, these two are well on the way.

December 4, 2002

Next up was the Prix de Lausanne, to which Tim would be bringing Jessica Tretter, another advanced dancer of his professional division and Rochester City Ballet. Accompanying them would be Jessica's mother, Deborah, who had worn many hats in the studio over the years. Tim was particularly enthusiastic about making the trip as a most special way to celebrate the fortieth birthday of Katherine Ertsgaard, his dear friend who had served him loyally over many years. And with that, the man who had somehow managed to become the centerpiece of so many people's lives was off on his last adventure.

Brittany Shinay as the Snow Queen in Rochester City Ballet's *The Nutcracker* in performance with the Rochester Philharmonic Orchestra, with Adam Kittelberger as the Snow King on the Eastman Theatre stage in 2006, 2007, and 2010. Photograph by Nancy Sands.

BRITTANY SHINAY

To this day, I remember the thoughts that used to run through my eleven- and twelve-year-old head before Tim Draper would teach my ballet class at the old Downtown Draper studio. His physical appearance and reputation of being "super strict" intimidated me, but at the same time, I had often stood in the doorway to the big studio from the time I was young, watching him rehearse the older dancers in such a nurturing and passionate way. I knew just how much he truly cared about all of them.

One particular day during the summer of 2000 stands out. Tim was walking into our funny-shaped studio in the old building that was accessed through the lounge and costume area, far off to the left. He dropped his bags below the stereo system and put a CD into the player. All of us dancers had become silent on his entrance due to a combination of nerves and excitement, so we just stood and waited for Tim to begin with *pliés*. I remember him staring at all of us before he began with the funniest half smile on his face that seemed to ask, "Why are you all SO quiet? What is wrong with you?" Actually, we were all FREAKING OUT on the inside because we so badly wanted to impress the artistic director during the short time we had with him! Tim was absolutely like a god to us preteens and teenagers. Brittany Monachino and I always stood next to each other during those classes because Tim liked to call us the BB's (Brittany + Brittany) when we danced together. She and I were the same age and were great friends. Tim always made us feel special by telling us that we had great potential, which made us want to try even harder.

The best moment of that day took place in the center floor, when Tim was demonstrating the pirouette combination with an energy drink in hand. He must have noticed Britt and me staring at it because he said to her, "Do you want to try a sip? It'll give you energy." She was too scared (or too wise) to taste it because she didn't know what was in it, so Tim turned to me and asked if I would try it. I took a sip and let me tell you, that was one ill-tasting carbonated concoction! He was happy that I tried it, though, and laughed at my reaction to the beverage! After that happened, I saw firsthand that he had a sense of humor and had a special way of connecting with the young dancers.

I will never forget Tim Draper and the dancer that he helped me become—he believed in my abilities and instilled a passion in me for this art form that seems to burn brighter each day I step into the studio.

Brittany Shinay performed numerous principal roles with Rochester City Ballet, including the title roles in *Cinderella* and *Firebird* and the Snow Queen in *The Nutcracker*. After she shared a gold medal with Jim Nowakowski for Jamey Leverett's *Symbion* at the 2007 Youth America Grand Prix, the three were invited to the fiftieth anniversary of the Spoleto Festival in Spoleto, Italy, where Brittany and Jim reprised *Symbion*. The dance critic Emma Manning wrote in *Dance Magazine Europe* that the "American Brittany Shinay was memorable for her spirited dancing." Brittany additionally studied at American Ballet Theatre-NY's summer intensive where she was nominated as a National Training Scholar, attended Juilliard's BFA program on scholarship and additionally trained with the Boston Ballet School. Brittany was Tim's last Clara in 2002, sharing the role with her friend, Brittany Monachino. She now dances with the Georgia Ballet.

16

HUGS, TIM

When Tim Draper signed off on an e-mail to someone he cared about, it would always end with the simple but endearing, "Hugs, Tim." It was present in the last e-mail that I, like so many others, had received from him over many years, this time as he was getting ready to board the plane at the Rochester airport for the last time. It had followed a series of back-and-forth communications in which I had fairly begged him to not go on the trip. I just didn't have good feelings about it. The subject heading itself was foreboding, "Nothing Will Be Good If You Go." But his note was sweet and upbeat, particularly when it came to my daughter: "Tell her she was a great Clara." Then, "Hugs, Tim."

No one's funeral is packed to overflow capacity with mourners crying uncontrollably unless that individual has been well loved. Tim was most certainly that. And testimonials do not pour in from around the world unless that individual has made a difference at a most profound level. Tim certainly achieved that. As *Dance Magazine*'s editor in chief, Wendy Perron, noted in her beautiful tribute, "Timothy Draper saw his dream realized before he died. Under the leadership of its acting artistic director, Jamey Leverett, the Timothy M. Draper Center for Dance Education and the Rochester City Ballet seem well poised to live out Draper's wishes and continue his dream."

Life wasn't easy for Tim Draper. Not many people can survive ridicule over one's sexual preference in a less-enlightened era, an estranged father, a career ending injury in one's twenties, and the knowledge that one has had his life stolen from him at a young age, without being consumed by anger and bitterness. But Tim was deep down a good person with a good soul (if not a healthy heart), and thus channeled his own personal disappointments into bringing forth the gifts he had been given to help the next generation experience all that he had loved so very much. Not having any children of his own, he considered his dancers in a sense his children, with the hopes and dreams that all parents experience, especially when the children are young and haven't yet pushed back to create their own identities. It appears that when gifted dancers or those with tremendous potential came to Tim later in life, when they were as fiercely intent on their achievement as was he, there was a perfect alignment of thought and a scripted path for success. The discipline worked, and the tears of training could always be forgiven in pursuit of the greater good. But when dancers with the same enormous potential came to him so young, so tender, so excited, and with very high expectations because of their enormous talent, the sheer length of training sometimes became too much to sustain over the long haul, when the natural desire to experience all that life had to offer was always beckoning just beyond the studio walls. This is when the problems developed between Tim and those he cherished so dearly—when there wasn't a congruence of thought, and all that Tim could envision was that the talent would be wasted and a life would remain forever unfulfilled. What made this scenario all the more complicated was Tim's firsthand knowledge that dancers have a very short shelf life as performers—if they are lucky, they might manage to dance into their late twenties or early thirties if they can remain injury free, and if the stars are aligned. Dance is so different from any other field, where it is indeed possible to take a break, live life, see the world, and then come back with renewed fervor to put one's innate talents to work. Tim knew that those who strayed might never have the chance to come back when they were ready, and that knowledge weighed heavily on him. But his intensity, born of a fear that his time would run out before he could fully achieve his vision, colored his relationships in ways sometimes unbearable, whether in the studio, in the boardroom, in the advertising agency, in the newsroom, or at home. This was not something that he could turn on and turn off at will, and it tended to provoke just the opposite reaction in those he most wanted to help and in those whose help he most needed.

But his intentions, if not his execution, would always be forgiven, because he had pushed and inspired and believed in his young dancers in a way that no one else ever had or probably would again.

Tim, Jamey, and Sari, Prix de Lausanne, 2000. Courtesy of Jacquelyn Ostrum.

SARI OSTRUM

Tim was always like my second father. I began my ballet lessons when I was three years old, and before I knew it, the Draper Center became my second home. The majority of my waking hours apart from school were spent at the studio and always around Tim. When I was quite young, perhaps around six or seven, I remember my teacher, Sally Stepnes, taking me up to Tim and showing him my feet. He seemed quite excited with my potential talent. I think I reminded him of my mom, who had great extension and good arches. He danced with her a lot in his younger years with Olive McCue and the Mercury Ballet Company here in Rochester. At a very young age, I was hooked. I loved to dance. I loved the teachers, and I loved the studio. I would have slept there if it were allowed!

Jamey took me under her wing during these young years and always had a competition in sight that required constant rehearsing. She got Tim excited about the competitions as well, and he started watching rehearsals. Come competition day, he was always present at the performances. If we danced to the best of our ability and won the top awards, he would let us know how proud he was. I can remember him giving me a big hug after my solos. Nothing could have made me happier than pleasing him, because it was never easy to do so. Not only was I taking class every day during those early years but I was constantly rehearsing after hours for one thing or another. I went very rapidly through the levels and made it to the professional division by the age of twelve. Tim made me feel as if he was always so proud of me. Once I got into level 6, the professional division, he would insist that I demonstrate every combination. Fortunately, I could pick up combinations quickly. (It now seems much harder for me!) He began to have pet names for me. Penelope or Henrietta were his favorites, depending on his mood. I was always scared of level 6 because the girls were so much older than I was, and Tim gave me so much attention. I felt that the older girls resented this and didn't like me. But as I grew in the level, I gradually became friends with everyone.

During one class Tim asking me to come to the center to do a pirouette. He told me that I had to do more than a triple. I was so nervous, but I placed myself in fourth position and proceeded to do five turns! I looked at him and he said casually, "See, I told you you could do it!" When rehearsing a new ballet, it was quite humorous, because Tim would never know the ballet himself. He would simply give us a tape to watch, sit in his chair, and wait for us to learn it. It was a good thing I picked ballets up quickly because he would invariably say, "Now watch Sari." Tim would sit next to Jamey during rehearsals. Jamey had a habit of rapidly bouncing her foot and leg up and down. It would drive Tim wild! He couldn't concentrate and would slap her leg to make her stop. It always made our class smile (hiding it, of course).

I remember when I was rehearsing with Jimmy [Rodriguez] for *Gershwin in the Park*. Jamey and Tim were conducting rehearsal. I was very young then, and he would constantly tell me I had to look at Jimmy (who I knew was gay) as if I were in love with him. At this point, I had never even kissed a guy, and it was very hard for me to look "in love" at first. Tim would say, "Look at Jimmy as if he's Brad Pitt, and Jimmy, look at Sari as if she's some famous hot man!" That was very awkward for me. In class two weeks before the Gershwin performance, on a *glissade*, I fell on my ankle, and it swelled up like a tennis ball! Tim was so upset that he took me up in front with him and put my ankle on his lap, stroking it gently while finishing his class. He was so worried about me and took care of me like a father would his own child. He would make me stay late at the studio many times just to talk.

I also remember when I was in my early teens (before I started having to watch my weight), I danced all day at the studio. Tim noticed that I hadn't eaten anything on one particular day and practically forced me to eat half of his sub. He was always taking care of me. One year on April Fool's Day, all of level six wanted to trick him somehow. Instead of starting with the right side on every combination, we all started on the left. He didn't realize it until twenty minutes had passed! Then he decided to trick me. Everything I did he would say "Sari, that's horrible," "Sari, that's not high enough," "Sari, that's not rotated enough," and so on.

Another memory that sticks in my mind is that he always had about ten dollars worth of quarters in the side pocket of his dance bag. He would regularly ask me to go get seventy-five cents for his Diet Pepsi downstairs in the pop machine.

When Tim taught class, he often got the timing completely messed up! He would be doing a combination in eight counts but used music that was counted in threes! He would get so frustrated that it wouldn't turn out right! We would all laugh, but we had to be careful, because he hated it when we were right and he was wrong!

I remember when I danced the role of the Snow Queen in *The Nutcracker* ballet for the first time. I learned so much artistry from him. He would explain that when I reached for the Snow King, I should so gently place my hand in his and look at him with loving and caring eyes as if we were really in love with each other and not just acting on stage.

Jamey was not just my teacher when I was growing up, but she was really my very best friend! At the time she lived on Meigs Street, right next door to Tim. I was always over at her house and we would occasionally go over to Tim's. Tim would love it when we came.

When I reached my teens, it started getting harder to please Tim. In fact, he was always much harder on all the older girls. He would throw me out of the studio on a regular basis, it seemed, making a spectacle of me in front of the class. One time it was just because I gave him a wrong look. He was very big on being respectful to one's teachers! His reasoning was usually somewhat irrational from my point of view when I would get in trouble. I think he expected so much of me and wanted me to be so perfect. When I wasn't, he just couldn't handle it. When people asked him how he was in such great shape he would say, "It's because of Sari. She makes me so mad that I have to go to the gym to work off my anger." But after the storm, he would call me late at night and tell me how much he loved me. The conversation would always end with the threat that I had better be in class bright and early the following day. Even though he would usually apologize, his criticism started taking its toll on me. His anger gradually grew and when he was angry, he would say horrible, belittling things. It was almost as if he had two personalities. When he was in a good mood, his charm would be so magnetic that you would do everything in your power to stay close to him. Unfortunately, it became a regular scenario that I would be humiliated for some reason or another in front of the class. We would have many good days in between, but I found myself gradually changing. My enthusiasm and confidence slowly waned and my self worth went down to pennies.

One Friday night I had slept over at Jamey's house. The next morning, Tim took me out to breakfast at his favorite place, the Highland Diner, on South Clinton. I remember class started at noon and we didn't leave the restaurant until after noon! I said frantically to Tim that we were going to be late! He said, "I'm the teacher and class doesn't begin until I'm there!" Heaven forbid if I or anyone else were late even just one minute! That was another typical reason why many of us were thrown out of class.

I remember how he lectured the level 6 girls on why we should all be Democrats and not Republicans, because the Democrats favored the Arts. I would marvel at how he tried to mold us and EXPECTED us to change to his way of thinking.

My relationship with Tim took an abrupt turn after he and Jamey accompanied me to the international Prix de Lausanne Ballet Competition in Switzerland when I was a junior in high school. I can remember desperately wanting to dance in a reputable competition the previous year, but he told me that I wasn't ready and had to wait another year. By the time I was able to go, my enthusiasm had somewhat diminished, probably because my confidence was not what it used to be. I was going through the motions, but my heart wasn't in it. At this time I had put on an extra five pounds. I didn't look as thin as I usually did. Tim started out excited and very enthusiastic. He said that he wanted to educate me while we were in Europe. He told me he was going to take me to Paris to see the famous sights and most important, to take me to all the art galleries. He felt it vitally important that I was well versed in art through the ages and ended up giving Jamey and me an art appreciation course of a lifetime. I must admit I was grateful for that.

Tim and Jamey rehearsed me on the necessary solos I was required to learn for the competition. Because it was the first time Tim had taken one of his students to a competition of this caliber, he followed the original choreography exactly on my classical solo. During the competition, we all realized that most students added many spectacular tricks to their solos, making them much more impressive to watch. Tim was used to me winning competitions, and when I didn't win, he was beside himself. I always wondered if I had been a few pounds thinner, if things would have turned out differently. Even though I didn't win, I was offered scholarships to the Vienna State Opera and the

Stuttgart Ballet schools, but I was not at all interested in being so far away from my home and family. Tim was quite perturbed with me over this, and from that moment on, our trip was a disaster. He would alternate his anger between Jamey and myself. One day he would be mad at me, and the next day, Jamey. If either one of us was on the "off" day, it was hell to pay! He was constantly asking me what my goals were. I was confused and not clear on them at the time, and my answers were never satisfactory! This would infuriate him beyond reason! He wanted me to have clear objectives, and he wanted me to have the same goals he wanted for me. When I showed uncertainty, he became enraged! He would say to me often, "If I had your looks and body, I would be famous by now!" He told me that one of my short-term goals should be to play the role of Cinderella in Rochester City Ballet's premiere full-length performance of the ballet *Cinderella*, which was coming up in the spring. Another goal, he said, should be to join American Ballet Theatre. Fortunately, I had planned to meet a good friend of mine, David Hallberg, in Paris, where he was enrolled at the Paris Opera Ballet School. We had become close friends in the ABT summer intensive programs and had kept in close touch. If it hadn't been for meeting him in Paris, and giving me a breather from Tim, I don't know what I would have done. After returning, Tim and I always had an on again, off again relationship. I did end up playing the role of Cinderella in the spring, but I was beginning to burn out. I was tired of dancing all the time. I had very few friends at school. I always had to forfeit birthday parties and overnights as a child. I think I only went to one school dance as a teenager in high school because ballet always conflicted. I wanted to have more friends. I wanted to date a boy. I wanted to have some fun.

It was during this frame of mind that I graduated from high school early to pursue a career in dance. I had planned for this for so many years but now that it was here, I wasn't too excited about it. Nonetheless, Tim got me an audition with the ABT Studio Company and I was offered a job. It was with reluctance that I took it, because I finally had a new boyfriend and would be leaving him indefinitely. The experience with the Studio Company was wonderful, though. There were six boys and six girls, and we were constantly traveling and performing. We all became like brothers and sisters, and these relationships are what I valued most. I soon became an apprentice with the main company and traveled and danced in many ballets with them. However, my heart was still not in it. I had five to ten pounds to lose and I didn't take that seriously. In fact, I didn't appreciate even being there. I wanted a long vacation. I was tired of living, moving, and breathing dance. I wanted more. One of the ballet mistresses loved me and told me that I didn't have many pounds to lose. She encouraged me in every way, but I didn't want to try hard enough. The artistic director, Kevin McKenzie, told me that I was a great performer, and that when I was on stage, he couldn't take his eyes off me. He also said that they didn't have anyone with my "look." But I had to lose the weight. They even encouraged me to stop my menstrual cycle as I had too much water gain at that time of the month. I was *not* interested in the slightest in even entertaining the idea!

At first, Tim seemed to be proud of me for being a part of ABT. He frantically called my mom to see if I was in the city during the 9/11 disaster. He had been so concerned and worried about me. He asked me to come guest dance the Sugar Plum Fairy in his *Nutcracker* with a good friend of mine from ABT, John Michael Schert. After I performed, Tim said that I danced beautifully but could lose a few pounds. Shortly after that, I was still unhappy in New York City, had not lost the weight, and was even skipping company class on occasion. ABT gave me plenty of time but I could not show them I was serious enough, so I left the company. At this time, Tim must have been frustrated beyond belief with me. I would hear many rumors about me circulating in my hometown. They were all so farfetched that it was actually humorous! I was also told that Tim was the one who was spreading these rumors. I wondered whether he had to save face in the eyes of the public and let them know that my failing had nothing to do with him or his teaching. He was constantly calling my mom and friends to find out where I was. After all the lies I had been hearing, I became very angry with him and wanted to get as far away from him as I could. I heard Tim made several trips into the city to look for me. He would go into Steps and ask if anyone had seen me. My mom just told him that I wanted to be left alone for a while, and that made him even more furious! My parents told me that I had to do something constructive if I wasn't dancing, so I hid out in Brooklyn for a while and went to college. I needed something different in my life. Even though I was not doing anything earth shattering, I learned a lot. It was during the middle of my first year in college that I heard about Tim's passing. The news was almost more than I could bear, because we had not resolved our differences. I felt a multitude of emotions. I missed him, I was angry with him, I felt alone, I felt great sadness, I felt a type of relief, but most of all I felt the deepest love for him. After my year of school was completed, I couldn't wait to get home. I wanted to get back to the studio, but this time without so much pressure. I thought I might like to teach for a while as well as dance. I wanted to help support Tim's studio—the studio he spent his lifetime building.

Jamey was also feeling a great sense of loss without him and decided to choreograph a ballet in his honor. It was a ballet about her relationship with him, their history together, their ups and their downs. When she asked me to play the lead role, I didn't know what I was in for. I found myself in Jamey's role. Tim's and my history together had so many similarities to Jamey's history with him. In the end, I was able to play out all my emotions, to speak my mind to him through the dance. I was able to finally be free of pain. I was able to find peace. I had been healed.

SARI'S POEM TO TIM

Draper Studio was home,
Home to my heart
My love for dancing
Here's where it starts.

Tim was my teacher
Like my father in fact,
He demanded the best
Taught me how to act.

No matter how hard I tried
He always wanted more.
At times I couldn't take it
And walked out the door.

We had many fights,
Many traumas we shared
But always in the end
We knew that we cared.

The argues, the make-ups,
The long days of dance,
Tim only wanted the best
And for me took a chance,

He created a dancer
That he wanted to succeed
But at times I was pushed
Not knowing what to believe.

The grueling rehearsals,
The performance, then after,
We all kept strong
Hoping for his praise and laughter.

No matter the situation,
He was always right.
Off the music he would count
As we all danced in fright.

For all of his students
He only wanted the best
I wish we'd had one last chance
To put our differences to rest.

As of now I am not
Dancing professionally today.
He might be disappointed
But still proud in a way.

My talent I am giving
To students who learn
I enjoy teaching now
And have taken a turn.

A turn that really makes me,
Makes me so strong
I only wish Tim
Is not thinking I'm wrong.

I want him now
To accept me as I am
I hope he's looking down
With joy to my life's plan.

I'm sorry that I
Never got total peace.
Though times when I hurt
My love never ceased.

We both knew our relations
Were more than just fights
We weren't teacher and student
We were family, that's right.

We shared many memories
That we will always hold
I'll keep next to my heart
Forever in a mold.

Tim I miss you.
Draper studio was my life.
Time may have changed
Our past of much strife.

But you will always be
A part of me inside.
You gave me a gift
That I'm beginning to realize.

Teaching I love
And look forward to each day!
I owe my success to you,
You showed me the way.

The way too of dancing,
Of not caring who was there
When I dance I'm alone
Fear nothing—so rare!

You taught me that dance
Was an art and a feeling
That whenever life is low
To start dancing and believing.

I know now Tim
You are in a better place
I want to ask for peace
To put an end to all strife.

I wish I could have told you
How much I really do care.
I hope you can feel
My light and love beaming you there.

Draper studio was my home
And that will always be,
The start of my dancing
That has set both you and me free.

Love,
Sari (your Penelope and Henrietta)

Following an exceptional career with Rochester City Ballet, Sari Ostrum was invited in 2000 to join the American Ballet Theatre's Studio Company and in 2001 the American Ballet Theatre, where she performed in such ballets as *Swan Lake, Giselle, Onegin, La Bayadere, Don Quixote, Symphony in C,* and the *Nutcracker.* In 2006, she choreographed and performed Mozart's *Romance* with organist Hans Davidsson in Goteborg, Sweden, for Swedish royalty, Princess Desiree. Sari is now a much sought-after ballet teacher and coach, as well as a young wife and mother.

Sari Ostrum (*center*) enjoying some light moments with fellow dancers from the world-famous ABT Studio Company. *Top left to right:* Craig Salstein, Erin Ackert, Megan Knickerbocker, John Michael Schert, Catherine Sebring, Masayoshi Onuki, Patrick James Ogle, Angela Snow, and Misty Copeland. *Bottom left to right:* John Meehan (artistic director), Dartanion Reed, and David Hallberg. Courtesy of Jacquelyn Ostrum.

17

TOO YOUNG, TOO SOON

On Sunday, February 16, 2003, Tim boarded a plane in London, to begin his journey home. Shortly after takeoff, he began to suffer a diabetic episode as a result of his adult-onset diabetes, a complication from the medicines that he had been given for his enlarged heart. The plane was diverted immediately to Shannon Airport in County Clare, Ireland, so that Tim could be stabilized at the nearest hospital. Reportedly, the imbalance in his blood sugars was enough to cause a heart attack that night as he slept. According to Randy Stringer, "From what his doctor told me, he simply went to sleep that night somewhat tired from the episode and never woke up again. As deaths go, it was mercifully 'an easy one.' The time of his death was recorded at 3:00 a.m., February 17, 2003."

His nearest and dearest had known for a long time how critically ill Tim was. He had been on a wait list for a heart transplant, according to his sister, Donna. Despite his vibrant exterior and rigorous workout schedule, he often voiced his fear that the end was near. As Randy Stringer explained,

> He worked out aggressively for two reasons—one, since he could no longer dance, he needed and wanted to do something physical. Two, had he not worked out, eventually his heart condition would have left him breathless and poorly oxygenated, quite likely, bed-ridden. The exercise strengthened his heart, ironically, so he could lead an active life right up to the end. He would have gone insane being bed-ridden. He was fearful the end was coming during the entire time of our relationship—it was always on his mind in one form or another.

Nevertheless, it was still horribly shocking to all when his life ended so tragically at the age of forty-nine. It seemed unthinkable that someone who looked like the epitome of health could possibly be so ill as he said he was. When the dancers were called to attend an emergency meeting at the studio, no one wanted to believe that anything of a tragic nature was about to be revealed to them, so the rationalizations began: "It's probably about some last-minute scheduling change for Ballet Builders. You know how this place obsesses about everything." For all who were used to seeing him bound up and down the stairs to teach class, get a soft drink, or make a joke with the parents waiting to pick up their kids, it was impossible to contemplate anything more serious.

On arriving at the studio, dancers and parents were instructed to go upstairs to the main studio to await an announcement that would be forthcoming at the appropriate time. No more effective crepe could have been arranged for what was to follow; quite simply, there was no way to intellectually dismiss the swollen, red eyes of the teachers, the staff, and a fourteen-year-old dancer. After a very long wait, a procession of studio officials mounted the stairs to the main studio. All were in tears or had been—executive director, Kathy Ertsgaard; associate artistic director, Jamey Leverett; chairman of the board, Dr. Roberto Corales; and various support staff. The young dancer, who had been informed of the tragedy earlier in the day, was sitting on the floor, sobbing silently. However, even she remained mum as she had been instructed to do when her friends beseeched her to tell them what was wrong. Most tried to believe that she had just had a bad day, as was so often the case with teenagers trying to juggle academics and dance with too little time available in their day. Then the chairman of the board moved to the center of the floor and began speaking slowly with quiet elegance. "I have some very sad news to tell you all. Timothy Draper, who was both my patient and friend, passed away at three o'clock this morning in Ireland after having a heart attack from which he couldn't recover. I will answer any and all questions that you may have." Within milliseconds that felt like hours, stunned silence gave way to deafening tears and hysteria. The dancers screamed in disbelief, pleading to know more. Mothers and fathers were gently reminded that if their children were in the room, they should feel free to go and comfort them. In fact, so profound was the grief among the parents— many of whom felt that they, too, had been kicked in the stomach with such horrible news—lost sight of the most vulnerable members of the assembly needing consolation: their babies. For the next two numbing and gut-wrenching hours, the woman who had been his artistic compatriot drew on exceptional inner strength to begin the healing process by first speaking to the gathering and then going around the room to each dancer to say exactly what he or she had meant to Tim. This was an enormous act of grace on Jamey Leverett's part and exactly what was needed at the moment. In fact, no one other than Jamey would have been tolerated in the aftermath of such excruciating news. Afterward, the group dispersed, mostly to go home or to friends' houses for therapeutic sleepovers. Some dancers could not leave the room. My baby of thirteen stood bravely at the barre and did a series of deep *pliés*, almost as if she were telling Tim that it was going to be all right, that life and dance would go on in his memory. No one knew what to do next or what should follow. Some parents offered to phone the rest of the studio so that they could be spared the added distress of learning about Tim's death on television. Most media outlets agreed to hold the news for twenty-four hours to allow this courtesy to take place, but one did not, leaving many at home to recoil in shock over what greeted them on the 6:00 and 11:00 o'clock news.

If the studio at 320-A North Goodman Street had a heart and soul, it, too, died on that sorrowful Monday afternoon.

As heartbreaking as it was for his current students to learn of Tim's death in this manner, it had to be even worse for his former students, who no longer had the built-in support system of multiple shoulders to cry on when they heard the news. Kathy Joslyn recalls with extreme sadness receiving a telephone call from her sister, telling her to turn on the television. Rebekah von Rathonyi was so devastated after her friend and colleague, Adam Kittelberger, called her in tears to relay the news that she remembers being unable to process what he was saying. Despite the many times Adam told her, "He's gone, Becky," in that moment her mind could allow only that he was away in Europe.

Herb Simpson expressed well the sentiments of all who had known Tim personally or by reputation, in an article for Rochester's *City Newspaper*.

> It's shocking to hear that Timothy M. Draper, founder and artistic director of the Rochester City Ballet, died Monday, February 17, at 49. The report stated that he went into diabetic shock on a flight from London to the United States, and died of cardiac arrest in a hospital in Ireland, where the plane made an emergency landing. I knew that Tim was a diabetic; so am I. But I never thought of him as ill or vulnerable; he was incredibly healthy looking. Working seriously at gyms, Tim developed such a trim, powerfully muscular body that I remember kidding him about where all those muscles had come from. Tim looked stronger than he had when he returned to his

native Rochester from a career as a ballet dancer and began teaching
here. First he got his own school; then, in 1987, he founded Rochester
City Ballet. It may sound insensitive, but I feel that even more shocking than the tragically untimely death of this fine young man is the
disastrous loss to our region's arts and culture. To be tactlessly frank,
I must say that although for decades many talented people made worthy efforts to create a significant ballet company in this area, only
Tim Draper succeeded in doing so. He developed a ballet company
good enough to appear with the Rochester Philharmonic Orchestra
in their annual *Nutcracker* performances, and to dance them better
than the well-known professional companies the RPO had brought
in before. Furthermore, year after year, he trained very young dancers to be such exceptionally beautiful, gracious artists onstage that a
significant number of his protégés are now performing in New York
City Ballet, American Ballet Theatre, the Joffrey Ballet, and several
other fine companies. World-famous teachers and artistic directors of
major ballet companies have commented on Draper's extraordinary
training abilities. This year's graduate, Sarah Lane, won a position
with American Ballet Theatre's studio company and won top prizes in
two international ballet competitions.

What will become of ballet in Rochester without Tim Draper? I
have no idea.

—Herbert M. Simpson

The loss to the dance world was deeply felt, from North Goodman
Street to Ukraine. Cards and flowers began pouring in from all over
the world. The legends of the international dance community had
long admired the man who, from little Rochester, was sending his
dancers to perform on the world's greatest stages. One cannot begin
to even imagine the devastation of his own family and the closest
members of his dance family. Jamey channeled her grief into the
creation of a new ballet that delineated her loving and complex
relationship with Tim, entitled *Pedestal*, set on Sari Ostrum and Jonathan Davidsson with a small ensemble including Chelsea Bonosky,
Kelsey Buchanan, Jordan Drew, Katie Lally, Hayley Meier, and Brittany Shinay, all of whom were members of the professional division.
The emotional tribute was performed locally and led to Jamey Leverett's third trip to New Choreographers on Point: Ballet Builders,
which was reviewed by Dr. Roberta E. Zlokower, publisher of Rober-
taOnTheArts.com on April 10, 2005: "I found this piece the most
moving and memorable, with its recorded crying and visual grief,
choreographed by Jamey Leverett, Artistic Director of Rochester

City Ballet, in memory of the company's founder. The unfolding segments included fascinating choreography that meshed with Barber's renowned *Adagio for Strings*. It was obvious that the company is still mourning its loss, and this Dance was a fitting tribute."

Dr. Zlokower was well aware of the quiet sobbing that took place in the audience that night, raw emotion that could never be contained, no matter how many times the work was performed.

Tim accomplished so very much in his forty-nine years, but one is left to ponder what his life might have been like had he not been cut down at such a young age. Assuredly, his dancers would have continued to make brilliant names for themselves and for him. As Randy Stringer noted,

> I think the thing of which he was most proud toward the end of his life was finally seeing professional success and validation that he was indeed producing some of America's future ballet stars. In the end, he was respected by ABT's Kevin McKenzie and other artistic directors who were beginning to see, and want, the quality dancers his teaching methods were producing. Had he lived another ten or fifteen years, I think he would have actually been known as the "Ballet Master of America."

As one looks at Tim's life from the perspective of time, it becomes apparent that although his career as a dancer was important, it was not extraordinary. What makes Tim Draper a legend is that in just seventeen years, he built a school and a company from scratch. He nurtured dancers who routinely enthralled the international dance community and who went on to perform on the great stages of the world and in significant films. And he accomplished these feats strictly with volunteers and on a shoestring budget—in a mid-size city, not a major metropolis where dance students and dollars abound. If ballet were a sport, it would be the equivalent of a local high school baseball team sending three or four players to the New York Yankees. If it were science, it would be the equivalent of a local community college professor winning a Nobel Prize.

Tim died too young, too soon, like so many other artists through the centuries. But he did die at the top of his game.

Kristi Boone, soloist, American Ballet Theatre. Photograph by Jade Young.

KRISTI BOONE

Every time I think about Tim Draper and what he and his studio did for me, it truly amazes me. I would not be a soloist with American Ballet Theatre today, and have experienced all the wonderful things my dance career has given me, without the training I received at "Draper."

His guidance and knowledge about the art form truly guided me to be the dancer I am today. He was what inspired me to always emote and show the passion and maturity behind each move. I always felt that gave me a huge advantage on the stage and also in the studio. The ability he gave all of us dancers was to express ourselves. He could be a bit strong at times, as we all know, but it set me up for having the proper etiquette and perseverance in a major professional company that not many new professionals have. I'm thankful that at the age of thirteen (which is a relatively late start for a ballet dancer), I came to study under him and made the transformation in one year's time to a proper ballet student striving for a life as a ballerina.

I made it because of my passion to be a dancer, but I got there because of him. I miss that he can't come to New York City to see me dance, because I know what pride it gave him to see any of his dancers succeed in life. I think of him before every big premiere I have and feel his presence in my dancing always. I know that he is looking down at all his dancers with pride, as I know everyone is thankful for what they learned in their years in his studio, in life and in dance.

Kristi is a soloist at American Ballet Theatre. Seeing her perform there was one of the great joys of Tim's life. He especially delighted in telling everyone he knew (and even those he didn't) that when she was still only a member of the corps, she was selected to perform leading roles.

18

THE SCHOOL AND THE COMPANY GO ON

Grief continued unabated in the aftermath of Tim's death, but the board of directors needed to tackle the thorny issue of succession. Some on the board, as well as other interested parties, felt that a big New York name was needed to preserve the Rochester City Ballet brand. In other instances when a founder and artistic director of a dance company died, the company often lasted less than five years. Others, however, who had worked with Jamey Leverett day in and day out through her role as Tim's associate artistic director knew that not only had he trained her eminently well, but that she and she alone was equipped to take over the company that her mentor and friend had created seventeen years earlier. Not only was she Tim's designated heir apparent as well as his close collaborator for many years, she was also the only one capable of furthering and preserving his teaching method with a level of passion that matched his own. In addition, she was singularly able to curate his ballets down to the gesture, develop new choreography, excite the community, maintain the critical relationships so essential to a not-for-profit organization, and be able to work well with Kathy Ertsgaard, the executive director, as well as the board of directors. Jamey and Kathy had known each other since 1987, and although Kathy had come to the company and studio as a young adult while Jamey was still a teenager, they shared important history, and over time they had become very close friends.

More important than any other consideration, however, was the fact that Jamey had the implicit trust of her company. Had the proverbial push come to shove and the board decided to exert a heavy hand by finding an external successor, the company would likely have ceased to exist, because the dancers wouldn't dance for anyone other than Jamey. Her opinion had long meant as much to them as had Tim's. During this catastrophic time, she was needed more than ever. Dancers simply would have followed her anywhere she chose to go. At some

point in its deliberations, the board apparently came to the same conclusion. Without the exceptional dancers who were the RCB, everything else was irrelevant. Jamey was initially appointed interim artistic
director and became permanent artistic director in August of 2003.

After the funeral and the stoically inspired Ballet Builders performance in the days and months that followed Tim's death, Jamey carried the entire studio's heartbreak on her small shoulders. She never
let on how very difficult it was suddenly to do the work of two people.
But she did it without missing a beat and brought a level of renewed
vigor and decisiveness to each project she undertook. This was all the
more remarkable because she was also a very hands-on mom to her
young son, T. J. The multiply versatile Brian Norris had also by this
time become a part of the artistic triumvirate, teaching and rehearsing
the dancers as ballet master.

Although the studio was still in shock, its pace did continue on
track. The studio itself was once again renamed, this time honoring
the name of its founder in full. The Timothy M. Draper Center for
Dance Education continued to dominate every competition it entered,
future productions and school demonstrations were thrilling, and the
dancers continued to be trained to the highest possible standard. Tim's
often-stated desire to have a paid company came to fruition on Jamey
and Kathy's watch with significant assistance from the company's photographer cum benefactor, Nancy Sands, who ensured that the company not only would remain solid but would grow at a remarkable rate.

The dynamic artistic director, who merits a biography of her own
for the extraordinary gifts she brings to the profession and the people
who inhabit it, knew intuitively what to do to preserve Tim's contributions. Her bold, collaborative style enabled her to take the company
forward. Among her most significant contributions in the years that
followed were, first and foremost, providing the leadership to stabi-
lize the school and company. Without her passion for ensuring continued excellence in the development and showcasing of her dancers
in accordance with the highest professional standards; creating new
ballets; and making important collaborations both internally and
externally at the local, national, and international levels, it is unlikely
that the funding would have been available to ensure a new home, a
thirty-four-week paid contract available to company members, and a
strategy for the future. A thumbnail sketch of these accomplishments
surely would include the expansion of the company to eighteen contracted dancers; the hiring of Beth Bartholomew and Fidel Orrillo as

ballet mistress and ballet master; building on the excellent relationships that had been established with the RPO, resulting in enhanced *Nutcrackers* and additional collaborations at both CMAC/Constellation Brands Marvin Sands Performing Arts Center and the Eastman Theatre; a home season with multiple performances at the Nazareth Arts Center and a New York City debut season in 2010; and the creation of more than fourteen new works for the company, including *A Common Thread, Bravo! Colorado, LumaVoce, Gershwin Preludes, Pedestal, Respect, How to Break a Heart, An Intimate Portrait, Peter and the Wolf*, and the critically acclaimed full-length ballet *The Blood Countess*. Jamey's works have been performed at the USA Jackson International Ballet Competition and at the fiftieth Anniversary of Gian Carlo Menotti's Festival dei Due Mondi in Spoleto, Italy. She has worked with some of the greatest artists of the day, including Jeff Tyzik and the Rochester Philharmonic Orchestra, Cello Divas, Stephen Kennedy, Deborah Fox, Hans Davidsson and the Eastman Rochester Organ Initiative, Arabesque Winds, the Ying Quartet, and the pianist Elinor Freer. Choreographic collaborations have included works with Inma Rubio Thomas, Patrick Corbin, Daniel Gwirtzman, and Edward Ellison, who have set work on the Rochester City Ballet. In 2009, the company performed works by George Balanchine (*Serenade*) under the direction of former Balanchine dancer, Leslie Peck, a recognized authority on Balanchine ballets and one of the few authorized by the Balanchine Trust to stage Balanchine ballets, as well as Gerald Arpino's *Valentine*. Peck returned in 2013 to reprise her earlier work for the company's twenty-fifth-anniversary program.

To Leverett's great credit, rare among artistic directors today, she has a passion for developing outstanding dancers, who may or may not fit the singular aesthetic that has resulted in a homogenization throughout much of the professional dance world today. There is a place in her company for dancers of shorter stature or a body type that doesn't necessarily fit the scripted mold if they are exceptional artists. As has been stated in recent years, some of the greatest dancers this art form has ever known probably would never make it today because of the very narrow restrictions that permeate the industry. Grace Edwards notes, "Margot Fonteyn wouldn't meet today's 'standards.' Her thighs are too big. Mikhail Baryshnikov may well not have had his legendary career had he stayed in the USSR, where he was considered too short. . . . It's enough to make you wonder, how many Baryshnikovs and Fonteyns are rejected by elite schools each year?"[1] Although neither Tim nor Jamey were impervious to the desire for a healthy, slim aesthetic in their dancers and would guide them accordingly, they focused more on an appreciation for what dancers could do with their bodies than on whether they adhered to the strict "look of the day." They also invested the time to encourage their outstanding dancers toward healthy choices rather than leaving them to wither on the vine.

In the years following Tim's death, Jamey created artists of her own, and their numbers continue to grow. Those who continued to train in the years immediately following Tim's death, as members of the professional division and company members of Rochester City Ballet, went on to achieve stunning success in the field. Chelsea Bonosky went to NYU's Tisch School of the Arts and now enjoys a significant reputation as an emerging choreographer. Kelsey Coventry danced with Dance Theatre of Harlem and is presently with Ballet NY. Jonathan Davidsson performed with Houston Ballet and the National Ballet of Canada, and now dances with the Estonian Ballet. Gabe Davidsson went to Kansas City Ballet and is also presently with Estonian Ballet. Jordan Drew attended Alonzo King's LINES Ballet Training Program and now dances with the Dawson/Wallace Dance Project. Sarah Hillmon graduated from NYU Tisch School of the Arts. Hayley Meier is with River North after a trail-blazing tenure at the University of Arizona. Brittany Monachino graduated from SUNY Purchase College and now dances with Philadanco! Jim Nowakowski went to Houston Ballet. Brittany Shinay went to Juilliard on scholarship, the first dancer ever to be accepted there from the Draper School.

It did not happen by chance. Notwithstanding her multiple concurrent responsibilities as artistic director of the Rochester City Ballet and Timothy M. Draper Center for Dance Education, Jamey worked tirelessly to provide every possible performance opportunity in the repertoire, through regular Rochester City Ballet productions and via regional and international competitions, to showcase her dancers and provide them with outstanding opportunities and connections in addition to the world-class training they were receiving at their home school. In 2004 and 2007, she took many dancers to the prestigious international Youth America Grand Prix competitions. They won coveted medals, beating out dancers from other elite competitors worldwide and taking home Outstanding Choreographer, Outstanding School, and Outstanding Teacher awards. Dancers were invited to appear at Rochester's version of Oscar Night and many other

Brittany Shinay stars as Cinderella in Rochester City Ballet's 2008 production. Photograph by Nancy Sands.

Jamey Leverett, Jim Nowakowski, and Brittany Shinay tour Rome between performances of the fiftieth anniversary of the Festival dei Due Mondi in 2007, where they were invited to perform after winning a gold medal for Jamey's *Symbion* in the international YAGP NYC Finals, topping more than six hundred dancers who represented over 150 ballet schools from across the world. Author's collection.

high-profile venues. And although Tim had missed by only weeks the 1980 trip to Spoleto with Trockadero, three of his protégés, Jamey Leverett, Jim Nowakowski, and Brittany Shinay did it for him, twenty-seven years later.

Jamey is a powerful combination—artistic director, choreographer, spokesperson, fund-raiser, and her dancers' best champion. A signature work that had its debut in 2011, *The Blood Countess*, a full-length original ballet based on the true story of the sixteenth-century beauty and female serial killer, Elizabeth Bathory, Countess of Transylvania, will someday soon make her a household name.

Jim Nowakowski, demi-soloist with Houston Ballet. Photograph by
Ken Riemer.

JIM NOWAKOWSKI

There are numerous people throughout my life who have had great significance to me. I look to them as heroes and mentors. They have guided me through life and have helped me to become a part of who I am today. One person in particular who had this impact on my life was my dance coach, Timothy M. Draper. As my dance career evolved, it was he who trained and taught me the essentials of becoming a great artist. After he passed away on February 17, 2003, it made me work harder toward becoming the successful dancer he knew I had the potential to become.

Timothy Draper was the founder of the Rochester City Ballet in Rochester, New York. He had performed all over the world with the Israel Ballet, with the Puerto Rican Dance Theatre in New York City, with the Fusion Dance Company in South Florida, and with Les Ballets Trockadero de Monte Carlo and the Garden State Ballet. He then turned his attention to teaching. In that capacity he was codirector of the Fort Lauderdale Ballet, ballet master of Dance Miami and Ballet Etudes, and a guest teacher in New York City for Nancy Bielski at Harkness House, Hebrew School of the Arts, and Steps.

From the very beginning, Mr. Draper was a hero in my eyes because of his immense success in the dance world. His great success had only come from his hard work as a dancer, and I admired him so much for that. It was not until I met him when I was eleven that he actually started to have an impact my life. With the physique of a body builder, Tim Draper came off initially as very intimidating. However, he was truly the total opposite, with the greatest sense of humor, and a heart of a lion.

His dance classes were inspiring. There was not a day I when I did not look forward to his teaching. Tim Draper taught me some of the most important things in becoming a great artist that have helped me become the dancer I am today. Tim taught us not only the technique of ballet dancing but also the beauty and history behind it. Mr. Draper was a very intellectual man, full of knowledge that was inspiring to listen to. He would always make jokes in class, thereby making it fun to learn and making the joy of dancing become even more joyful.

Perhaps Tim Draper's greatest gift was that not only did he teach me about dance but he gave me advice about life and prepared me for the real world.

Mr. Draper had coached me on my very first international competition, the Youth America Grand Prix. That he chose me to compete at the YAPG, with its high standard of competitive talent, told me that he had seen the potential in me and had faith. I was honored to receive the chance to compete in such an impressive event. However, at times, the hard work to prepare for this became frustrating. Tim would always give me the words of advice to help me through these frustrating moments during rehearsal and he was always there for support. When the big moment came at last, I gave it my all, with the corrections, words of advice, and support he had given to me in rehearsals. During the awards ceremony, I was presented with the 2002 Junior Grand Prix Award, the highest award given in the junior division. At the end of the ceremony he came toward me, grinning ear to ear and gave me the biggest hug. From that moment on, I knew that I had made him proud.

A few months later, Tim Draper and I were invited to go to Ukraine, where I performed in a festival called Ballet Stars of the World. Getting the opportunity to travel overseas for the first time with Tim was very special to me. We were able to observe parts of the world together that we had never before seen. We also received the pleasure of seeing three ballets performed that were new to me. Traveling to Ukraine with Tim had allowed us to get to know each other better, and caused me to become very close to him. On February 17, 2003, however, a horrible disaster occurred. My teacher, Timothy Draper, passed away. No words could describe my pain at such a time. He had been a part of me, and a part of my life was no longer there. Over time, I came to realize that although he was not with me anymore, he would be still with me in spirit, watching over me from a better place. The loss of Tim has only pushed me to work harder toward becoming the dancer I knew he wanted me to become. Every word of advice about dance and life will always remain with me while I grow as a young man. I thank Tim Draper for his love, support, encouragement, and his great sense of humor in ballet class. I hope that I will continue to make him proud and that he is still grinning from ear to ear, as I remember he always did, while he watches over me. He will remain in my heart as my journey through life continues.

Jim Nowakowski is a demi-soloist with Stanton Welch's Houston Ballet. He was a prodigy in dance. Jim's parents had to eventually bring along an old-fashioned wagon to the various competitions in which he participated just to cart the trophies home. Jim came to the Draper Studio a star. Under Tim and Jamey's watchful eyes, he left an artist. He was thrilled to receive the 2007 National Foundation for Advancement in the Arts Gold Award from Mikhail Baryshnikov in New York City.

19

OUR MUSES

And now, we come full circle—to the muses of the Eastman Theatre Ballet, who were the backdrop and inspiration to Timothy M.
Draper in all that he was to accomplish. They continue to live on in the
hearts and minds of artists, as does Tim, and for those who never knew
them but for whom ballet will always be the beautiful satin ribbon that
binds. One may safely assume that they, and Tim, can look down with
pride over what they have wrought.

Olive McCue
A tribute by Jacquelyn Ostrum

I close my eyes and begin to think back to the time in my life that
was spent with Olive McCue, and the mental pictures flood my
mind. I can almost hear her voice, as if she were standing in front
of me. The hundreds of hours spent with her in rehearsal and
ballet class left profound memories. I began taking ballet lessons
with her in 1966, when she was around the age of fifty-nine, and
studied and danced in her company until 1974. She was nothing
less than dramatic in appearance, with fine, thin flaming red hair
hanging just below her chin. She almost always wore a tight, form-
fitting black dress to the knee, skin-colored stockings and black
flats. She loved a wide, scooped neckline with short sleeves baring
her shoulders. Her skin and complexion were exceptionally pale,
with darker, penciled-in eyebrows and the brightest of orangey red
lips. Many times it looked as though she had smudged her lipstick
across her mouth with her finger, missing the outline of the lip
altogether. Her figure was one of slender hips and lean, beautiful legs but fuller in the bust and stomach. I'm certain though, in
her performing years, her body was nothing less than George Balanchine's idea of perfection. The moment she entered the studio,
her presence commanded attention. Her manner, her confidence,
and erect posture were in the truest sense royal in quality, therefore unequivocally receiving immediate respect. She was a star in
every sense of the word.

Enid Knapp Botsford
A tribute by Mary M. Wilson and Donna Schoenherr

Enid Knapp Botsford was a remarkable pioneer. As a young dancer she assisted George Eastman, of Eastman Kodak, in realizing his full ambition for the Eastman Theatre. By her own persuasion, she convinced the single-minded Mr. Eastman to bring the world of ballet and modern dance to Rochester at a time when classical dance in America was still in its nascent stage and considered by some to be an oddity. She went on not only to teach dance in her studios and prepare young dancers for performances in the Eastman Theatre but also to advance dance education and community outreach programs among the schools throughout the city and its suburbs. This was an enlightened pursuit. Later in her career she became a renowned leader of preprofessional dance education at a world-class level. She was, in the truest sense, a twentieth-century visionary who left a legacy that resides among the world's most influential. Reflecting back on those years with her now, we remember Enid's presence, her consistency, her style, and her character. She cultivated her life's work with infectious passion, rigor, integrity, discipline, and respect. Enid was the very best of role models; one who had artistic talent, a purpose in life, drive, sound business acumen, and a compelling vision for the dance life in Rochester and beyond.[1]

Thelma Biracree
A tribute by Katherine Wilson Whitelaw with Lana Gitlin Rouff, Tara Stepenberg, and Eleanor Gitlin Lange

I think we feel we were blessed to have real theater teachers. Thelma could read a music score and play piano and knew what gels to use for curtain lighting effects. Earl Kage and she were real theater people along with so many interesting characters who hung around the Swan Street Alley. It was such a rich time in music, dance, and art. The Eastman days were character building. We were fortunate that it was before the dance craze of today, with everyone dancing and getting degrees but not really knowing the greats of ballet or theater. We entered 50 Swan Street on the ground level, climbing up the stairs to the third floor. The harps were sitting there on the second level in a big room. We'd put on *pointe* shoes and then run down a flight to wet the heels and even pose for an artist. We heard this incredible orchestra led by such luminaries as Howard Hanson, Eric Leinsdorf, and Frederick Fennell—Miss Biracree would call him "Freddie"! He conducted the RPO for the Mercury Ballet performances. He was British and just terrific. We were so lucky—it was texture and character during a time when Sadler's Wells and American Ballet Theatre and the Ballets Russes were all coming to the Eastman Theatre. Howard Hanson used to park his car in the garage below the rehearsal halls [in

Miss Biracree and friends in the Tower. Author's collection.

the Theatre Annex] and somehow, the garage deteriorated, which was why they tore the building down. Paul White of the Rochester Civic Orchestra usually conducted at Christmas. Clarence Hall had a set-design room on the same floor as the RPO's rehearsal studio. Earl was one of the Ted Shawn men who built the original barn at Jacob's Pillow. Thelma's uniqueness was her style of ballet, which included a lot of flow and perhaps some nontraditional stylistic components as well. She emphasized the importance of DANCING—not of performing steps, but of using dance forms to express something, which could be abstract expression. She was assuredly influenced by her experience in Martha Graham's first company, performing St. Denis–like movement. Miss Biracree was like a second mother, coming to New York to see me in *Mame* in 1967 and asking me if I would come back to take over the school and each year sending Christmas cards. Blind by then, she would say "My darlings, life is so good to me—I am so grateful." She was so dear. We are still students of hers. . . .

As the well-known *Times-Union* theater critic Hamilton Allen pointed out to Miss Biracree prior to her retirement in 1967, she had trained over four thousand students over an illustrious career.[2] The impact of a wonderful teacher is truly inestimable. And the Tower, which hasn't changed a bit since 1922 (save for a stray bobby pin or two), has never looked better. Those would be Rochester City Ballet's bobby pins.

Tim would be proud.

NOTES

Introduction

1. "Ballet Studio atop Eastman School of Music Center Wing under Way in Next Two Weeks," *Herald,* June 24, 1923.

2. John Pitcher, "Dancer Timothy Draper Dies," *Democrat and Chronicle,* February 17, 2003.

Chapter Two

1. Tim's mother, Hazel Draper, shared in a conversation with me how Tim's great-uncle, Kenny Draper, had performed on the Vaudeville circuit. See also "500 Attend Firechiefs' Banquet; Demonstration by Old Forge," *Utica Daily Press,* May 25, 1944.

2. "Passages, Earl Kage," *Memorial Art Gallery MAGazine,* Fall 2008, 11.

3. Vincent Lenti, *For the Enrichment of Community Life: George Eastman and the Founding of the Eastman School of Music* (Rochester, NY), 83.

4. "Motion Picture News," February 3, 1923, 602. Housed in 1923 Scrapbook, Sibley Music Library Special Collections Department.

5. *Musical Leader Review,* September 6, 1922.

6. Lenti, *For the Enrichment of Community Life,* 141.

7. Martha Graham website, http://marthagraham.org/about-us/our-history (accessed May 22, 2014).

8. "Eastman School of Dance Established to Broaden Activities of Theatre and School of Music," *New York Times,* July 3, 1925.

9. Mary M. Wilson and Donna Schoenherr, "Remembering the Enid Knapp Botsford School of Dance," *Democrat and Chronicle,* May 16, 2012.

10. "George Cukor Facts," in *Encyclopedia of World Biography,* ed. Paula K. Byers (Detroit: Gale, 2004).

11. Clips are available for viewing at the National Film Preservation Foundation website, http://www.filmpreservation.org/dvds-and-books/clips/the-flute-of-krishna-1926 (accessed May 19, 2014); and on YouTube as "Martha Graham—The Flute of Krishna," posted October 30, 2009, by planetbenjamin, https://www.youtube.com/watch?v=T4OIX4eiEq8.

12. *Penn Yan Democrat,* June 12, 1931, 5.

13. *Cornell Daily Sun,* vol. 69, no. 129, March 23, 1953, 1.

14. "In the Name of Auguste Ventris: An Interview with George Clouser on Injury Prevention," June 20, 2005, http://auguste.vestris.free.fr/Interviews/JamesClouser.html.

Chapter Three

1. *Nutcracker* program, Draper Dance Theatre, December 10 and 11, 1988. In later years, the title of this character changed to "Maid."

Chapter Four

1. ArtsAlive.ca, Meet the Artists: Peter Boneham, http://www.artsalive.ca/en/dan/meet/bios/artistDetail.asp?artistID=86 (accessed May 22, 2014).

2. Pamela Wilkens-White, interview with author.

3. Agrippina Vaganova, *Basic Principles of Classical Ballet* (Mineola, NY: Dover, 1969).

4. The late Edward A. Charbonneau III provided this information in a personal communication.

Chapter Five

1. John Dwyer, "Ballet's Soft-Spoken Inspiration," *Buffalo Evening News,* September 24, 1971, 35.

2. Ibid.

3. Ibid.

4. "Officers, Directors Elected by New Dance Group." *Tonawanda Evening News,* April 4, 1972.

5. Dwyer, "Ballet's Soft-Spoken Inspiration."

6. Ibid.

7. "Children's Yule Festival Set by Performing Ballets." *South Buffalo–West Seneca News,* December 18, 1969, 13.

8. "Ballet Group to Suspend Operations," *Tonawanda News,* December 21, 1971, 4.

9. "Officers, Directors Elected by New Dance Group," *Tonawanda News,* April 4, 1972. *Buffalo Evening News,* September 24, 1971, 35.

10. Ibid.

11. Dennis Harrison, "Lively Audience Applauds Ballet," Lockport *Union-Sun Journal*, December 2, 1972, 1.

12. George H. Kimball, "Dame Margot, Festival Ballet Score at Eastman," *Rochester Times-Union*, April 1, 1973.

13. "Festival Ballet Folds; Director to Disband It," *Utica Daily Press*, April 28, 1973, 3.

14. *The Bulletin*, April 16, 1977, 10.

15. George Jackson, "Back on the Map," *DanceViewTimes*, March 2, 2009, http://www.danceviewtimes.com/2009/03/back-on-the-map.html.

16. "Western New York Ballet Company," press release, January 1979.

17. "Kathleen Crofton, 76, a Dancer, Ex-Director of Maryland Ballet," *New York Times*, December 5, 1979.

Chapter Six

1. Wendy Perron, "Curtain Up," *Dance Magazine*, August 2006, http://www.dancemagazine.com/issues/August-2006/Curtain-Up.

2. "Mrs. Botsford to Begin Classes," *Avon Herald-News*, September 10, 1959.

3. Pam Whittemore, "New Stories," Brighton High School Class of 1960, http://bhs1960.net/Stories%20we%20can%20tell%20after%20reunion.html (accessed May 22, 2014).

4. Endorsements, Donna Ross School of Ballet, http://www.donnaross-ballet.com/endorsements.php (accessed May 22, 2014).

5. Sebby Wilson Jacobson, "Visions of Sugar Plums," *Rochester Times-Union*, December 17, 1987.

6. Donna Schoenherr, personal communication.

7. Walter Terry, *Ballet News*, January 1980, quoted in "Features: Puerto Rican Ballet Comes to Vassar," *Miscellany News*, April 25, 1980, vol. 69: 8.

8. Jennifer Dunning, "Riverside Dance to Close," *New York Times*, February 10, 1987.

9. Sanjoy Roy, "Step-by-Step Guide to Dance: Les Ballets Trockadero de Monte Carlo," *Guardian*, February 17, 2009.

10. Joan Acocella, "Ladies and Gentlemen: The Trocks," *New Yorker*, January 10, 2005.

11. Jill Sykes, "The Trocks," *Sydney Morning Herald*, October 8, 2005, http://www.smh.com.au/news/arts-reviews/the-trocks/2005/10/07/1128562992707.html.

12. Jann Parry, "Paul Ghiselin, aka Ida Nevasayneva. Les Ballets Trock-aderode Monte Carlo." *Balletco Magazine*, April/May 2011, http://www.bal-let.co.uk/magazines/yr_11/apr11/interview-paul-ghiselin.htm.

13. "Jocks of the Trocks," *Sunday Magazine Australia*, quoted at Les Ballets Trockadero de Monte Carlo, http://www.trockadero.org/jocks-of-the-trocks.html (accessed May 22, 2014).

14. Jennifer Chung, "Boys Will Be Boys . . . Except When They're Dancing as Girls!" *Gay & Lesbian Times*, January 6, 2005, http://www.gaylesbian-times.com/?id=4217.

15. Donald Rosenberg, "All-Male Les Ballets Trockadero de Monte Carlo Brings Its Ballet Parodies to PlayHouse Square," *Cleveland Plain Dealer*, January 28, 2011.

16. Bertram Coleman, "Ballets Trockadero de Monte Carlo: A History of the Company, 1974 to 1990" (PhD diss., University of Texas at Austin, 1993).

17. Interview with Michael Patrick McKinley (former Trockadero dancer), October 2012.

18. Coleman, "Ballets Trockadero."

19. Quoted in ibid.

20. Coleman, "Ballets Trockadero."

21. Quoted in ibid.

22. Quoted in ibid.

23. Quoted in ibid.

24. Coleman, "Ballets Trockadero."

25. Quoted in ibid.

Chapter Seven

1. *Boca Raton News*, August 15, 1985.

2. Jacobson, "Visions of Sugar Plums."

3. Ibid.

Chapter Eight

1. Sebby Wilson Jacobson, "Visions of Sugarplums," *Rochester Times-Union*, December 17, 1987.

2. Kathy Ertsgaard, eulogy for Tim, February 26, 2003.

3. Sarah Lentini, *Metropolitan* magazine, Spring 2009: 19.

4. Interview with Kathy Joslyn, September 28, 2012.

5. See Cory English's website for more information: http://www.cory-english.com (accessed May 19, 2014).

6. Heidi Lux, "The Timothy Draper Dance Theatre: Creating New Performance Outlets for Dancers," *Brighton-Pittsford Post*, December 9, 1987.

7. Jacobson, "Visions of Sugarplums."

8. Kristine Bruneau, *Rochester Woman* magazine, November 2012: 12.

Chapter Nine

1. Hamilton Allen, "She Set City's Feet a'Dancing," *Rochester Times-Union*, June 29, 1967.

2. Sebby Wilson Jacobson, "Missing Miss McCue," *Rochester Times-Union*, June 3, 1988.

3. Robert V. Palmer, "Draper Dancers Off with Right Foot on Premiere," *Democrat and Chronicle*, June 6, 1988.

4. Sebby Wilson Jacobson, "Three 'Nutcrackers' in Town?! Here Are the Whys and Hows behind the Embattled Ballets," *Rochester Times-Union*, December 1, 1988.

5. Heidi Lux, *Wolfe Publications*, December 5, 6, 7, 1989.

6. Interview with Sally Stepnes, Sepember 12, 2012.

7. Herbert M. Simpson, "Draper Dance Theatre Fires Up 'Firebird,'" *Democrat and Chronicle*, May 8, 1989.

8. Karen Flynn, "Draper Dancers' Potential Shines with 'Firebird,'" *Rochester Times-Union*, May 8, 1989.

9. Lesley A. Rex, Timothy J. Murnen, Jack Hobbs, and David McEachen, "Teachers' Pedagogical Stories and the Shaping of Classroom Participation: 'The Dancer' and 'Graveyard Shift at the 7-11," *American Educational Research Journal* 39, no. 3 (2002): 765–96.

10. Stewart Sweeney, "An Interview with Howard Sayette: On Staging Bronislava Nijinska's *Les Noces*," CriticalDance.com, July 2003, http://www.criticaldance.com/interviews/2003/howardsayette20030700.html.

Chapter Ten

1. "Draper Dance Comes to Smith," *Finger Lakes Times* (Geneva, NY), January 5, 1990, 6.

2. Robert V. Palmer, "Grieg, Vivaldi Meet Pink Floyd: Introductions by Draper Dance," *Democrat and Chronicle*, 1991.

3. "The Studio of Dance, Class Schedule," 1991.

4. "Draper Dance Theatre," *Democrat and Chronicle*, date unknown. A copy of the article is on file at the Rochester Public Library, Local History Division, in a folder titled "Dancers and Dancing, Teachers and Schools of Rochester, 1979–1993."

5. Sharon McDaniel, "New Mayor, New Name among the Sugarplums in this 'Nutcracker.'" *Democrat and Chronicle*, December 15, 1993, 1C, 6C.

6. Zan Dubin, "The Trocks Toe the Line between Art and Camp Dance: The All-Male Les Ballets Trockadero de Monte Carlo Parodies the Classics with Technical and Dramatic Skill," *Los Angeles Times*, January 21, 1995.

7. Dubin, "The Trocks Toe the Line."

8. Gia Kourlas, "Where Are All the Black Swans?," *New York Times*, May 6, 2007.

9. "Dancers in Flight," *Democrat and Chronicle*, September 9, 1995.

10. Sharon McDaniel, "Despite Setbacks, Rochester City Ballet Is Stepping Up Its Effort to Crack the Big Time," *Democrat and Chronicle*, September 9, 1995.

11. McDaniel, "Despite Setbacks."

12. Sharon McDaniel, "A Tough Nut," *Democrat and Chronicle*, December 14, 1995.

13. McDaniel, "Despite Setbacks."

Chapter Eleven

1. Sharon McDaniel, "City Ballet's 'Nutcracker' Rehearsal Outperforms Expectations," *Democrat and Chronicle*, December 13, 1997.

2. Ibid.

3. Herbert M. Simpson, "Youth on Pointe [*sic*]," *Rochester City Newspaper*, December 16–22, 1998.

1. Chapter Twelve

Quoted in Kristine Bruneau, "Artist View: An Intimate Look at the *Nutcracker*," *Rochester Woman Magazine* (1999): 12.

2. Sharon McDaniel, "RPO, City Ballet's Nutcracker Sparkles with Energy," *Democrat and Chronicle*, November 27, 1999.

3. Sharon McDaniel, "Two Local Ballerinas Hitting New Heights," *Democrat and Chronicle*, September 6, 2000.

Chapter Thirteen

1. Herbert M. Simpson, "RCB Attends the Grand Ball," *Rochester City Newspaper*, May 10–16, 2000.

Chapter Fourteen

1. Stuart Low, "Ballet Troupe on Slippery Ground," *Democrat and Chronicle*, February 14, 2001.

Chapter Fifteen

1. Attributed to dance superstar, Rasta Thomas, whose company is Rasta Thomas' Bad Boys of Dance. Thomas said this to Tim Draper at the night of the YAGP Gala. It was overheard by Connie Nowakowski, Jim's mother, who passed it on to me. Personal communication, April 26, 2014.

2. USA International Ballet Competition, http://www.usaibc.com/about-us/about-2/quotes/ (accessed May 19, 2014).

Chapter Eighteen

1. Grace Edwards, "The Body of Ballet," *Trespass Magazine*, December 14, 2009, http://www.trespassmag.com/the-body-of-ballet/.

Chapter Nineteen

1. A part of this tribute was published in Wilson and Schoenherr, "Remembering the Enid Knapp Botsford School of Dance."

2. Allen, "She Set City's Feet a'Dancing."

INDEX

An italicized page number indicates a photograph.